YOU
ARE
CALLED

ALSO BY JOHN BEVERE

The Awe of God

The Bait of Satan

Driven by Eternity

God, Where Are You?

Killing Kryptonite

The Holy Spirit: An Introduction

Under Cover

Honor's Reward

The Story of Marriage (with Lisa Bevere)

The Fear of the Lord

Relentless

Breaking Intimidation

Drawing Near

How to Respond When You Feel Mistreated

Extraordinary

A Heart Ablaze

Enemy Access Denied

Thus Saith the Lord?

Good or God?

Everyday Courage

YOU ARE
CALLED

DISCOVER YOUR
GOD-GIVEN GIFTS
TO **FULFILL**
YOUR **PURPOSE**

JOHN BEVERE

W PUBLISHING GROUP

AN IMPRINT OF THOMAS NELSON

ISBN 978-1-4003-5028-5 (audiobook)

ISBN 978-1-4003-4253-2 (ePub)

ISBN 978-1-4003-5026-1 (TP)

Library of Congress Cataloging-in-Publication Data

ISBN 978-1-4003-5026-1

Printed in the United States of America

25 26 27 28 29 LBC 5 4 3 2 1

CONTENTS

A SPECIAL MESSAGE FROM JOHN

Throughout these pages, you'll find biblical insights and strategies that will empower you to discover your purpose, ignite your passion, and realize your God-given potential. Within each chapter, you'll also see questions and prompts to help you think about and personalize what you're learning.

As you go on this journey to discover and step into your calling, I want to make sure you know about the *CALLED* course, which serves as an excellent companion resource to this book. In the MessengerX App, we've made this full-length course available to you at no cost.

Inside the free MessengerX App, you'll also have access to dozens of full-length courses, audiobooks, sermons, and other discipleship resources to help you grow in your faith every day. We've made this app available for free in over 130 languages because we believe everyone should have access to life-transforming biblical teaching, regardless of their location, language, or financial position. (The story behind this outreach is something you'll learn more about in the pages of this book.)

Download the free MessengerX app today in the Apple App Store or on Google Play and begin taking advantage of this powerful tool to help you get even more as you journey through these pages.

Cheering you on!

John

Download the free MessengerX App and get the full-length CALLED course.

CHAPTER 1

CONNECTING THE DOTS

Fear of the LORD is the foundation of wisdom . . .

Wisdom will multiply your days

and add years to your life.

If you become wise, you will be the one to benefit.

PROVERBS 9:10–12

The year was 2012. I was scheduled to speak in the Los Angeles area for a church's weekend services. My normal pattern is to fly in late Saturday afternoon, minister Saturday evening and Sunday morning, and return home Sunday afternoon. This routine was about to change.

One of our ministry partners—I'll call him Stan—in discovering I was scheduled in the LA area, called and asked if I would like to play the golf course at the famous Riviera Country Club. This is an exclusive and private club, very difficult to get into. I didn't have to think twice. I enthusiastically responded, "Absolutely yes, I'd love to!"

Stan picked me up early Saturday morning for the dream round. I started out the first four holes being three over par (nerves got the best of me), but ended the round at two under par. Stan and I had a great time together; it was a memorable morning, to say the least.

On the drive back to my hotel in downtown Los Angeles, Stan asked a heartfelt question: "John, can I ask you about an issue I've been wrestling with?"

"Sure."

In a vulnerable and sincere manner, he set up his question: "John, I've worked tirelessly and diligently, giving many hours to building my businesses over the past couple of decades. My net worth is now approximately $9 million. Everything's running smoothly with my current clients. The result of years of hard work is that my wife and children are financially set for life."

Then came his question: "Now that I'm entering my fifties, why should I work at the same pace? Why should I struggle to build my businesses to $35 million over the next ten years?"

> Before you read on, consider this question: Like Stan, have you wrestled personally with a "why should I" question—without yet fully answering it? If so, mentally complete any of the following phrases that reflect your struggle: *(Feel free to write out your response in the space provided.)*
> - Why should I keep caring about . . .
> - Why should I keep devoting time to . . .
> - Why should I keep on . . .
> - Why shouldn't I give up on . . .

There with Stan, the Holy Spirit instantly gave me wisdom on how to answer. "Let me pose a scenario," I said. "Suppose I was to say to you, 'Stan, I've spent years working hard to write seventeen books that are now in over eighty languages with copies numbering in the multiple millions. I've flown over ten million miles in the past twenty-five years, fought jet lag, experienced a variety of cultures and strange foods, and stayed in tiny hotel rooms—all so I could minister the gospel all over the globe. The ministry is doing well, and finances are stable; Lisa and my children are set too. Why should I continue to work at this same rate?'"

It was a perfect setup. With a slight chuckle, he answered, "I wouldn't want to be in your shoes when you face Jesus one day."

"Stan," I said, "that's exactly what you were talking about regarding your own businesses."

The smile immediately left his face. He turned his eyes away from the highway and toward me with a look of shock. "How do you mean?" he asked.

I then explained to Stan that God has divinely gifted every one of His children to build His kingdom. However, we are stewards, and we can therefore choose at any given time to use these gifts in one of three ways:

1. We can use the gifts to build God's kingdom.
2. We can use the gifts to build ourselves.
3. Or we can neglect the gifts altogether.

Take a moment to pray, acknowledging before God what you want your future to look like regarding your most important gifts from Him (even if you're not yet certain what those gifts really are). Ask for His help and guidance. You may want to use the following phrases if they match your genuine desire to follow Him.

- Lord God, as You make me more fully aware of my gifts from You, help me to embrace and not neglect them.
- Help me, heavenly Father, to use my gifts to build up Your kingdom.
- Meanwhile, I trust You, Lord God, to provide security and well-being in the future for my family and me, according to Your own love and wisdom.
- (Or write your different response here:)

I had Stan's attention, so I continued: "Some of my obvious gifts are writing and speaking; your gifts are related to business and giving. You can see how my gifts are used to build the kingdom, but you don't see how *your* gifts can be used to build the kingdom. However, here's the truth: Your gifts, Stan, are just as important for building God's kingdom as mine are. In fact, yours may be *more* important—and yet you haven't connected the dots!"

We continued to talk along these lines. From our conversation, I found it both fulfilling and enjoyable to see the rapid change in Stan's thoughts and attitude.

THE UPDATE

Six months later, I called Stan to touch base. We had another unforgettable chat.

"Hey, Stan, how you doing?"

"You want the honest truth?" His answer caught me off guard.

"Yes, of course."

"I've been haunted, in a good way, by the words you spoke to me six months ago."

"What are you doing about it?"

With a laugh, he quickly stated, "I'm busting my rear end to build my businesses up to $35 million for the sake of building the kingdom."

"Good for you!"

Then in 2022—ten years after our initial conversation—I received a text from Stan, which he signed: "70 million dollar Stan."

Stan has grasped the reality that he's not a spectator in advancing God's kingdom, but a vital participant. He caught the vision, which eludes so many, that his unique abilities are valuable for the eternal, not just the temporal. Now he fully understands he's gifted for a greater purpose than himself and his family.

I'm so grateful he was blunt, sincere, and humble. These traits opened him up to receive the truth that would change his life—and due to his testimony, the lives of so many others in turn.

Just recently, I received this text from Stan:

Years ago, after I played golf with you at Riviera, I started a new company with three Jewish men. Again, this was after you and I had a long talk. Now here's the news I told you I was going to share when I could: This morning, we closed on the sale of the company to a private equity group out of NY. Very exciting. We ended up selling for $555mil. Thank you for your words of wisdom!

Stan's enlightenment has now become his motivation to multiply his efforts, and it exemplifies the primary purpose of this book. In conversing with believers throughout my years of travel, the vast number who think no differently than Stan did is a shocking reality. In fact, if I were backed into a corner, I would have to say it's the majority. However, many are not as forthright as Stan in admitting it.

But as conversations ensue, the disconnect is uncovered.

In light of Stan's story, how do you view your own gifts and abilities? Which of the following statements best reflects your honest response?

- I believe God wants to use my gifts and abilities for building His kingdom.
- I fail to see a close connection between building God's kingdom and my own gifts and abilities.
- (Or write a different response here:)

A PARADIGM SHIFT

If you question your purpose or have similar thoughts, I'm so happy you have this book in your hands. My sincere hope is that your paradigm will also shift.

As with Stan, be honest with yourself; doing so will help you connect your dots. In this posture of humility, you'll discover and firmly believe in *multiplying* your unique gifts for building the kingdom. (This concept of multiplying is one we'll explore in depth as we go along.) You're just as called by God as your pastor or anyone else is. Your calling is just as legitimate as that of the late Billy Graham, or of any well-known minister today.

You're just as called by God as your pastor or anyone else is. Your calling is just as legitimate as that of the late Billy Graham, or of any well-known minister today.

Think for a moment about how fully you can embrace this statement: "I'm just as called by God as anyone else on earth." Which of the following responses best reflects your present belief and honest mindset about this?

- I can clearly recognize that some people are more called by God than I am.

- I want to believe that I'm just as called by God as anyone else—but I'm not there yet.
- Yes, I mentally accept that I'm called by God, but my heart doesn't really feel it.
- Yes, in my mind and heart I believe I'm just as called by God as anyone.
- *(Or write a different response here:)*

If you struggle to believe that you're just as called by God as anyone else—what can you identify as the root reasons for your resistance to this? *(Here—as with all the reflection sections in this book—you're invited to use the space that follows to jot down your response—your further thoughts, prayers, and questions.)*

In this guidebook, we'll explore how to discover, develop, and most importantly *multiply* your gifts to enhance your specific calling. The Word of God and the stories contained in these pages will build your faith to greatly increase your effectiveness.

I know this firsthand; it happened with me as I was creating this book.

BORN ON PURPOSE, FOR A PURPOSE

Let's begin by examining a familiar portion of Scripture:

For by *grace* you have been saved through faith, and that not of yourselves; it is *the gift of God*, not of works, lest anyone should boast. (Ephesians 2:8–9 NKJV)

The focus of these two verses is the *grace of God*. It's clear—abundantly clear—that we're saved by grace, which is a gift from God. The twenty-first-century church has done an excellent job of communicating this truth. We can never work hard enough, live pure enough, or sacrifice enough to earn the privilege of spending eternity with our Creator, Almighty God. This familiar scripture has been the most looked-to reference to reveal this important truth.

However, we may have neglected what comes next:

> *For* we are His workmanship, created in Christ Jesus for good works, which God prepared beforehand that we should *walk in them*. (Ephesians 2:10 NKJV)

Notice that the next word after the ninth verse is *for*. This word is a *conjunction*, which joins the two statements together. This tells us that the beginning of Paul's statement (verses 8 and 9) is not complete on its own. The word *for* means "because of this," so verse 10 should not be left out when citing verses 8 and 9; otherwise, we don't get the complete meaning of what's being communicated.

you experienced—or would you expect to experience—in seeking to know and live out God's unique plans for you?

- What could you do to overcome these hindrances?

In a simple statement addressed to God, let Him know how much you desire to know with certainty His plans for you and how He expects you to live them out.

Paul states in Ephesians 2:10 that we are His handiwork created for a specific purpose—to produce good works. To summarize, in these three verses combined (8, 9, and 10 in Ephesians 2), Paul in essence is saying: "We're saved by grace to first *be someone*—a child of God—and we're equally empowered by that same grace to *do something*."

We should never overemphasize one truth to the neglect of another truth. But let me emphasize up front that who we are in Christ Jesus is paramount to what we do—because *anything we do should be an outflow of who we are.*

Think about your typical activities—what you've actually been doing—during your awake time over the past week or so. What statements do these activities make about who you truly are?

It's tempting to shy away from the "do something" aspect, since it relieves us from any pressure of laboring to build the kingdom. But the serious reality is this: *Our labor energizes us.* Jesus says, "My food is to do the will of Him who sent Me, and to finish His work" (John 4:34 NKJV). He also says, "As the Father has sent Me, I also send you" (John 20:21 NKJV). Putting His two statements together, we clearly see that our food is to do and finish the will of Jesus, who sends us. Food strengthens us. If we don't eat, we become weak and are good for very little.

A few additional worthwhile questions to ponder:

- In what kinds of tasks or working situations have you experienced being energized by your efforts and labor?
- Through your relationship with Christ, and as you remember His words, what would it mean in your life today to say (as He did), "My food is to do God's will and to finish His work"? What would that work involve?
- What does being "sent" by Jesus (as He teaches us in John 20:21) mean to you?
- Doing the will of God strengthens us. Is what you're doing with your life strengthening you?
- How passionate are you about the work you're now doing? If you're lacking passion, assess your situation carefully. Why do you think you're lacking fulfillment in this area?

STRENGTH FOR DOING WHAT GOD HAS PLANNED

Let's now bring this over to our spiritual life. If we don't do the will of Jesus who sends us, we become weak. That makes us more vulnerable to temptation.

In more than forty years of walking with Jesus, I've noticed that one of the primary causes of people slipping away from the faith is a lack of "doing." They become lazy and idle regarding their calling, and before they know it, they find themselves in complacent drunkenness, immorality, or given to interests that pull them back into the world's way of living. They lose their spiritual strength.

Here's the bottom line: What we do for God strengthens us.

How would you honestly describe the overall present condition of your spiritual strength?

In what specific ways do you sense the need for *greater* spiritual strength?

Allow me to restate the truth of these three verses (8, 9, and 10 in Ephesians 2): You were born again by the free gift of grace to be a child of God, and you were equally empowered by that same grace to do something.

Scripture declares that God planned each of our works beforehand. Addressing the Lord, David writes:

> You saw me before I was born. Every day of my life was recorded in your book. Every moment was laid out before a single day had passed. (Psalm 139:16)

God designed things for you to do *before you were born*. He actually recorded these works in a book! We can only imagine how huge this book is, because every moment of our lives is recorded in it. These assignments He planned for us revolve around building His kingdom.

Regarding our specific calling, we won't be judged on what we did, but rather on what we were called to do. That's both sobering and invigorating.

His deepest desire is that we fulfill His plans for our life—but it's not guaranteed that we will. Notice in Ephesians 2:10 the word *should*. It doesn't say "that we *would* walk in them"; it says "that we *should* walk in them." Here's where our free will enters the game. He prearranged our works—but it's up to us to walk in what He planned.

I'm firmly convinced that when we stand before Jesus at the believer's judgment seat (where we'll be rewarded for our labor as Christians or suffer loss for our neglect), He will open His book and say, "Let's compare how you actually lived to the original plan My Father and I had in mind for you." (In regard to the judgment, it's written in two different places in Scripture that the "books were opened"—see Daniel 7:10 and Revelation 20:12.) I believe these books were written by God about our life before we were born. Regarding our specific calling, we won't be judged on what we did, but rather on *what we were called to do*. That's both sobering and invigorating.

> Envision yourself standing before the Lord after your present earthly life is past, and your eternal rewards have been granted—having been determined by your faithfulness to God's original plan for your life, and for your

unique calling and purpose. What do you think you'll want to praise and thank Him for most?

What do you think you'll want most to hear from Him?

Keep thinking further about the truth that God has a unique, original plan and calling for each of us. What does this say about our heavenly Father's character—especially about His wisdom, His compassion, His grace, and His mercy? As you reflect on this, feel free in this moment to give Him your worship and praise.

DESIGN, CHOICE, AND REWARD

At this point, you may be feeling a little panicked. Please don't! There are three important things to note:

First, God is more passionate about you completing what He's called you to do than you are, so He's not going to hide His plans from you. *He* desires that you know your calling more than *you* do!

For the good of your mind and heart and soul, express realistically in prayer your personal gratitude for how passionate God is about your calling, and for how strongly he desires for your to know and understand it.

Second, the process of growing into the fullness of your calling is a journey, not a one-time event, so fight the urge to give in to impatience.

Communicate to the Lord your willingness and commitment to persevere patiently in the journey of discovering and living out his calling on your life.

Third, in this book you'll find insights from both Scripture and experience to help you discover and develop your calling.

> Speak to the Lord also about how eager you are to learn all you can from this book and from Scripture about your calling.

Consider this illustration. Suppose I'm a city planner, and I desire to build a spectacular residential, recreational, and retail complex near the city center. Being the city planner makes me the chief designer, so I organize the master plan with skilled developers and architects. In this complex, I want play areas, amusement rides, sports courts, fountains, sitting areas, and walking trails. I also want restaurants, movie theaters, shops with upstairs condominiums, and other creative accents to make our complex unique.

Once the design is complete, I then determine what contractors I'll need to accomplish the different aspects of the master plan. I hire these various contractors and give them a timeline for their assignments. The project is set to commence.

If all the contractors do exactly what I ask, the massive project will be built seamlessly and smoothly. However, what if some of the contractors don't make this project a priority? What if they accept the assignment but then use their skills to work on other jobs instead? What if they go fishing or golfing or attend sporting events too often, so the project gets neglected? What if others are lazy and don't take their work seriously? If I totally depend on these original contractors, the project won't get done on schedule. In fact, it may never be done.

The choice belongs to the contractors in what to do with their time and talents. However, as the city planner, I'm not going to settle for major delays or the possibility of the project never being finished. Instead, I'll bring in others to do the work.

What's the result? The original contractors don't get the reward of being a part of the team that builds the beautiful complex. They won't be able to show their children, grandchildren, and friends the part they played in the beautiful focus of the city center. Their children won't be able to tell others about what their parents accomplished. They'll also lose the reward of being paid for the assignment.

FAILING TO FULFILL GOD'S PLAN

You can see this same principle exemplified all through Scripture. God has a master plan for the building of His kingdom. Yet throughout history, God has had to work with people who haven't fulfilled His desires. Therefore, He's frequently had to adjust His original plan. (I speak in human terms because God knows the end from the beginning; He's not bound to time.) "Changing" the plan is not a shock to Him. He knew what His laborers would choose beforehand. He was already prepared with their replacements.

Here are a few of many examples of this in Scripture. You see this with Abraham's father, Terah. (Our youngest son, Arden, recently reminded me of this truth.) Most of us know that Abraham was born and grew up in Ur of the Chaldeans before God called him to travel to Canaan. But if you look closely at the story, the lesser-known detail you'll discover is that Terah was more likely the original one called to do this. We read:

> One day Terah took his son Abram, his daughter-in-law Sarai (his son Abram's wife), and his grandson Lot (his son Haran's child) and moved away from Ur of the Chaldeans. He was *headed for the land of Canaan*, but they stopped at Haran and *settled there*. Terah lived for 205 years and died while still in Haran. (Genesis 11:31–32)

Here are two things to consider. First, why would a man, for no reason, uproot his family from Ur and travel over six hundred miles toward, of all places, the land of Canaan? A trip by camel is slow and arduous. With women and children, it probably took at least a few months. It's not like Terah could go online and see pictures and read articles about Canaan being a great place to live and work. He didn't discover it through posts on social media. He would have had a reason for this distinct and distant move.

Second, if he was headed for Canaan, why did he settle in Haran? Why didn't he complete his journey to the destination? Could it be that he was tempted to not finish? Could he have run up against interfering desires, hardships, a family member who was fed up with traveling, or other distracting circumstances? Could it have been that he saw more chances for opportunity in Haran and didn't want to risk losing out on them simply over a word from God?

In considering all this, could we possibly conclude that Terah was God's first choice to be "the father of many nations"? Was he also originally assigned to be the *father of faith*, a term now ascribed to Abraham (Romans 4:16–17)?

Terah decided not to go the distance; he settled in Haran. I believe if he'd stayed the course, today we would read about his adventures and covenant with God. I believe Israel would have called him their father of faith, and that Jesus would have been referred to as the seed of Terah instead of the seed of Abraham (Galatians 3:16).

> For contrast, you may want to consider the actions of Terah's son Abram (later called Abraham). You can find evidence of this man's true responsiveness to God by looking up these Bible passages: Genesis 12:4–9; 13:14–18; and 15:1–6. Look to Abram's actions as a pattern and example for your own life, as you pursue your calling and purpose.

Another example of a change in God's master plan is the judge and head priest Eli. He and his descendants were assigned to be the priests who would approach God for the people. However, a prophet sent to Eli declared:

> The LORD, the God of Israel, says: I promised that your branch of the tribe of Levi would always be my priests. But I will honor those who honor me, and I will despise those who think lightly of me. The time is coming when I will

put an end to your family, so it will no longer serve as my priests. (1 Samuel 2:30–31)

Eli's disobedience affected both him and his descendants. Had he walked honorably before God, the priesthood would have continued with Eli's clan.

> As a contrast to Eli, consider the example of Samuel, who as a boy lived under Eli's care. Look in your Bible at 1 Samuel 3:19-21. Notice how God was at work to confirm Samuel's calling and purpose as God's prophet and priest for Israel. What honest expectations do you have for how God will communicate and confirm His calling and purpose in your own life?

Still another example is all the kings of Israel. The first would be David's son Solomon. God said to him, "Since you have not kept my covenant and have disobeyed my decrees, I will surely tear the kingdom away from you and give it to one of your servants" (1 Kings 11:11). Had Solomon stayed true, the kingdom never would have been ripped away later from his son Rehoboam.

The majority of the kingdom was given to Jeroboam, yet later he also failed in being faithful. God told him:

I promoted you from the ranks of the common people and made you ruler over my people Israel. I ripped the kingdom away from the family of David and gave it to you. But you have not been like my servant David, who obeyed my commands and followed me with all his heart and always did whatever I wanted . . . And since you have turned your back on me, I will bring disaster on your dynasty. (1 Kings 14:7–10)

Jeroboam would have had an enduring dynasty had he not misused his position and gifts to benefit himself instead of God's kingdom. A similar message was given to King Baasha of Israel (1 Kings 15:25–16:7), as well as to others entrusted with kingdom responsibilities.

Here's my point: Often our unfaithfulness to the call of God affects not only us, but also our descendants. With Terah it didn't, but with many others it did.

We see a similar situation among the prophets. Elisha served Elijah and received a double portion of what was on Elijah's life. But years later, Elisha's servant, Gehazi, who was next in line to walk in the prophetic gifting, lost focus of what was important and pulled away. He became a leper and left the service he was originally called to (2 Kings 5:14–27). A new servant (not named) moved into his place to assist Elisha.

In the New Testament, you see this with Judas Iscariot. Because he misused his calling and the gifts entrusted to him, he had to be replaced. Peter said to the disciples in the upper room, "This was written in the book of Psalms, where it says . . . 'Let someone else take his position.' So now we must choose a replacement for Judas" (Acts 1:20–21).

How sad, how tragic! Imagine the regrets so many will have because they chose not to steward the calling or gifts upon their lives in a worthy manner.

In returning to the positive aspect—hear again that you were born *on* purpose and *for* a purpose. Your life has great value in building the eternal. It's not the will of a mere man or woman, but determined by God Himself.

YOU DETERMINE YOUR EFFECTIVENESS

Here's the startling reality: *How effective you are is not up to God, but up to you.* That may sound irreverent if you've put all your life achievements in the basket of "God's sovereignty." However, I assure you it is not irreverent, nor does this statement take anything away from the sovereignty of God. It's a testimony of His trust in us, and His desire for His sons and daughters to exercise the free will He's given us.

Let's look again at a portion of the Scripture that opened this chapter:

> Wisdom will *multiply your days* and add years to your life. If you become wise, you will be the one to benefit. (Proverbs 9:11–12)

This truth is so encouraging and powerful! What does it mean to *multiply your days*? It surely means more than lengthening your life; this is already covered by the statement "and add years to your life." Rather, it must mean *increasing your effectiveness* each and every day. In other words, you'll get more out of the day than someone without God's wisdom.

You've most likely heard the proverb, "If the ax is dull, and one does not sharpen the edge, then he must use more strength; but wisdom brings success" (Ecclesiastes 10:10 NKJV). Wisdom is the focus here. You won't be as effective or productive with a dull ax (a lack of wisdom). Conversely, you'll be able to cut down many more trees with an ax that's sharpened (by living wisely). You'll multiply your efforts using the same strength.

God's wisdom is so important. I'll share a story later in the book of a friend of mine who was unproductive as a believer for decades and eventually became fed up with his lethargic state. The first thing he did was to immerse himself in Scripture for six months. This gave him the wisdom to be more effective, and you'll be amazed by his life story.

And it's not just true of my friend; we're all told, "Getting wisdom is the most important thing you can do" (Proverbs 4:7 GNT). I love this statement. Once you really believe it, you'll give your time and energy to acquiring wisdom. But the great truth of Proverbs 9:11–12 is this: Once you obtain wisdom, *you are the one who benefits.*

> Take a moment to pray in a way that rightly expresses your true commitment to seeking and depending on God's wisdom regarding your life's calling and purpose.

The wisdom of God that I write about in this book took years of seeking, searching, and listening to come by—coupled with both positive and negative experiences. But as you'll discover, it's not only me, but also others that I've had the privilege to interview who've walked wisely and borne tremendous fruit. I can only hope that in a short amount of time you'll receive what took me years to obtain, and that you'll go much further with this wisdom than I have.

It's a kingdom matter. We are all one, so if you benefit, then I benefit. If you go further than me, it's also to my advantage. We are all working for a common purpose and for the glory of our King.

REFLECTION FOR RENEWAL

(Each chapter will include space at the end—like what follows here—where you can jot down concluding thoughts and responses as you review and reflect upon what you've just read.)

In this chapter, what statements or Scripture passages seemed most meaningful for you?

How would you restate them in your own words? (Personalize your answer as a prayer of response to God.)

What are your thoughts about what God wants you to do now in response to what you've seen and reflected upon in this chapter?

IMPARTED ABILITIES

Having then gifts differing
according to the grace that is given to us,
let us use them.

ROMANS 12:6 NKJV

I have a friend named Jim who coached a high school girls' basketball team for eighteen years. In all that time, they weren't able to win the state championship. Year after year, the team was either beaten in the regional finals or eliminated in the state tournament before the final round.

Jim shared with me, "I was frustrated and ready to quit, but around that time period, I discovered the power of God's grace."

Jim made a firm decision. He would no longer coach in his own strength as he'd done for eighteen years, but would completely rely on *the grace of God*. He asked the Lord what to do, and God's response was, *Restructure your practices. Instead of ninety minutes on the floor, spend forty-five minutes in the locker room reading the Bible, sharing, and praying, then spend the last forty-five minutes on the floor.*

Jim told me, "John, this seemed counterproductive. We needed to work on skills and run plays; I needed every bit of the ninety minutes for practice. But I knew I'd heard from God."

He explained the new strategy to the girls. "They thought it was a bit religious and seemed like a silly idea," Jim said. "Some were even frustrated when they first heard it, but after further sharing my heart, they bought in."

With a smile on his face, he continued his story. "That year we won the state basketball championship for the first time. If that wasn't enough, the next year we won it again." And that second state championship "was mind-blowing," he said. "We missed every layup in the final game. We should never have won with all those missed shots. However, after reviewing the stats, we realized we set a record in that game for three-point baskets. The three-pointers compensated for all the missed layups and gave us the score we needed to win."

EMPOWERMENT

Jim tapped into divine wisdom; in fact, it was the same insight the apostle Paul discovered—one that statistically eludes over 90 percent of the twenty-first-century church. That insight is this: Biblical grace is not only God's gift of salvation, but also His *empowerment* for our lives. Examine the following words that Paul wrote, quoting exactly from the mouth of the Lord: "My grace is all you need, for my power is greatest when you are weak" (2 Corinthians 12:9 GNT).

There's no question or gray area here. God directly refers to His grace as being His empowerment. The word *weak* in the above verse means "inability." The Lord declares to Paul—and also to you and to me: "My empowerment—My grace—is optimized in situations that are beyond your natural ability."

> Consider again carefully those words from the Lord: "My grace is all you need, for my power is greatest when you are weak" (2 Corinthians 12:9 GNT). What kinds of inherent weakness on your part have you recognized in areas where you most want to serve God and others? And what kinds of empowerment do you most long for in these areas?
>
> In your life, what would it look like to fully trust God for this kind of empowerment?
>
> How can you personally access God's empowering grace, which is available to you in abundance?

For my friend Jim—trying on his own, with all he had, to lead his girls into a championship—what did eighteen years of hard work yield? Nothing but years of falling short. But it was well worth the agony and multiple disappointments for the wisdom Jim would finally discover: *God's grace empowers us to go beyond our natural ability.*

In a different letter, Paul makes a rather bold statement: "I have worked harder than any of the other apostles." Wow, did he really write this? Think of who's included in this list: Peter, James, John, Barnabas, Apollos, and a slew of other great ones. Sounds a little arrogant, but if you read the rest of his statement, you realize it isn't:

> I have worked harder than any of the other apostles, although it was not really my own doing, but God's grace working with me. (1 Corinthians 15:10 GNT)

Paul is boasting of God's empowerment, not his own ability, so there's no personal bragging involved. He relied on grace to accomplish his divine mission.

After years of frustration and eventual enlightenment as a coach, Jim now depends on God's empowerment (grace) to go further than his own ability. He's carried this wisdom into all aspects of his life; his ax (remember Ecclesiastes 10:10) has been sharpened!

With this in mind, let's return to our individual mission. Again, God's Word declares, "For we are His workmanship, created in Christ Jesus for good works, which God prepared beforehand that we should walk in them" (Ephesians 2:10 NKJV). God Himself prepared your assignment, even before your birth. This crafted calling is what will bring you *true* fulfillment; no other work or play will. Your purpose is remarkable in magnitude. In fact, in regard to accomplishing it, here's a critical truth:

Your destiny, which God prepared for you, is beyond your natural ability.

Let me make this abundantly clear. It's utterly impossible for us to fulfill our divine assignment in our own ability. How do I know this to be true? Because God firmly declares that He will share His glory with *no one* (Isaiah 48:11). If any of us were to accomplish

It's utterly impossible for us to fulfill our divine assignment in our own ability, because God firmly declares that He will share His glory with no one.

our divine destiny in our own ability, then God would have to share His glory with us, which He will not do! God intentionally made your calling beyond your natural ability so you would have to depend on His *grace* to fulfill it.

> How convinced are you that the destiny God has prepared for you is beyond your natural ability?
>
> To fully attain this God-prepared destiny, which of your natural strengths and abilities do you think He will want you to move beyond, as you trust in His empowering grace?

SPECIFIC ABILITIES

Next, we should ask whether there are specific endowments of grace. In other words, in the same way grace empowers us to live beyond our natural ability, does God equip us with unique capabilities to accomplish our specific mission?

Allow me to answer with several examples. Your favorite pro tennis star could never have become one of the world's greatest tennis players if he or she had no access to a tennis racket and balls. Without the proper tools, the finest woodworking craftsman around would never have discovered his or her ability. You would never have known who Michelangelo was had he never had access to a chisel, a brush, or paint. Is the same true for our divine callings?

Two quick stories will help clarify.

When I first started in ministry, I met an exceptional praise and worship leader. This gentleman led worship for a world-renowned evangelist in the mid-1900s. The evangelist passed away in the 1970s, and this worship leader branched out into his own ministry. He frequented our church in the 1980s, and I often found myself just staring and listening with awe—he was so gifted! He could play the piano like few I'd heard, and with no apparent effort. In no time flat, he could motivate thirty-five hundred people to get on their feet, singing and dancing. When he praised God, the entire atmosphere changed; it became charged with God's presence.

The last few times he came to minister, I had the privilege of hosting him. Having this time together, I asked questions because I wanted to know about his God-given abilities. I discovered that his mother, a godly and devout woman, prayed many hours a day. He said, "John, when I was in my mother's womb, a man" (his mother believed it was an angel) "came to the house one day. This man, who my mother had never seen before, said, 'Your son will lead multitudes into the presence of God and will play the piano skillfully at a young age.'"

Then came the part of his story that astounded me, making it unforgettable. As a toddler, he sat down at his parents' piano one day and began to play perfectly, without any previous lessons or practice. He didn't play "Chopsticks," but rather a complex piece that only experienced piano students could tackle. And, of course, he did it without any sheet music.

From that day forward, he played skillfully, not once reading a note of music; he played every song by ear. He had the ability to hear a song and play it within moments.

His ministry began as a young boy playing in the main services of his hometown church. Eventually, his gift opened the door to playing for the famous evangelist.

He obviously had a gift—a divine ability.

Another well-known gifted person, Akiane Kramarik, started drawing exceptionally at the age of four without any art lessons. By age six, she advanced to painting complex objects as well as her unique visions. At the age of eight, she painted the now famous *Prince of Peace*, a portrait that hangs in my office.

She obviously has a gift—a divine ability.

It's easy to wonder: Why do only some get gifts?

Or is that actually the case?

The question we should ask is this: Do some, or many, or even all of God's children receive gifts?

In what you've come to understand in your Christian life, what seems to be the best answer to the question just asked?

Among the fellow believers in Christ you know best, what are some gifts from God that seem especially strong in their lives? (Give Him thanks and praise for these!)

Do other believers you know seem, from your perspective, to be less gifted (or not gifted)? If so, in what ways might your perspective be too limited?

Let's look again at this chapter's opening verse of Scripture from the New Living Translation:

In his *grace*, God has given us different *gifts* for doing certain things well. (Romans 12:6)

We see two very important but distinct words in this verse. We've already discussed the first, *grace,* which is the Greek word *charis.* Let's add a *ma* onto *charis,* and we come up with another Greek word, *charisma*; it's the word for gifts in the previously mentioned verse. *Charisma* will be our focus.

In the years of studying Greek dictionaries and examining the context of how *charisma* is used in the New Testament, I've come up with a definition: *specific endowment of grace that empowers an individual with a special ability.*

This ability is actually a divine capability that God entrusts to an individual, and it always exceeds mainstream natural ability. Some gifts are clearly supernatural. On the other hand, others seem like natural human abilities, but in reality are extraordinary. Some gifts were given at birth, and others are given at a specific time at the Lord's word.

WRITING CHARISMA

Let me begin our exploration of *charisma* by using my life as an example. (I've written briefly about these personal stories in a previous book, *Driven by Eternity.*)

A *charisma* on my life is writing. Unless you've followed our ministry for years, you probably don't know that English, creative writing, and foreign language were my worst subjects in school. I sometimes think my English teachers passed me just so they wouldn't have to endure another year with me.

When our class was given a writing assignment of merely a page or two, it would take me hours to accomplish what should have been a quick task. I would write a sentence, stare at it for a few minutes, and with every passing moment, grow more and more disgusted by how choppy and pathetic it looked. Eventually, I'd crumple up the paper only to start the process again. I would repeat this cycle, wasting a lot of good paper, time, and mental energy. I recall occasions in which I'd write for an hour without completing the first two paragraphs.

If you doubt my personal assessment, then let me cite my SAT score. As you likely know, the SAT is a required examination prior to entering many colleges or universities. Back when I took the test, it covered two major areas—mathematics and verbal. The verbal was, in essence, an English exam testing reading and writing abilities. The highest you could score was 800 points. My score for the verbal was 370. (Yes, you read that correctly.) If you looked at the percentage, I scored a whopping 42 percent—an F on most grade curves. In all my travels during the past thirty-plus years, I've met only two individuals who scored lower than I did on the verbal SAT (one of whom only guessed at all the answers because he didn't want to take the test).

Now let's fast-forward to my early thirties. One summer morning in 1991, while I was out praying in a remote, deserted place, God spoke to me: *Son, I want you to write.*

I laughed within myself. *God, You must have so many of us sons and daughters on this earth that You're getting us confused with one another. You don't want me to write; just ask my English teachers from high school.*

I heard no response. Just silence.

I took His silence as agreement. I convinced myself I'd gotten out of it because there was no answer from Him. But my heart knew better. Ten months later, within two weeks of each other, two different women came to me from two different states and spoke the exact same words: "John Bevere, if you don't write what God is giving you to write, He'll give the messages to someone else, and one day you'll have to give an account for it."

When the second woman from Texas repeated what the first woman from Florida had said, the holy fear of God came on me, and I acted. Since this was in 1992, there were no iPads—just pen and paper. So I took a sheet of notebook paper and wrote CONTRACT in bold letters on the top. I then scribed:

Father, I can't write. So in order to obey You, I need grace! If I do write, then my request is that every word would be inspired by Your Spirit and would be flooded with Your anointing. I ask that the words would change men, women, children, churches, cities, and nations. I vow in advance to give You all the honor, praise, glory, and thanksgiving. I seal this contract (covenant) with You in Jesus's mighty name. Your son and servant, John Bevere

Let's fast-forward again to today, almost thirty years later. Currently, I've written over twenty-five books, and they number in the tens of millions of copies. Many of them have been on several bestseller lists in both general and Christian markets, both nationally and internationally. The books are in over 125 languages all over the world, and in several nations they are the most published books in both secular and Christian categories.

In almost every book I've written, I hadn't previously heard, read, or thought of 20 to 30 percent of the written content. The words came to me while typing on the keyboard. I recall several times being in either my home office or hotel room and becoming overwhelmed by what was being typed out. A few of those times I jumped up shouting, "Wow, that's so good!"

You may ask: How could you say that? That's prideful.

My answer is that I know where this content came from—*not me*. I fully believe my name is on these books only because I was the first person outside of heaven to get to read them. I know the words came from the Holy Spirit. It's not unlike the apostle Paul, who also sounded a little arrogant when he penned the words, "I have worked harder than any of the other apostles." Doesn't that sound a bit like someone who's competitive, egotistical, or even narcissistic? However, we know from Scripture that Paul was bragging on God's gift of grace rather than his own ability.

I personally believe that when God spoke to me in prayer that summer morning, the *charisma* to write was *released* into my life. But it wasn't until I made the decision to obey God that it was *activated* in my life. Some would argue this point, but permit me to say up front that it's not important enough to debate. I realize I could be wrong in my belief, so let me give voice to what others would counter.

Some would contend that the gift was given the moment I was born again in 1979. I can't address this discussion by experience because I didn't try writing anything between 1979 and the day I wrote the contract in 1992. One thing I can say for certain: I wasn't born with this gift, like the pianist I described earlier in this chapter. His example does, however, settle the point that some gifts are given right from conception. For example, we know from Scripture that John the Baptist was filled with the Spirit of God (who gives gifts) even before his birth, because he recognized the living Christ in Mary's womb while he himself was still in his mother Elizabeth's womb (Luke 1:41). Thirty years later, when Jesus came to be baptized by John in the Jordan River (John 1:29), this same gift in John was able to recognize Jesus before anyone else did.

On the other hand, some gifts come later. Saul, son of Kish, was a man who did not begin his life prophesying. He didn't prophesy until his young manhood when Samuel anointed him with oil to be the first king of Israel. Samuel stated that Saul would later see a group of men who would be playing instruments and prophesying. To quote Samuel directly, "At that time the Spirit of the LORD will come powerfully upon you, and you will prophesy with them. You will be changed into a different person" (1 Samuel 10:6).

In looking at these two different testimonies from Scripture, we clearly see how some gifts are given right from a mother's womb and others are given later.

Pause for a moment to express to God your trust in His perfect timing in this matter of revealing and manifesting to you His calling and gifting.

Also, take a moment to read and ponder James 1:17—and thank God for His goodness and perfection, as well as for what is good and perfect about His unique gifts to you.

SPEAKING CHARISMA

Another *charisma* on my life is public speaking. Sharing about this gift will strengthen our understanding.

A very memorable occasion for me was the first time my wife, Lisa, heard me speak the Word of God in a service setting. To put it mildly, it was a colossal failure, and I'm not exaggerating. She fell sound asleep within the first five minutes of my message and continued in and out of sleep the entire time. The message was awful. In fact, her best friend, Amy, sitting next to her, fell into such a deep sleep that I saw her drooling from her wide-open mouth while she was in la-la land. Honestly, I was a pathetic public communicator.

At that time I was serving in my local church as an assistant to my pastor and his wife. (Our church was large—with over four hundred paid staff members—and had a nationwide influence.) My post was to take care of my pastor's family's needs and all guest ministers who came to our church. No gray area here; my kingdom responsibility was not the oracle gift, but rather to serve behind the scenes. (I'll speak of this in a later chapter.) Yet I was trying to start my own ministry because God had shown me that I would proclaim His Word to the nations of the world.

My error then was this: I was doing it in my own strength. Also, I was still in the season of primarily serving another person's ministry—being "faithful [to] what is another man's" (Luke 16:12 NKJV). I did use all my free time and energy to produce, package, and market my messages. (It would have been so much better if I'd focused on being a better servant and husband to my wife during that time, but we sometimes have to learn from the school of hard knocks.)

In short, I was birthing an "Ishmael ministry." Why do I call it that? There's a parallel in Scripture. God told Abram (Abraham), who was seventy-five years of age, that he would be father to a promised son, and that through him he would eventually become the father of many nations. Ten years after the promise was made, there was still no baby, and he was now eighty-five years old. So Abraham and his wife, Sarai, devised a plan to "help" God bring to pass what He'd promised. From this vain human effort, Ishmael was born. Hence, I identify this type of endeavor as an Ishmael ministry.

It's hard to believe, but some people actually gave me money. I sold them on my self-appointed mission, Bevere Ministries. Our tagline was "Reaching the World through His Marvelous Light." I'm laughing at my stupidity and immaturity as I'm typing this. Our Ishmael ministry's first four-part cassette-tape series even contained the message that put my wife and her best friend to sleep. How many others were lulled into sleep and drooling as they listened to that tape series? I shudder thinking about it.

Yet the story gets worse. During this time my hero was the great evangelist T. L. Osborn, who's now in heaven. He and his wife led over fifty million people into salvation in their lifetime. I wanted to pattern my preaching after his. I would listen to his messages for hours on end, learning his voice pitch, inflections, teachings, power statements, and even his humor. I wasn't even an original boring preacher but an awful copy of someone else.

T. L. was a master communicator. When he spoke at our church, everyone listened intently to every word. Once he was telling about a great move of God in one of their massive crusades in Africa. While sharing with us, he was so overwhelmed by the notable miracles that he excitedly exclaimed, "Wow!" Then he paused—leaving us all on the edge of our seats—and in jest he blurted out, "That word is so amazing that it's the same backward: Wow!" Everyone laughed; it came out in a way that only he could make happen.

Being silly and naive, I picked that one up and started saying "wow" regularly. I did it the same way T. L. had done in that one unique incident. The only problem? No one ever laughed. But of course, I didn't get it.

After falling on my face time and again in my personal strivings, I eventually broke. Then an amazing change happened. I once again started to enjoy my current position of serving.

After falling flat on my face time and time again in my personal strivings, I eventually broke. But then an amazing change happened. I once again started to enjoy my current position of serving. I now gave my free time to my marriage and friends. Life was fuller, richer, and more complete once the striving was past. Once I found true contentment, it became obvious that all my efforts were futile, making it easy to scrap Bevere Ministries. I knew God would bring forth what He'd promised one day, but it wouldn't happen by my initiation.

Within months of getting to this place of peace and serenity, you guessed it: God promoted me. I was asked to be the youth pastor of one of the fastest growing churches in the United States.

I'll never forget the first Sunday. Our church's pastor was world-renowned. People would line up every Sunday for over an hour in the hot sun to get a good seat in our auditorium, which was packed every service. Visitors from other states and nations were always attending our services.

The service was in full swing. We'd had a magnificent time of worship. One of the first things our pastor did when taking the platform was to inform the church of the new youth pastor—me. To my surprise, he then asked me to come up for a couple of minutes and address this Sunday morning crowd—which was twenty-eight hundred people!

At that moment, unbeknownst to me, my wife panicked. I probably would have, too, had I taken time to think about it. *Shock!* Lisa dreaded the outcome, because from past experiences she knew what was coming. How would we recover from this looming disaster? It would probably be the last time most in the sanctuary would hear me, because after this I'd certainly never be asked to speak to the main service again. All these fears mounted in her as I walked up to the platform. She told me afterward that she anxiously prayed that I wouldn't do my T. L. Osborn imitation, especially my "default awkward moment" routine of saying "wow" backward.

Once I was on the platform, our senior pastor turned over the microphone. Within sixty seconds, the entire church was on their feet cheering, applauding, and shouting in excitement about what I was saying. I spoke for four to five minutes, with the twenty-eight hundred people on their feet the entire time. I then handed the microphone back to my pastor and returned to my seat. I shook for the next five minutes from the adrenaline, or the presence of God, or probably both. My wife was stunned, in disbelief of what had just happened. She told me after the service, "John, I thought, *Who just inhabited my husband's body?*"

We'd lived in Texas during my first ministry position, but this new church was in Florida. For years, Lisa described the change this way to those who asked: "John turned into another man the moment we crossed the Florida line." Her statement was much like the one made regarding Saul, once the gift of God came on his life (1 Samuel 10:6).

Ever since that time, I've been preaching, teaching, and speaking before audiences, and most of the time I've done so with ease. (I'll describe the difficult times in a later chapter.) It's no longer a labor to do so. Speaking comes without the striving I experienced in my Ishmael days. The differences between the Ishmael and Isaac times have been as vast as night and day.

Let's fast-forward another eight to ten years from that first Sunday in Florida. By this time, Messenger International was well established. We were doing some spring cleaning in our garage. While going through boxes and tubs, we came upon the original masters of that tape series, including the message that had lulled Lisa and her friend to sleep. Without hesitating, I turned to throw it in the garbage bin.

Suddenly I heard the Holy Spirit address me: *Son, do not throw away that master tape.*

I quickly countered, *Why not? It's awful. No one should ever have to listen to that message again. It should be destroyed.*

Again, I heard, *Don't do it.*

Knowing full well I'd heard from God, I asked Him why.

The Lord answered so clearly in my heart: *It's protection for you.*

Protection?

Then came this wisdom: *Son, I always want you to know how terrible a communicator you are without Me.*

With each passing year, I recognize more fully the "protection" factor. In the past three decades, the gift has operated powerfully, producing an abundance of fruit. In countless incidents, I've witnessed atmospheres shift, eruptions of praise after revelations, countless lives saved, and the manifestation of numerous miracles. Many have commented on how their lives or churches have permanently changed. With all this fruit, I might have easily thought I had something to do with it—but I can honestly say with the apostle Paul, "It was not I but God who was working through me by his grace" (1 Corinthians 15:10). In all these years, I haven't forgotten how awful I was without God's *charisma*.

ARE YOU GIFTED?

Writing and speaking are two of the God-given gifts that are upon my life to serve and build others. Can you relate to the struggles I experienced? Perhaps they make your own struggles in locating the *charisma* on your life seem more normal. Or, maybe as you read these accounts, your frustration has grown because you're thinking, *I don't have any gifts.* I assure you that you *do* have gifts—and this will become clear in the next two chapters.

I promised to answer the question of whether some, or many, or even all of God's children receive gifts. The immediate answer is yes! And I'll prove this from Scripture shortly. Not only will this question be thoroughly covered, but before the end of this book, you'll have a firm grasp on how to locate your *charisma*, develop and operate in it, and thus multiply your effectiveness in building God's kingdom.

REFLECTION FOR RENEWAL

In this chapter, what statements or Scripture passages seemed most meaningful for you?

How would you restate them in your own words? (Personalize your answer as a prayer of response to God.)

What are your thoughts about what God wants you to do now in response to what you've seen and reflected upon in this chapter?

ASSESS YOURSELF HONESTLY

Be honest in your evaluation of yourselves.

ROMANS 12:3

N ow that I've shared the struggle of having to both identify and walk in the *charisma* on my life, I want to briefly share what I'm *not* gifted at.

It would be impossible to make an exhaustive list—there are just too many examples. First on the list is singing and playing musical instruments. Anytime I sing at home, my wife and children ask me politely but firmly to sing to myself.

During high school athletics, while in the locker room showers, I sang only once. The reaction was intense; a handful of guys in unison shouted at me to zip it, and one guy in jest threw a shampoo bottle my way.

My parents gave all of us Bevere children piano lessons. My teacher was a professional pianist, quite renowned in our hometown. She'd made a career of teaching piano and was good at it. But after four hard years of lessons, she approached my parents and pleaded with them to allow me to quit. I was that bad.

As time passed, I thought maybe I was just bad at the piano. So a few years later I tried a different instrument. After we bought a classical guitar, we found a well-known teacher. He was patient and worked meticulously with me. I gave it my full effort and practiced diligently. But I struggled. It took another year and a half of lessons before I could admit I just didn't have musical ability.

What's the long-term outcome? Let's just say that for me, nothing has happened musically through the years. It's completely different from the story of my writing. At no time has any musical ability suddenly manifested in my life.

SELF-EVALUATION

I could carry on listing the things I'm not gifted at, but you get the point. It's safe to say that we all tend to know what we don't do well. Sometimes I wish it were as easy to identify our gifts as it is to pinpoint what we're *not* gifted at.

With that in mind, let's move on to more of Paul's instructions:

> Because of the privilege and authority God has given me, I give each of you this warning: Don't think you are better than you really are. Be honest in your evaluation of yourselves, measuring yourselves by the faith God has given us. Just as our bodies have many parts and each part has a special function, so it is with Christ's body. We are many parts of one body, and we all belong to each other. In his grace, God has given us different gifts for doing certain things well. (Romans 12:3–6)

Paul begins by positioning what he's about to write as a *warning*. Let's isolate and emphasize this warning:

> Don't think you are better than you really are. Be honest in your evaluation of yourselves. (12:3)

Here we're told to do an honest self-evaluation. Of what? Of the gifts God has placed on our lives in *real time*.

Why do I use the words *real time*? Simple. Think of the biblical example used earlier. Saul's honest assessment before he met Samuel would have been, "I cannot prophesy." This would have been true and accurate for Saul at the time. However, once he met Samuel and the gift of God came on his life, his honest assessment would have changed to this: "I can prophesy."

Oh, how I wish I'd read this verse about honest self-assessment more closely when I was trying to birth my Ishmael ministry. If I'd been honest with myself, I would have acknowledged back then that I was out of my element in public speaking, though I was gifted to serve my pastor. In my natural ability, however, I was trying to bring forth what had been clearly spoken to me, revealed in prayer, and prophesied by leaders of *what would come*. It wasn't *real time* yet, and I wasn't ready—which was obvious, had I only heeded this command in Scripture and done an honest assessment. I could have saved a lot of time, resources, and energy. I also could have been more effective in what I *was* gifted to do *in that time period*.

In real time—this present season of your life—what's your current understanding of the most important things God has called and gifted you to do?

Regarding different gifts, Paul's words are crystal clear: "Just as our bodies have many parts and each part has a special function, so it is with Christ's body" (Romans 12:4–5). Simply consider your own body: Your fingers can do things your nose can't; your nose can do things your ears can't; your ears can do things your stomach can't; your stomach can do things your liver can't; and the list goes on.

Here's the main point:

- Happy and blessed are those who know their gifts and operate in them.
- Miserable and stressed is anyone who tries to operate in someone else's gifts.

What experiences have you had while expending effort and action in an area you later realized was outside your gifting? What was that like for you emotionally? What lessons did you draw from those experiences?

Wouldn't it be strange if one morning you woke up and your thumb said, "I've had it! Mouth, you've been speaking for years, but I'll do the talking today." That would be ridiculous. The thumb has no capability to produce sound the way the mouth can. However, the thumb does have unique abilities the mouth doesn't have. Suppose the mouth were to say, "I want to type on the computer today!" Again, ridiculous.

Can you fully trust God's unique calling upon your life?

To answer that question, consider the wisdom the Holy Spirit gave to David about the super intimate way in which God knows every person in His family. Read about this in Psalm 139, especially verses 1–6 and 13–16. Reflect richly on these verses; what specific reasons do you see there for having full confidence in God's perfect design of both you and your life's calling?

Finally, use the last two verses in Psalm 139 as your personal prayer, seeking God's direction for your lifelong faithfulness to His calling.

ONLY ON THE PLATFORM?

Here's the next important question: Why do we put such a premium on the "platform gifts"? Why do we think ministers who speak and worship leaders who lead congregations possess the ultimate gifts? Listen to Paul's words to the Corinthian church on this subject: "Some parts of the body that seem weakest and least important are actually the most necessary" (1 Corinthians 12:22).

Let me give a practical example. Have you ever noticed that legs get attention? People make statements such as, "She's got some great legs," or, "Wow, his calf muscles are huge!" When I was a teenager, I recall my dad doing something completely out of character one day. Although he was very conservative, disciplined, and quiet—practically never calling attention to himself—he blurted out, "Son, you have a good-looking set of legs."

Shocked, I just stared at him with no response and a curious smile, wondering where he was going with this. He continued, "Do you want to know why? It's because *I've* got a good set of legs. You inherited them from me."

I was so caught off guard, I didn't know whether to fall over laughing or simply acknowledge his statement. I just laughed and said, "Thanks, Dad, for giving me a good set of legs."

It's true; legs get attention. But have you considered how people can live without legs? I know a man who lost one leg in a car accident, but he still lives a normal life.

The liver, however, is a different story. No one can live without a liver. It's an extremely important organ, much more important than a leg. But have you ever heard anyone say, "Wow, that's a gorgeous liver you have"? It won't happen.

Listen to Paul's words again: "Some parts of the body that seem weakest and least important are actually the most necessary" (1 Corinthians 12:22).

Again I ask: Why do we put such a premium on the platform gifts? They're highly visible parts, and they're necessary—but according to the Word of God, they're not the most important.

My friend Stan (from the first chapter) has a gift of reaching people in the business world, as well as earning and giving financially. In our established church culture, his gift seems less valuable than a platform gift, and this gets communicated nonverbally. The typical underlying message in the church is this: "Those on the platform are the chosen ones who really have a calling on their life."

Think about it. When someone says they have a calling on their life, everyone immediately thinks of a pastor, worship leader, youth leader, Christian author, missionary, or the like. Upon hearing this statement, very few would say, "He's called to the medical field, and he's discovering new ways to cure cancer," or, "She's in government to establish laws to protect the advancement of God's kingdom," or, "He's in education, seeding young minds with the knowledge and wisdom of God," or, "She's called to the marketplace, to reach the lost there and to finance the building of the kingdom."

The consequences of our narrow mindset on gifts are evident. Stan had been in church for years without realizing he's just as called as I am. His God-given abilities didn't seem as important to him because of this unspoken understanding that "church-related" gifts are more crucial than others. This needs to change! We're all called, and we all carry unique gifts that are needed to fulfill our kingdom assignment.

Here's the fuller context of what Paul said about this to the Corinthian church:

> Our bodies have many parts, and God has put each part just where he wants it. How strange a body would be if it had only one part! Yes, there are many parts, but only one body. The eye can never say to the hand, "I don't need you." The head can't say to the feet, "I don't need you." In fact, some parts of the body that seem weakest and least important are actually the most necessary. And the parts we regard as less honorable are those we clothe with the greatest care. So we carefully protect those parts that should not be seen, while the more honorable parts do not require this special care. So God has put the body together such that extra honor and care are given to those parts that have less dignity. This makes for harmony among the members, so that all the members care for each other. (1 Corinthians 12:18–25)

Maybe the reason we honor church-related gifts more than others is because we limit Paul's discussion to church or conference settings. In such an atmosphere, it's obvious that preaching or teaching gifts are more in demand. But kingdom work happens everywhere, so this is another paradigm that must shift radically. The Greek word for church is *ekklēsias*, which means "called out." The Greek dictionary definition adds this: "the called people, or those called out or assembled in the public affairs of a free state; the body of free citizens called together by a herald."[1]

We are the church, and we're equipped with giftings to build the kingdom wherever we are —twenty-four hours a day, seven days a week, 365 days a year.

Are we the church only when we're gathered within a building? Are we the church only when we pray, worship, preach, or minister together? This paradigm causes people to act one way in this type of setting and revert to a different behavior when out in society. We *are* the church, and we're equipped with giftings to build the kingdom wherever we are—twenty-four hours a day, seven days a week, 365 days a year.

I met recently with a multibillionaire. He was conducting what he called his "God tour." He and his team had flown to various cities and attended churches and conferences to meet with certain ministers. His goal was to be sharpened and further equipped for his work. My meeting with him was set up in advance by a good friend. It occurred in Dallas, where I was speaking at a conference. As it turned out, this man and I had a great three-hour lunch, and I came away feeling I got more out of it than he did.

He shared that he'd floundered in the business world early in his career, but the day came when his eyes were opened. The enlightenment began when he questioned why kingdom activity should happen only in church or conference settings—why not everywhere? He knew he was called to the marketplace, but why was he conducting himself in that arena in a way that was no different from how unbelievers act? Nothing separated him from the world.

He determined he would "walk with God" in the marketplace and listen to the Holy Spirit's voice, just as a minister would on a platform. In essence, he faced squarely the calling question, and he decided he was just as called by God as any pastor. He then identified his God-given gifts and determined to purposefully operate in them. He would listen to God's voice in his quiet times, as well as in business meetings. Sure enough, God gave him words of knowledge and wisdom for his marketplace affairs.

For this man, the results are evident: He's no longer floundering! He shared some of the specific words he received from God, which often seemed insignificant—but he was determined to obey, even if the divine instructions went against conventional business wisdom and were uncomfortable to follow. He related the questionings, raised eyebrows, concerns, and even resistance he encountered from both clients and his own team members. But the fruit of his steadfast confidence in the words from God proved to be worth billions. I was mesmerized by the miraculous stories he shared.

Wherever you might find yourself as a result of the Lord's calling and gifting, He offers rich assurance that He will clearly and continually lead you. Experience this as you come before Him and meditate on some or all of these passages: Psalms 23:3; 25:9; 31:3; 73:24; 139:10; Proverbs 3:5–6; Isaiah 30:21; 42:16; 48:17; John 8:12; 2 Corinthians 2:14.

DISCIPLES OF NATIONS

If we can flip this cultural mindset about gifting in today's church, what will the outcome be? If we effectively communicate to all who hear our messages that *every person is called, gifted, and valuable to the building of the kingdom*—what will happen? That's easy to answer. Everyone would work with the purpose and passion of Billy Graham, Oral Roberts, Mother Teresa, and the apostle Paul. I observed this purpose and passion in the multibillionaire in our meeting. He knew his mission and the importance of his God-given gifts to accomplish it.

This is the paradigm we must have for nations to be discipled. But let's dig a little deeper into this point. In Matthew 28:19, Jesus doesn't say, "Make disciples of all church attendees"; rather, He commands us to "make disciples of all the nations." The Greek word for nations is *ethnos*, which is defined as "a body of persons united by kinship, culture, and common traditions."[2] This certainly includes actual nations, tribes, territories, and ethnic groups. But it can also encompass persons with a particular commonality—such as cyclists, actors, physicians, business owners, pilots, lawyers, stay-at-home moms, government workers, athletes, and many more. The list is virtually endless. We're to make disciples of the men and women in all these different circles of life.

What are some commonality groups you would most like to see impacted by the kingdom of God (regardless of whether you have particular influence in these circles)?

Ask God to be at work in these groupings and to reveal evidence of Himself.

Let's take it one step further. Jesus doesn't say, "Make disciples of the people in all nations." He says, "Make disciples of all the nations." It's important to catch the difference. Through the Word of God, we're to foster change in *how* these different circles operate. Of course, this occurs first and foremost by reaching the individual people of these different circles. However, it goes deeper. Not only the people, but also their cultural patterns and modes of operation are to be baptized (immersed) in the ways of the Father, Son, and Holy Spirit. We are to assist in transforming the thinking of those involved in the marketplace, government, healthcare, athletics, and so forth. This is just the tip of the iceberg.

Consider Zacchaeus. He's described as a chief tax collector—no doubt one of the best in the region. In essence, he was head of the mafia in the area. He most likely was hated by the people because he did what most tax collectors did: leveraged his position for selfish gain. He probably robbed, swindled, cheated, intimidated, and dominated the citizens. He was a notoriously influential figure, so his example most likely flowed down through the ranks.

I've witnessed this in a few of the nations I've visited. The leader of the nation is corrupt, and he requires his officials to slip money to him under the table. This same behavior trickles down. Now the immigration official at the airport needs a bribe, or else you can't get his approval to leave the country.

Back to Zacchaeus. Jesus called him by name and—interestingly—spoke these words to him: "Quick, come down! I must be a guest in your home today" (Luke 19:5).

There in his own home, Zacchaeus stood before the Master and responded, "I will give half my wealth to the poor, Lord, and if I have cheated people on their taxes, I will give them back four times as much!" (Luke 19:8).

What happened in that region in regard to tax collecting? The chief role model's mode of operations shifted from dark, worldly techniques to kingdom practices. This area of business and government would now be conducted much more closely to the way heaven operates. A shift in society had occurred. This change didn't happen during a church service, nor did Jesus preach a message in a conference, convincing Zacchaeus to be a follower. It happened in the city center. Zacchaeus had an encounter with Jesus, and his methods of operation suddenly changed.

This should happen every time people encounter us in our different "nations"—the circles of influence we're called to—because this same Jesus lives in us.

> How would you best describe the "nation"—the circle or circles of influence—where you believe God has called you to live?
>
> How might you be used by Him to have a spiritual impact on the people in these circles?

I'm currently coaching a former NFL football player who has a large social media audience of bodybuilders. He's instructing these bodybuilders in such a way that the culture of the kingdom of heaven is flowing into this nation (*ethnos* group) regardless of whether this man's followers are yet committed to Jesus's lordship. He's speaking to them in a way that demonstrates kingdom ways and methods.

Our gifts aren't only for the gathering of saints in a building, although they are valid and important. I certainly don't want to downplay our gatherings. The intention here is to expand our view of the operation of God's gifts. If we're called to labor outside the church, which is the case for most of us, we're called to operate supernaturally through our gifts within our circle of influence—among our *ethnos* group. If you've separated the secular from the sacred, that mentality needs to change.

> What are your present thoughts about whether your own gifting from God should operate primarily within the church or outside the church?
>
> What factors and reasons contribute to your conclusions about this?

When you walk into the room, no matter where it is—the hospital ward for your work as a surgeon or nurse, the public school classroom for your teaching, the factory for your skilled labor as a machinist, and so forth—you've been gifted to bring the sacred into that atmosphere and to disciple it in the name of the Father, Son, and Holy Spirit. You have divine backing and authority to bring heaven to earth, just as Jesus did with Zacchaeus and others. You're called to multiply the kingdom's mode of operation throughout your arena of influence.

Doesn't this make going to the office or school so much more of an adventure?

Do you feel a sense of adventure about what the Lord has called you to do? What about where He has called you to do it? If so, express to the Lord your sincere gratitude for this.

If you don't feel that sense of adventure, what questions or doubts are blocking this? Talk to the Lord about your feelings.

REFLECTION FOR RENEWAL

In this chapter, what statements or Scripture passages seemed most meaningful for you?

How would you restate them in your own words? (Personalize your answer as a prayer of response to God.)

What are your thoughts about what God wants you to do now in response to what you've seen and reflected upon in this chapter?

STEWARDS

Let a man so consider us, as servants of Christ
and stewards of the mysteries of God.

1 CORINTHIANS 4:1 NKJV

We've showcased the words *grace* and *gift*; now we'll turn our focus toward *stewardship*. After we establish an understanding of that term, we can join all three of these words together from Scripture to discover a clear mandate for our lives.

Merriam-Webster defines stewardship as "the careful and responsible management of something entrusted to one's care." The Greek word for steward in the above verse is *oikonomos*, and it's defined as "one who has the authority and responsibility for something—one who is in charge of, one who is responsible for, administrator, manager."[1]

From both definitions, we derive three clear aspects of stewardship:

- overseeing what belongs to another;
- carrying authority to manage what has been entrusted;
- being responsible and giving an account to the owner.

God created and owns everything. Psalm 24:1 declares, "The earth is the LORD's, and all its fullness" (NKJV). This makes us stewards over everything in this realm. We're to manage the earth—all land, water, air, resources, animals, fish, and fowl. We're responsible to care for the good of human beings spiritually, emotionally, intellectually, and physically. This includes all godly and beneficial knowledge, wisdom, and understanding. In essence, we're responsible for *everything* on earth, both seen and unseen.

This comprehensive idea of stewardship can be hard for us to grasp and buy in to. It's easy for negative attitudes such as pride, self-centeredness, greed, and entitlement to creep in and block our understanding and acceptance. Allow the teaching in the following passages to help you guard against such wrong and negative thinking: John 3:27; 1 Corinthians 4:7; James 1:16–17.

Let's drill down to the precise usage of stewardship in Paul's statement in 1 Corinthians 4:1. He writes of being "stewards of the mysteries of God" (NKJV). The New Living Translation of this verse says we "have been *put in charge* of explaining God's mysteries." One of the gifts (*charismas*) on Paul's life was revelation; it was the ability to communicate mysteries—hidden truths that had not yet been revealed. Therefore, the exact *stewardship* he refers to is not managing money, time, or resources (all valid stewardships), but rather managing the gift (*charisma*) on his life. Does this also apply to us?

Peter writes: "As each one has received a *gift*, minister it to one another, as good *stewards* of the manifold *grace* of God" (1 Peter 4:10 NKJV). All our highlighted words are found in this one verse (gift: *charisma*; stewards: *oikonomos*; and grace: *charis*). Peter informs us, no differently than Paul, of our entrusted stewardship of *charisma*. Much is revealed in this one statement, so we should examine it carefully.

Notice how Peter said "each one" has received a gift. It's important to point out that he didn't say "each minister," "each pastor," "each worship leader," or any other oracle ministry gift, but rather "each one." If you're born again, you have a gift or gifts that have been imparted and entrusted to you. This is Scripture's answer to our question from two chapters ago. To reiterate, *these gifts you have are specific endowments of grace that empower you with special abilities.*

To show the importance of your gifts, let's use Paul's attitude as a template. He regarded his stewardship seriously—quite seriously, in fact. A little later in this letter to the Corinthians, he writes:

If I preach the gospel, I have nothing to boast of, for necessity is laid upon me; yes, *woe is me* if I do not preach the gospel! For if I do this willingly, I have a reward; but if against my will, I have been *entrusted with a stewardship.* (1 Corinthians 9:16–17 NKJV)

Immediately my attention is captured by the phrase "woe is me." These are strong words, stronger than most of us comprehend. The Greek word for woe is *ouaí*, defined as "disaster, horror."[2] Another dictionary lists its meaning as "interjection of grief or indignation."[3] Each occurrence of this word in the New Testament implies a serious and terrifying judgment that awaits those it's ascribed to. When Paul says, "Woe is me," it's akin to calling a curse upon himself. This should get our attention at once. To neglect our God-given gifts is a severe matter.

Paul knew God had entrusted him with something of great value. Here's the far-reaching truth: If he didn't administer it properly, then others would not experience the benefit of what God intended for them to receive and would suffer loss instead. Paul knew the gift wasn't given *for* him; it was given *through* him *to* others. In other words, he carried what God wanted others to have. This was the reason for the severity behind declaring "woe" onto himself for neglecting his stewardship.

Let's revert to you and me. There are two interesting points to highlight.

First, Paul's gift was a "noticeable" gift. Recall that God has chosen less overt gifts to be held in greater honor than those that are more prominent. If Paul treated his noticeable gift with such a high degree of seriousness, we should never devalue the gift God has placed on us, especially if that gift isn't noticeable.

Even more important is the second takeaway: The gifts of God on your life are not for you; they're for *others* to benefit *through* you. You carry what God wants others to have.

The gift of writing I've received is not for me, but for you; the gift of speaking is not for me, but for those I speak to; the gift of leading is not for me, but for those I lead—and so forth.

The gifts of God on your life are not for you; they're for others to benefit through you. You carry what God wants others to have.

Your gifts from God are for others, not for yourself. With this truth in mind, ponder what's at stake if you neglect your stewardship of these gifts. Try making a list of the possible or likely negative consequences of such neglect on your part.

WE CHOOSE HOW TO USE THE GIFT

We can use the gift on our life well, or we can misuse it. The choice is ours. The gift will still operate even if it's not used according to its original divine intent to build the kingdom. Adolf Hitler was a gifted leader who could have led his nation in a way that would have benefited millions of Germans, Jews, Russians, Frenchmen, Britons, and so forth. Did he use this gift for God's glory—or to benefit only himself and those he favored? Did he use his gift to bring harm—to plunder, devastate, torture, and put to death millions of Jews and others? Did he misuse the gift of leadership on his life? The answers to these questions need no discussion; they're crystal clear.

Let me also discuss two other well-known personalities from the past who may not be as obvious. First, Whitney Houston, an artist who had one of the greatest voices I've heard in my lifetime. The touch of God was evident upon her life. When Whitney sang, all who heard her were deeply stirred. She was ethereal, seemingly angelic, and quite powerful.

A second example would be Freddie Mercury, lead singer of the rock group Queen. He had the ability to move entire stadiums with his gifts of composing and singing. His ability was far from common, and some might even say supernatural. He could arouse a crowd to follow his lead in almost any setting. Years after his death, his songs are still sung widely.

Did either Whitney or Freddie manage their gifts well? No doubt, many would argue that they did. But let's view this question through Jesus's words:

Wisdom is shown to be right by its *results*. (Matthew 11:19)

And again:

Wisdom is shown to be right by the *lives of those who follow it*. (Luke 7:35)

Let's examine the fruit of these two amazing entertainers, in both the short-term and long-term results of their stewardship. Did Whitney use her gift to lead people into the presence of God? After listening to her sing, were her audiences moved toward godliness? Did her songs strengthen marriage covenants, or did they foster discontent by creating an unrealistic romantic expectation? Did Freddie use his gift to move his audiences toward righteousness? Did he compel people to honor their Creator?

How did Whitney and Freddie depart this earth? Are their legacies enduring or fleeting? Will those legacies last forever, or will they perish with this world?

Jesus encourages us to examine the outcome—so if you know their stories, I'll let you determine the results of Whitney's and Freddie's stewardship. However, the ultimate examination will come in the presence of our Creator. Each will give an account at the judgment.

I realize that if you're a fan of either Whitney or Freddie, you may be uncomfortable with this discussion. But let's ask a question that will shed more light on how their stewardship will be assessed at the judgment. Let's view their legacies from the vantage point of ten million years from now. How will Whitney and Freddie look back at how they managed their God-given gifts? Examining the eternal perspective may change your original view.

Life is all about perspective. If we view something through the lens of eighty years, we'll see it one way. However, if we view it with an eternal perspective, things look different.

Consider this scenario: You're invited to have dinner at a cafeteria. You pay one price, then eat all you desire. There's a large dessert buffet filled with all kinds of delicious offerings. If you look at it with a one-day perspective, what will you do? You might want to try some of every dessert on the table. What if

Life is all about perspective. If we view it with an eternal perspective, things look different.

you look at it with a one-year perspective? You'd probably eat only one dessert, or maybe none. Why? Because you don't want an upset stomach tomorrow morning, ten pounds of fat added to your body by next week, and compromised long-term health.

When we look at Whitney's and Freddie's fruit from the eternal perspective, the wisdom of their stewardship becomes clearer.

It's nonthreatening to speak of Adolf Hitler, or even Freddie Mercury or Whitney Houston. But here's the reality: You and I will also have to give an account of our entrusted gifts when we stand before the Judge. Our gifts will be seen through the perspective of eternity, and not just seventy or eighty years. Our gifts will be examined in the light of God's eternal Word that commissions us to build His kingdom. Will our legacy be enduring—or will it pass away with the world's system?

> What helps you most to have an eternal perspective of your life? And for you, what distractions or temptations can make it easy to lose that perspective?

A CLOSE LOOK AT MOTIVATION

Let me restate what was discussed in the first chapter. You can steward your gift at any given time in one of three ways:

- You can use it to build the kingdom.
- You can use it to benefit yourself.
- You can neglect it by not using it at all.

It's important to amplify the second point, which can be deceiving. Many may think they're benefiting others, even for the kingdom's sake, yet they are operating with the motive of personal gain.

To help you be more alert to how you might be motivated to serve others for the sake of your own benefit, think over the truths and principles (and their implications) you see in the following passages: Philippians 2:3–4; Matthew 11:19; Romans 12:3; 12:9–10; 1 Corinthians 13:1–5; James 3:13–18.

I unknowingly fell into this motivation of personal benefit. Years ago, in my early days of ministry, I consistently spoke nice and pleasing words to everyone on our team and at church, and to anyone else in my world. I'd utter happy and pleasant statements, even if they weren't true. Word got back to me of how kind and loving people thought I was. These compliments certainly encouraged my behavior.

One day in prayer, I heard this question from God: People say you're a loving, caring, and kind person, don't they?

I would normally take His words as an affirmation, but the way the Holy Spirit spoke didn't seem to be going this direction. I cautiously replied, Yes, they do.

He immediately asked, Do you know why you say only nice things to people?

Even more cautiously, I responded, Why?

His answer: Because you fear their rejection. Who's the focus of your love—you or them?

Knowing my motives were completely and utterly exposed, I admitted my selfish focus.

Then He said, If you really loved people, you would tell them the truth—even at the risk of being rejected.

Can we misuse the gifts of God on our lives in a similar way? It may appear to others that our gifts are being used to build God's kingdom—but in reality, are they being used for self-seeking purposes? Once again I'll use myself as an example, then look also at scriptural examples.

Normally, I don't get a direct word from the Lord as far as what to speak about at a conference or church service, but I always listen to my heart for the leading of the Spirit. Sometimes, however, I definitely get specific words from the Lord regarding what to speak on. I refer here to one of those few occasions.

I was scheduled to minister at a conference in the Midwest. When I awoke in my hotel room on my scheduled day to speak, I undoubtedly heard the Holy Spirit tell me to minister on *The Bait of Satan*—a book I wrote in 1994 about overcoming offenses and freely forgiving those who've hurt us.

All day I wrestled with His instructions. *The Bait of Satan* message had been out for several years. It was a bestselling book, and because I'd preached its message all over the country for an extended season, a lot of people had already heard it. What made this direction from the Spirit even more difficult was that I was in the process of working on a new manuscript. When you're in the midst of writing about something for months, those particular truths are the strongest and freshest in your heart. Bottom line: I really didn't want to speak the older message. But I had a direct word from the Holy Spirit.

Upon arriving at the auditorium that evening, I was informed by the conference coordinators that people had traveled long distances to hear me. I supposed there was a good chance that a healthy percentage of these travelers had already read *The Bait of Satan*, and I shuddered to think of them getting only a repeat message.

Upon walking into the auditorium, I noticed the atmosphere was energized. The anticipation of the people was obvious—which made obeying the Lord's instructions I'd received that morning even more difficult. Somehow, I just didn't want to disappoint the people—so I yielded to the pressure and decided to speak the "fresh" message.

I was delighted with how it went. The preaching was strong, and the people responded enthusiastically. Some even stood to their feet, affirming the strong points I was making. It looked as if I'd "gotten away with it"—or perhaps I had *not* actually heard from God that morning. Either way, I was happy. Afterward, the people I was around were pumped and thankful for a great message.

Typically, I leave a city with a sense of satisfaction and joy; it's almost as if God smiles inside my heart. This was definitely not the case for me the next morning. I woke up heavy in heart. I lacked energy and was even fighting depression. I immediately knew why: I'd disobeyed God. I got down on my knees, repented, and asked for forgiveness. I pleaded for the blood of Jesus to cleanse me.

However, I felt no relief. I carried the heaviness all day—during my remaining time in the hotel, on the trip to the airport, at the airport for a delayed flight, and through the trip to the West Coast. The sadness and depression were almost unbearable. Finally, when we were circling San Diego, all of it lifted off me.

I questioned Him: *Father, I repented and asked for forgiveness this morning. Why haven't You restored my joy, peace, and contentment until now?*

I heard the Lord say, *I allowed you to carry the weight of your disobedience so you could understand its severity. There was a pastor in the service last night who needed to hear the message I've entrusted to you about the bait of Satan. It's a critical time in his life and ministry. You disobeyed Me, and there are consequences. The weight you've felt is a warning to not let this happen again. This is a new city; now obey Me.*

Let's turn to incidents in Scripture to further illustrate the misuse of a divine gift.

Consider Moses. He was called to lead Israel to the promised land and was gifted to work renowned miracles to accomplish this mission.

> In Scripture's pages we see many examples of how servants of God were called in unique ways to their unique tasks. Take time to read over the calling of Moses as narrated in Exodus 3. As Moses received his assignment, what did he learn about God's character, God's ways, and God's purposes for His people?
>
> In what ways might those things relate to your own calling?

On one occasion, God instructed Moses to speak to the rock, so water would come out to give all the people a drink. But Moses struck the rock out of anger, directly disobeying the divine instructions.

However, water still came out in abundance—enough to give a drink to millions of people in the middle of the desert. It was another spectacular miracle for Moses's résumé. Once again, the people were in awe of their leader's gifting. However, Moses was afterward called to account for not handling the gift as God instructed. He was denied entrance to the promised land for his misuse. Sobering, when you think about it.

Another example would be Balaam. He went and prophesied over Israel, and his words are still recorded in Scripture to this day. Wow, what a great testimony—to have your prophecy in the eternal Word of God! But there's more to the story. God had specifically told him *not* to go—not to do what others wanted him to do. Yet Balaam's entrusted gift operated even though God had directly commanded him, "You shall not go" (Numbers 22:12 NKJV). Once again, the gift operated outside the original divine intent.

> *God is not a micromanager of His entrusted gifts. If He oversaw us in this manner, we wouldn't be called stewards. A steward is given authority to manage what's entrusted to him or her without direct supervision.*

Here's the bottom line. God is not a micromanager of His entrusted gifts. If He oversaw us in this manner, we wouldn't be called *stewards*. A steward is given authority to manage what's entrusted to him or her without direct supervision. A scriptural example of this would be Jesus's parable of the unjust steward:

> There was a certain rich man who had a steward, and an accusation was brought to him that this man was wasting his goods. So he called him and said to him, "What is this I hear about you? Give an account of your stewardship, for you can no longer be steward." (Luke 16:1–2 NKJV)

Since stewardship was a more common thing in Bible times than today, it's easy to miss something significant here. Notice there was a season in which the rich man was ignorant of what was transpiring. He wasn't watching the steward's movements day by day. Someone else had to get his attention by reporting the mismanagement that had been going on for a good while.

This is seen also with Joseph in the book of Genesis. In Egypt he started out as a slave in Potiphar's house, but eventually he was promoted and made a steward of the entire household: "Potiphar gave Joseph complete administrative responsibility over everything he owned. With Joseph there, he didn't worry about a thing—except what kind of food to eat" (Genesis 39:6). Potiphar didn't micromanage or supervise Joseph's work. He entrusted Joseph with a stewardship.

This is similar to the gifts God places in you and me. The apostle Peter charges us to be good stewards of the manifold grace of God—the *charisma*—on our lives.

UNOBVIOUS ETERNAL GIFTS

Let's drill deeper. First, let's refresh our memory of Peter's words: "As each one has received a gift, minister it to one another, as good stewards" (1 Peter 4:10 NKJV). As stewards we're expected to *minister* the gifts—to use them. Again, our gifts aren't for us, but for others. The word for minister is *diakoneō* and is defined this way: "to serve, wait upon, with emphasis on the work to be done."[4] We must maintain a serving attitude with our gifts. Our gifts were freely given, and we're to use these gifts willingly with the purpose of building up others' lives.

> How strong is your willingness to serve others with your gifts? Take a moment to talk honestly to God in prayer about this.

Recall again that Peter says we're to "minister" our entrusted gifts "to one another, as good stewards of the *manifold grace* of God" (1 Peter 4:10 NKJV). That word *manifold* here means "of various kinds."[5] It would take too many pages to list the various gifts God has given to His people. In fact, compiling such a list is probably not possible. Some gifts are obvious in their connection to building the kingdom. However, many more are challenging to identify.

Here's an example. I recently heard a well-known pastor talking about an interesting conversation that transpired just prior to his yearly conference, a popular and well-attended event. As the team was setting up the auditorium, the pastor saw a medical doctor, a member of his church, putting handouts on the seats for the conference delegates.

The pastor went to the doctor and apologized. "Doctor, you shouldn't be doing this," he said. "We have interns and other volunteers who can handle this."

According to the pastor, the doctor sternly but politely responded, "I take off from my medical practice every year for this conference. It's my most treasured week of the year because I get to do something to build the kingdom of God."

In listening to my pastor friend telling this story, I grieved for this doctor. I realized he hadn't connected the dots on the value of his gift in building God's kingdom. Again, some gifts connect directly, while most are indirect but are no less important.

This doctor was no different from Stan in the first chapter. What if there were no doctors? What would happen when people who are called in other areas to build the kingdom became sick or diseased? Without medical help, many would be taken out early.

Let's envision a hypothetical scenario illustrating the connection. A doctor uses his gift by assisting in restoring the health of a stay-at-home mom. Since this woman is no longer helplessly sick in bed or dying prematurely, she's able to flourish in her gift of raising her children in a godly way. One child is gifted in the area of innovation, and her mother encourages it. After this daughter graduates with a computer software degree, she takes a position working for a company that develops software.

This grown daughter, now fully operating in her gift, designs a new way of communicating that's far more effective than anything on the market. However, her innovation will not go far without her coworker in the advertising department. He uses his gift to make retailers and consumers aware of the potential of this new software package.

One of the retailers, a company owned by a gifted businesswoman, picks up the product. This retail store has a sales team, and one man exercises his gift to sell the software package to a ministry that's called to disciple the nations of the world.

This ministry has a gifted IT person who recognizes the potential of this software and recommends purchasing it. He integrates the software into their existing system. As a result, this ministry now has the global capability to impact pastors and leaders more effectively. Therefore, exponentially more men and women come to salvation and are discipled through the avenue of this software communication package.

At the judgment seat, the doctor who originally treated the stay-at-home mother will be in awe as Jesus shows him the multitudes of peoples he reached in the nations of the world. We can almost imagine what will then transpire. The doctor will protest: "No, that can't be me. I never went to those nations."

Jesus will then show him that because he was faithful to the gift on his life, a global chain reaction eventually led to the salvation of many, as well as the strengthening of many believers. Jesus will most likely say to this doctor, "You worked willingly in your medical practice as though working for the Lord rather than for people, and your fruit is evident. Many were impacted by your obedience. Well done, good and faithful servant!"

This is just one scenario. The possibilities of these kinds of connections or chain reactions are countless.

You may be questioning: Is this idea really supported in the Bible? Read this:

In all the work you are doing, work the best you can. Work as if you were doing it for the Lord, not for people. Remember that you will receive your reward from the Lord. (Colossians 3:23–24 NCV)

Think deeply about the scriptural command to do all your work for the Lord and not for people, while remembering that "you will receive your reward from the Lord." In the work you do, what actual difference is involved (especially in your mind and heart) when you're doing it for the Lord and not for yourself or others?

Also, what actual difference is involved when you stay mentally aware that you'll receive a reward from the Lord when doing the work specifically for Him?

Let's return to the actual story of my pastor friend and the doctor helping to serve at the pastor's annual conference. What if the doctor became fed up with feeling fulfilled only one week a year? (Of course, his lack of satisfaction is fueled by the ignorance of his gift's importance.) It's quite possible that eventually he'd walk away from the medical field, seeking to feel more fulfilled fifty-two weeks a year. Let's assume he accepts a position at his church teaching and developing curriculum for discipleship classes. What would happen at the judgment seat? Would he receive as great a reward, having walked away from his entrusted gift?

Sadly, I've often witnessed men and women struggle in positions of full-time ministry because they don't recognize how their gifts would flourish better in arenas outside the church environment.

It takes knowledge, spiritual sensitivity, and maturity to see the unobvious positions of kingdom service.

Here's the raw truth: Your gift—whether it operates best in healthcare, education, government, athletics, the marketplace, the arts, media, the home, or any other arena—has a connection to building the kingdom. The Master Planner designed it this way.

It's quite possible that we may not recognize the connections between our obedience and success until we actually stand before Jesus at the judgment seat. As Paul writes, "It is the same way with good works; even if they are not known at first, they will eventually be recognized and acknowledged" (1 Timothy 5:25 TPT).

So whether or not your gift is evident, your charge is this: "As the Lord has called each one, so let him walk" (1 Corinthians 7:17 NKJV).

How has this discussion expanded your perspective on the potential impact of your faithfulness to your true calling and giftedness?

MOTIVATION IS CRUCIAL

Let's return to Paul's words that we're using as a template for our stewardship:

> For necessity is laid upon me; yes, woe is me if I do not preach the gospel! For if I do this *willingly*, I have a *reward*. (1 Corinthians 9:16–17 NKJV)

The next truth to highlight is that our reward is directly connected to our willingness—or, in a more general sense, to our "attitude." Simply put, if our attitude is *selfless*, we receive a reward; if our attitude is *selfish*, we don't receive a reward.

The different scenarios of selfless *or* selfish motives are vast—too many to list. Let's highlight just a few comparisons. A selfless attitude could be: "What a privilege to serve others with my entrusted abilities." A selfish motive would sound more like this: "What can I gain from my ability?"

To put it more directly, the difference is between "What can I do for you?" and "What's in it for me?"

Another selfless attitude would be: "I'll do my very best, no matter what I get in return"; whereas a selfish motive is: "Why should I do a thorough job when there's not much in it for me?"

Still another selfless motive: "I must press on because there are so many people to impact." And the selfish motive: "I'm successful; now I can take it easy."

On the importance of attitudes and motives, Paul writes this: "Let a man so consider us, as servants of Christ and stewards" (1 Corinthians 4:1 NKJV). Those words are immediately followed by these:

> As for me, it matters very little how I might be evaluated by you or by any human authority. I don't even trust my own judgment on this point. My conscience is clear, but that doesn't prove I'm right. It is the Lord himself who will examine me and decide. So don't make judgments about anyone ahead of time—before the Lord returns. For he will bring our darkest secrets to light and will reveal our private motives. Then God will give to each one whatever praise is due. (1 Corinthians 4:3–5)

Paul is not concerned about the evaluations of his friends, critics, or any other self-appointed authority—not even his own opinion. These assessments are meaningless compared to what we'll all eventually face—the divine examination. What matters is how *Jesus* will evaluate our stewardship.

We'll all eventually face the divine examination. What matters is how Jesus will evaluate our stewardship.

To be sure, our obedient actions or works will certainly be important at the judgment. Jesus clearly states, "Look, I am coming soon, bringing my reward with me to repay all people according to their deeds" (Revelation 22:12). It's not an either/or scenario, but rather both/and—both motives *and* works will be examined at the judgment.

Some may think Paul is referencing the unbeliever's judgment—the "great white throne judgment"—where unbelievers will give an account for their sins due to not receiving the saving grace of Jesus Christ. This is definitely not the case, because at the great white throne judgment, no one will receive "praise" from God, as stated by Paul.

It's important to maintain the context of his subject matter; Paul is discussing *stewardship.* There's no doubt about what he's referencing. Our "darkest secrets" and "private motives" in handling our gifts will be revealed at the judgment (1 Corinthians 4:5). That really gets my attention!

> Pause a moment to give serious thought to the fact that the Lord not only knows your "darkest secrets" and "private motives" related to how you use your giftedness, but He will also openly expose these at our coming judgment.
>
> As you're able, offer genuine praise and thanksgiving to Him for these truths.

Let me make this crystal clear by using my previous story of disobeying the Lord on what I should preach. Those who attended that meeting most likely to this day believe I was obedient to God in speaking my "fresh" message. But I wasn't. Possibly, at the judgment, they'll learn of my disobedience, for Jesus states:

> The time is coming when everything that is covered up will be revealed, and all that is secret will be made known to all. Whatever you have said in the dark [our private motives and secrets] will be heard in the light, and what you have whispered behind closed doors will be shouted from the housetops for all to hear! (Luke 12:2–3)

At the judgment seat, I may be called upon to apologize to the pastor and others who didn't receive *The Bait of Satan* message that evening.

WHAT IS EXPECTED?

We've firmly established the importance of understanding stewardship. The most significant question now is: What's expected of us? In other words: What results will Jesus look for at the time of judgment when He examines how we handled His entrusted gifts? Can we know? Absolutely yes, for Jesus declares we "will be judged on the day of judgment by the truth I have spoken" (John 12:48).

We'll begin this revealing and empowering discussion in the next chapter. It's the major focus of this book.

REFLECTION FOR RENEWAL

In this chapter, what statements or Scripture passages seemed most meaningful for you?

How would you restate them in your own words? (Personalize your answer as a prayer of response to God.)

What are your thoughts about what God wants you to do now in response to what you've seen and reflected upon in this chapter?

FAITHFUL

Let a man so consider us, as servants of Christ
and stewards of the mysteries of God.
Moreover it is required in stewards
that one be found faithful.

1 CORINTHIANS 4:1–2 NKJV

The apostle Paul identifies Apollos and himself as *servants* of Jesus Christ and *stewards* of their entrusted gifts. In the previous chapter, we learned that this identity doesn't apply solely to these two great saints, or only to current church leaders—but to every believer. You and I are also servants of Jesus Christ, and a primary way we fulfill this role is to be good stewards of our entrusted gifts.

Like other servants of God we see in Scripture, the apostle Paul received his unique calling and assignment in a unique way. Look at how this unfolds in Acts 9:1–22. Notice also the various statements Paul makes about his calling in Romans 1:1, 1 Corinthians 1:1 and 15:9, and Galatians 1:15. What do these passages reveal about God's calling, God's character, God's ways, and God's purposes for His people?

How might those revelations relate to your own calling and purpose?

We turn our attention now to what's *required* of a steward—and in 1 Corinthians 4, only one attribute is listed: *faithfulness.* Let's ponder why there aren't two, three, or more characteristics listed here. Paul could have stated that stewards must exude joy, be strong, be scholars of the Scripture, be compassionate, or have any other godly trait. I'm not taking away from the importance of any of these attributes, of course. However, I'm pointing out that only one is listed—and it is *required*. So it's important to home in on this virtue if we're going to be good stewards and one day hear our Master say, "Well done."

THE DEFINITION OF FAITHFULNESS

I've had the privilege of addressing leadership teams all over the world—not just those in ministry, although ministry would be the majority—but also people on corporate, government, business, education, and athletic teams. I've often asked for team members to give a one-word definition of the word *faithful*. Being leaders, they're usually eager to speak up. After hearing similar answers in almost every setting, I decided to make a list of the most popular responses:

- Steadfast
- Consistent
- Dependable
- Reliable
- Loyal
- True
- Trustworthy
- Devoted
- Truthful
- Resolute
- Obedient

I've heard others, but these answers have been the most popular. Even more important, all these answers are in line with dictionary definitions and synonyms.

However, there's one important definition for *faithful* that I've never heard, not once in any setting. Here it is: *multiplication.*

You may immediately think, *Multiplication? That's not a synonym of* faithfulness*!* You also may be questioning my verbal skills, as my former English teachers did. However, I assure you that by the end of this chapter, you'll not only agree with me, but most likely see multiplication as one of the most important definitions of faithfulness.

THE PARABLE OF THE TALENTS

To introduce multiplication, let's go to Jesus's parable of the talents. Please read it carefully, even if you've read it numerous times before.

> The Kingdom of Heaven can be illustrated by the story of a man going on a long trip. He called together his servants and entrusted his money to them while he was gone. (Matthew 25:14)

First of all, this is a parable; it's therefore symbolic, not literal. So we need to interpret it in the light of biblical understanding—the overall counsel of God's Word. The man going on the long trip represents Jesus. This man has servants, who are symbolic of you and me. To each of these servants, something has been entrusted for them to steward.

Next, notice that the trip is long—which supports two facts. First, it has been almost two thousand years since Jesus left us in charge of building what He died for—the kingdom.

Jesus left us in charge of building what He died for—the kingdom. He hasn't yet returned, and it's been a long time.

Obviously, He hasn't returned yet, but even at this point in history, it's been a long time.

Second, this parable once again shows that stewardship is not micromanaged. The man in the parable is going away, and he won't be checking back every weekend or so on his servants' progress. According to the parable, he won't be inspecting their work until he finally returns from his long trip.

Let's continue this man's story as he's preparing to leave his servants:

> He gave five bags of silver to one, two bags of silver to another, and one bag of silver to the last—dividing it in proportion to their abilities. He then left on his trip. (25:15)

In this story, the entrustment is money. Most Bible translations use the word *talent*, and this word is actually the most accurate, for the Greek word is *tálanton*. A talent is a measure of weight used mostly for gold or silver. One talent is roughly seventy-five pounds. Some experts estimate a talent of silver to be worth roughly eighteen thousand dollars of US currency. (Other estimates vary, but not significantly.) The experts agree that the New Testament represents a "talent" as a large sum of money. A seventy-five-pound bag of silver is not chump change!

Based on my understanding now, I personally don't think the exact amount is important to the interpretation of this parable. What we can confidently conclude, however, is that one talent represented significant responsibility.

I don't believe Jesus is discussing money—although it could apply in principle. Rarely in a parable does Jesus use the exact representation of what's being discussed. He uses wheat for godly people, tares for evil people, seeds for words, thorns for the cares of life, a harvest for the end of the world, reapers for angels, and more. From the overall counsel of the New Testament, it's almost certain these talents represent *charisma*, or our entrusted gifts.

Another important point of this story is that each servant was not given the same amount. We'll cover this fact in more depth later, but this is why, at times, I've already referred to our entrustments as "gifts." Some have one, others two, and still others have more.

The different amounts could also represent the magnitude of our gifts. Let's be candid; some people have greater gifts than others. Many possess the gift of singing, and they inspire all who hear them. But all who sing don't have the level of talent that Céline Dion or Andrea Bocelli possesses. So if you back me into the corner, I would say each talent represents a certain gift, or could just as easily represent the magnitude of a gift.

Let's continue in the parable:

> The servant who received the five bags of silver began to invest the money and earned five more. The servant with two bags of silver also went to work and earned two more. But the servant who received the one bag of silver dug a hole in the ground and hid the master's money. (25:16–18)

Let me personalize the story by assigning names to these servants. Let's call the first one Allison, the second Bob, and the third Larry.

Allison started with five and multiplied her share, giving her ten.

Bob multiplied his two and ended up with four.

Larry, however, didn't multiply his entrusted gift; he only *maintained* it.

Let's spell all this out:

$$\text{Allison: } 5 \times 2 = 10$$
$$\text{Bob: } 2 \times 2 = 4$$
$$\text{Larry: } 1 = 1$$

(From this point forward, I'll personalize this passage in Matthew 25 with the names we've given each servant.)

THE JUDGMENT

Again, it's crucial to point out Jesus's emphasis of the word *long* in this parable. The story had begun with the description of a long trip; now, Jesus once again states, "After a *long time* their master returned from his trip and called them to give an account of how they had used his money" (Matthew 25:19). This "account" the master requires from each steward represents the judgment each of us will face for how we used our entrusted gifts.

Let's examine Allison first:

Alison, to whom he had entrusted the five bags of silver, came forward with five more and said, "Master, you gave me five bags of silver to invest, and I have earned five more." (25:20)

Listen to the judgment of her master:

The master was full of praise. "Well done, my good and faithful servant. *You have been faithful* in handling this small amount, so now I will give you many more responsibilities. Let's celebrate together!" (25:20–21)

This is a crucial point we must not miss: The master says, "You have been faithful." You can slice the master's response however you'd like, but there's no other interpretation: Jesus directly attributes *faithfulness* to *multiplication*.

This is a crucial point we must not miss: Jesus directly attributes faithfulness to multiplication.

Reread the master's comments carefully; nothing else Allison did was highlighted. He didn't say she was steadfast, dependable, loyal, devoted, truthful, or any other one-word definition for *faithful*. Don't misunderstand—all these admirable attributes go along with being faithful, but they aren't mentioned or emphasized in this parable. The master didn't point out any other virtue, action, or result of Allison's stewardship—except that she had multiplied. Therefore, he directly links *faithfulness* with *multiplication*.

The same is true with Bob. Read closely his account:

Bob, who had received the two bags of silver, came forward and said, "Master, you gave me two bags of silver to invest, and I have earned two more." (25:22)

Along the same lines, hear the judgment of his master:

The master said, "Well done, my good and faithful servant. *You have been faithful* in handling this small amount, so now I will give you many more responsibilities. Let's celebrate together!" (25:23)

Once again, Jesus directly identifies faithfulness with multiplication. Nothing else is highlighted—no other action, or virtue, or result.

Jesus doesn't want the master's emphasis diluted. There's only one takeaway: This man *multiplied* what was entrusted to him, which is clearly equated to his being faithful.

Also, the praise Bob receives is word-for-word what was stated to Allison. This reveals that on the judgment day, our multiplication "score" will be based on our labor. Jesus will be equally pleased with us regardless of the magnitude of our gifts. All that will matter is this: Did we multiply?

An example would be the stay-at-home mother who multiplied her effectiveness. She'll be as equally praised as the entrepreneur who multiplied his business and his giving to the kingdom.

How do you see Jesus Himself, in His life on earth, living up to this definition of faithfulness?

Jesus is called "the faithful witness" in Revelation 1:5, and in His present work in heaven, He's described in Hebrews 2:17 as "our merciful and faithful High Priest before God." How can and does the faithfulness of the Lord Jesus Himself help you to be faithful in your own work before God?

For your own faithfulness in stewarding God's gifts to you—what could multiplication look like? Express this in words as specifically as you can.

As the picture of this becomes more clear to you, ask God to bring about this multiplication in His own ways and timing.

Now let's turn our attention to Larry:

Then Larry, the servant with the one bag of silver came and said, "Master, I knew you were a harsh man, harvesting crops you didn't plant and gathering crops you didn't cultivate. I was afraid I would lose your money, so I hid it in the earth. Look, here is your money back." (Matthew 25:24–25)

Before moving on to Larry's judgment from the master, let's point out some important facts. First, Larry did *not* multiply; he merely maintained what was entrusted to him.

Also, notice *why* he didn't multiply. Larry didn't know the character of his master, so he incorrectly perceived him as harsh. Through years of ministering to believers from different parts of the world and all walks of life, I've noticed that one of their primary stumbling blocks to fruitfulness is not knowing God's nature. (I'll cover this in depth in a later chapter.)

When we perceive Him incorrectly, it often triggers what's behind a failure to multiply—*fear*. Larry was afraid. Fear, timidity, or intimidation will shut down the genuine gifts of God on our lives. This cannot be stressed enough. I know this firsthand, as I suffered with misperception for years. (I'll cover this also in a later chapter.)

> In what ways do you think you might be tempted to follow in Larry's footsteps?
>
> What will it mean for you to trust God to help you avoid such a failure? (Talk with the Lord in prayer about this.)

Now let's look at Larry's judgment:

But the master replied, "You wicked and lazy servant!" (25:26)

Wow! Let's pause and examine this statement before continuing. Remember all three are *servants*—not only Allison and Bob, but also Larry. They are not outsiders. It is *their* master who is assessing their labor.

Unlike the other two, Larry doesn't hear, "Well done, good and faithful servant." Instead he hears, "You wicked and lazy servant!" This is definitely an attention-grabber. Jesus isn't talking about salvation, but about the judgment of how we handle our gifts—either being rewarded for our labor or suffering loss.

Let's look carefully at both of the stern words from the master. We'll start with the easier one to swallow. The Greek word for lazy is *oknērós*, defined as "to delay; slow, tardy, slothful, lazy."[1] Another lexicon defines it as "shrinking from or hesitating to engage in something worthwhile, possibly implying lack of ambition."[2] My friend Rick Renner, who's an expert in the Greek language, says that *oknērós* "carries the idea of a person who has a do-nothing, lethargic, lackadaisical, apathetic, indifferent, lukewarm attitude toward life."

If you're fearful, you'll hesitate or refrain from engaging in an activity that should and could be done. If you're lethargic, you'll lack the drive to accomplish what should be done. If you're apathetic, you won't care enough to even consider acting. All these scenarios apply to this Greek word—yet the servant specifically confessed, "I was afraid." The other aspects of laziness could have come into play for this servant, but in the end, *hesitation from fear* was the overriding factor.

If we flirt with hesitation long enough, it can become a pattern that ultimately leads to complete avoidance and an unfruitful stewardship.

You may recall a time when you felt the urge to do something—you just couldn't shake it, especially when in prayer—but you faltered too long because you feared failing. Then you watched someone else do it, and afterward you thought, *I had that idea and should've acted on it*. This is Jesus's point regarding this servant. He repeatedly hesitated—not just once or twice, but throughout the entire period of his stewardship. It's acceptable a time or two, since we usually grow from these situations. But if we flirt with hesitation long enough, it can become a pattern that ultimately leads to complete avoidance and an unfruitful stewardship.

When the Lord first asked me to write, I hesitated for ten months. I was afraid of writing. I'd failed time and time again in school, and I'd even had a classmate in college who criticized my writing in front of everyone. An aspect of one assignment was to read each other's papers, and during class discussion, my classmate expressed his disapproval of my work to the professor. I was the only student who received criticism from a fellow classmate.

My fear of writing was well-founded. I had terrible SAT and ACT scores, numerous teachers' negative critiques, poor grades, and a critical classmate; history wasn't on my side. All of this only confirmed my hesitation. To write a book would take an enormous amount of time, and time is crucial. It would pull me away from other efforts to grow our young ministry. I had to lay these significant fears and concerns aside in order to obey His directive.

What if I'd hesitated too long and never obeyed? God would have given the talent to someone else—to an "Allison," so to speak, who would have fulfilled the mission. She would have received my assignment. Then where would I be today? Would I have ended up being called "lazy" before the Lord's judgment seat?

I know then how my destiny was wrapped up in writing. Had you said to me during my twenties, "John, God will send you to the nations of the world through your books," I would have said (while laughing you out of the room), "You've lost your mind! I can't even write a three-page paper." But now the books are national and international bestsellers, translated in over 125 languages, with tens of millions of copies in print. What if I hadn't obeyed? What if I'd allowed fear to hold me back? I shudder to think of the extent of my lost opportunity.

> How much can you identify with this kind of fear? In what situations have you experienced it or something like it? And what was the outcome for you?

Let's focus next on the more difficult word spoken by the master to the third servant. The word *wicked* may seem too intense, but Jesus never used words carelessly. The Greek word for wicked is *ponērós*, defined as "possessing a serious fault and consequently being worthless."[3]

In regard to how Larry handled what was entrusted to him, this definition fits. It's no different from Paul concluding "woe is me" if he'd ever become unfaithful to the gift of God on his life. Larry's misguided view of his master's character was a serious fault that fueled his fear. He was *worthless* to the working out of his entrusted gift.

These are strong statements. Nevertheless, if you compare Larry's behavior with Paul's words of potential nonuse of his own gift, they ring true.

Let me clearly remind you that this is not regarding our salvation, but rather how we handle our entrusted gifts. God's view is this:

- Those who *multiply* are good and faithful.
- Those who simply *maintain* possess a serious fault and are worthless and lazy.

Think about the gift or gifts God has entrusted you with. To what extent are you tempted to be content with only maintaining them—rather than multiplying? Evaluate yourself honestly in this.

Could it be that our view of faithfulness is incomplete?

Consider this example: There's a businessman who lives in an area with a strong and expanding economy. The business, a small shop the owner inherited from his father, is profitable but not growing. The man has had opportunities to open new branches of the business in other parts of the city, but despite his entrepreneurial gift, he has been content to "stay comfortable."

Could it be that our view of faithfulness is incomplete?

Now, let me push the envelope. In light of Larry's judgment in the parable, let's ask two important questions.

1. Should this businessman use his gift to start new shops and venture into other markets for the purpose of building the kingdom?
2. Is his desire to "play it safe" comparable to the unfaithful servant's strategy to merely maintain?

> From your perspective, what are the best answers to those two important questions?

To assess faithfulness, have we used the same criteria Jesus uses? Although the businessman is living a good life, isn't the overarching question whether he is multiplying or only maintaining his gifts?

Let's be honest in our assessment. Do we measure faithfulness only by reliability, without factoring in reproduction? Do we value steadiness apart from expansion? Consistency without attention to duplication? Have we missed the full scope of what it means to be faithful—to multiply whatever gifts we've been given?

Don't forget God's first commandment to mankind when He placed male and female on the earth: "Be fruitful and multiply" (Genesis 1:28). Of course, He was directing us to have babies and populate the earth. But also—and so much more—the command is this: *Whatever He puts in our care, we're to return to Him multiplied.* We are to procreate through multiplication. In the parable of the talents, Jesus specifically applies this initial Genesis command to our entrusted gifts.

NOT YOUR OWN ABILITY

Are you feeling uncomfortable? You probably are, but remember: *God's grace is all you need.* You aren't asked to do this in your own strength, but by the *charis* and *charisma* of God. The purpose of writing this message is not to discourage you, but to bring awareness to your God-given potential and to expand your faith in God's grace and the gifts on your life. I don't intend to put a heavy burden on you, something too difficult to lift. Paul cried out to God three different times to ease his load, but remember again how the Lord responded: "My grace is all you need. My power works best in weakness." Paul went on to write this:

So now I am glad to boast about my weaknesses, so that the power of Christ can work through me. That's why I take *pleasure* in my weaknesses. (2 Corinthians 12:9–10)

One of the definitions of the Greek word for weakness is "limitation." You and I aren't the only ones who feel overwhelmed at times. We all have limitations; even the apostle Paul had limitations. In the specific context of this verse, he refers to the resistance, opposition, and even physical persecutions he faced in every city (2 Corinthians 11:16–33), but this truth also applies to restrictions or impossibilities we may face—when the task seems undoable. Although multiplication is certainly not easy, this should cause us to deepen our resolve, to lean into His strength. Instead of *listening* to the limitations screaming in your mind, *speak* the promises of God. Do we listen to ourselves too much, when instead we should be speaking God's truth to ourselves?

Paul asked God to intervene three times, and each time God reminded Paul of *charis*. Paul got it the third time; he realized his constraints should only steer him to believe in God's grace and gifting on his life. This is why his tune changed from *God, take this away!* to "I take *pleasure* in my limitations." Did he really say "pleasure"? Yes! He now realized that the more impossible the challenge, the greater God's power would be manifested in and upon his life—*if he believed.*

Here's an important truth: *The grace we need to multiply can be accessed only by believing.* Paul writes, "We have access *by faith* into this grace" (Romans 5:2 NKJV). Imagine it this way: Faith is the pipeline that delivers to our heart the grace needed to multiply. When we hear this message, our faith or pipeline should enlarge, not diminish. But that's your choice. We are told:

The word which they heard did not profit them, not being mixed with faith in those who heard it. For we who have believed do enter that rest. (Hebrews 4:2–3 NKJV)

Don't view what you're reading in a way that brings no blessing, no profit; instead, mix it with faith. The same word from God accomplished two different results for the children of Israel. It was *profitable* to Moses, Joshua, and Caleb; they were strengthened by seeing it in a positive light. But the same word was *unprofitable* to the other Israelites because they viewed it in a negative way. This is the difference between belief and unbelief.

> Joshua was another faithful servant of God who received his unique assignment in a unique way. Look at how his calling unfolds in these passages: Numbers 27:15–23; Deuteronomy 31:1–8; Joshua 1:1–9. What do these passages reveal about God's character, God's ways, and God's purposes for His people?
>
> Also, how might those things relate to your own unique calling?

Believe that God has equipped you to go far beyond your own ability. He has given you no other option for strength and empowerment than to depend on His grace. When you do this, you'll enter the true "rest" mentioned in Hebrews 4:3—ceasing in your own efforts, no longer striving to produce results. What is this rest? It's cooperating with God's ability to accomplish your mission. When you enter rest, God will lead you to multiply.

God has equipped you to go far beyond your own ability. He has given you no other option for strength and empowerment than to depend on His grace.

This is one reason David was called a man after God's heart. He depended on God's strength, not his own. He repeatedly proclaimed, "The LORD is the strength of my life" (Psalm 27:1 NKJV). In everything he accomplished, there was one common denominator: David depended on God's ability in and through him.

This is why Timothy—who was battling fear and intimidation—received these words from Paul, his spiritual father: "You therefore, my son, be *strong in the grace* that is in Christ Jesus" (2 Timothy 2:1 NKJV).

This is why I devoted the second and third chapters of this book to firmly establishing *charis* and *charisma* before discussing Jesus's parable of the talents. It would be overwhelming and discouraging to face our stewardship in our own strength, apart from the gifts of God's grace.

> What helps you most to rely on the Lord's grace and strength? In what situations are you most tempted to rely instead on your own strength and abilities?

Please, never forget: Your calling is greater than your natural ability. This could be why we're told these truths:

> For you see your *calling*, brethren, that not many wise according to the flesh, not many mighty, not many noble, are *called*. But God has chosen the foolish things of the world to put to shame the wise, and God has chosen the weak things of the world to put to shame the things which are mighty; and the base things of the world and the things which are despised God has chosen, and the things which are not, to bring to nothing the things that are, that no flesh should glory in His presence. (1 Corinthians 1:26–29 NKJV)

Why is this? Why are there only a few wise, strong, and noble who are called? Could it be that it's easier for the naturally talented to "succeed" in their own strength? They're foolish! They compare themselves to others, and they win. Instead, they should see themselves in the light of their Creator's calling.

Paul was different. Although in measuring himself against his contemporaries he was wise and noble before being saved, there came a point when he counted all this natural ability to be nothing more than "dung" so he could enter into the power of Christ upon his life (Philippians 3:8 KJV). He was one of the few, because he learned that even though he was naturally wiser than most, he was unwise in comparison to God's wisdom.

SOCIALISTIC OR CAPITALISTIC?

Let's continue with Jesus's parable. Impossible though it seems, the story actually gets stronger and more shocking. Look what the master does next:

Then he ordered, "Take the money from this servant, and give it to the one with the ten bags of silver." (Matthew 25:28)

Wait a minute—did we read that correctly? The master actually orders the bag of silver (the talent) to be taken from Larry and given to Allison. Let's spell out their situation:

Allison: 5 x 2 = 10 + 1 (from Larry) = 11
Larry: 1–1 (to Allison) = 0

Allison ends up with eleven; Larry ends up with zero.

One morning in prayer, I was stunned by what I heard in my heart. Let me set this up. I hadn't thought about the parable of the talents for some time. But that morning I heard the Spirit of God say to me, *Son, I'm more capitalistic, not socialistic, in My thinking.*

What? I raised an eyebrow to this, but I've been walking with Him long enough to recognize when He reveals things to us that we don't know. Often it sounds contrary to religious or normal thinking—sometimes it even sounds absurd—as it did this time when I heard His words. I asked for understanding, because I'd thought that if anything, God was more socialistic in the way He did things.

That morning, He led me to this parable and showed me that if His thinking were socialistic, the parable would have gone differently. The story would have begun like this: All three would have received the same number of talents.

Allison: 3
Bob: 3
Larry: 3

Allison and Bob would have been faithful (multiplied), but Larry—because of his faults of being worthless and lazy—would have stayed true to form. The result would have been:

$$\text{Allison: } 3 \times 2 = 6$$
$$\text{Bob: } 3 \times 2 = 6$$
$$\text{Larry: } 3 = 3$$

The hypothetical "socialistic" God would have done the following:

$$\text{Allison: } 6{-}1 \text{ (to Larry)} = 5$$
$$\text{Bob: } 6{-}1 \text{ (to Larry)} = 5$$
$$\text{Larry: } 3 + 1 \text{ (from Allison)} + 1 \text{ (from Bob)} = 5$$

Everyone would have ended up with five talents! But this isn't what happened. God removed the one bag of silver from Larry and gave it to the one who had ten. Why? Jesus explains:

> To those who use well [who *multiply*] what they are given, *even more will be given*, and they will have an abundance. But from those who do nothing [who only *maintain*], even what little they have will be taken away. (Matthew 25:29)

I'm not saying God is a capitalist. No, never! It's just that capitalism, particularly here, is more in line with His thinking and ways than socialism. Our young people in America and elsewhere in the twenty-first century are being trained to think socialistically. Socialism is not godly and beneficial; in fact, it goes directly against the wisdom of God. It's an antichrist spirit masking as the common good, trying to reward laziness and penalize diligence, success, and abundance.

God's way is to reward those who multiply with more, and He has no problem with them having an abundance. Again Jesus says, "They will have an abundance." God desires you to have abundance *as long as your heart is to build the kingdom and use your abundance for others.*

You've probably heard it said before that God is not against abundance; He's against abundance having us. This is very true. To those whose hearts burn with God's passions, their satisfaction doesn't come from hoarding abundance or using it only for their lusts. Rather, it comes from walking with God and using the abundance He gives to build His kingdom. The abundance is only a tool for them to build up others. And obviously, if we're wise, we won't fall in love with our tools.

> In light of the superabundance of God's grace, how free are you to ask Him for abundance in multiplying your gifts for the sake of others and His kingdom?
>
> Take a moment to speak with God in prayer about this.

It's important to pause and stress an important truth: We're to take care of the poor and needy—those who are incapable of labor or those who need a kick start. Paul writes,

> Love empowers us to fulfill the law of the Anointed One as we carry each other's troubles. If you think you are somebody too important to stoop down to help another (when really you are not), you are living in deception. (Galatians 6:2–3 TPT)

When the leaders of the early church met, they realized what their different assignments were, and they even disagreed on minor points. But they certainly agreed about their responsibility to help those who were struggling. Paul writes of how those church leaders "simply requested one thing of me: that I would remember the poor and needy, which was the burden I was already carrying in my heart" (Galatians 2:10 TPT).

Leaders of the early church disagreed on minor points, but they certainly agreed about their responsibility to help those who were struggling.

With this stated, it's important to identify whether someone is truly in need or is just lazy. A socialist approach is to give equally to the lazy and to the poor. If we give to those in the lazy category, we only increase their dependence on us. Our goal is always to direct people to their God-given gifts, so they, too, can flourish and build God's kingdom.

Take a moment to thank and praise God for His own abundant faithfulness toward you. Read and reflect on Lamentations 3:22–23 for a rich portrait of His great faithfulness, and personalize those words in prayer to Him. (For further profitable reflection on this, explore Psalm 36:5 and 100:5, as well as 1 Thessalonians 5:23–24 and 1 John 1:9.)

Ask Him to let your faithfulness be a strong reflection of His faithfulness to others around you.

THE PRACTICAL APPLICATION

In any case, what's important is the fact that we've been entrusted with gifts, and we're expected to multiply them. If you love God, you'll passionately desire to use your gifts for His glory.

My main intent is to awaken you to your inward desire and potential. You've been created *on* purpose and *for* a purpose. You have the capability to multiply what you've been given for the glory of our King. This is the most important takeaway from this chapter.

Now that we've come to an understanding of the parable of the talents and what it represents, we're ready to move on to the practical matters. How does this multiplication play out? How does this translate into everyday life? Our journey will turn in this direction in the next chapter.

REFLECTION FOR RENEWAL

In this chapter, what statements or Scripture passages seemed most meaningful for you?

How would you restate them in your own words? (Personalize your answer as a prayer of response to God.)

What are your thoughts about what God wants you to do now in response to what you've seen and reflected upon in this chapter?

DILIGENCE AND MULTIPLICATION

The one who faithfully manages the little he has been given
will be promoted and trusted with greater responsibilities.

LUKE 16:10 TPT

According to the words of Jesus, if we are steadfast, dependable, trustworthy, honest, and diligent, and if we live by integrity and multiply what we currently manage, we'll be given greater responsibilities. Simply put, *when we multiply with integrity, God entrusts us with more responsibility.* He promotes us. It's a law of His kingdom.

Do a personal checkup. Do you have a multiplying outlook? Or have you carried more of a maintenance mentality? Have you coasted when you hit the level of success you viewed as higher than most—better than your parents, or enough to live on comfortably?

Be honest in your assessment. If you've been more of a maintainer than a multiplier, the great news is this: You still live on the earth and have time to change, multiply, and ultimately be given more responsibility.

Before reading on, answer fully and candidly those "personal checkup" questions for your own benefit.

TWO DIFFERENT OUTCOMES

Even when I was a young boy, it wasn't hard for me to recognize these two opposite motivations of maintainer versus multiplier, because my two grandfathers exemplified the differences right before my eyes. One retired at the age of sixty-five and entered a docile lifestyle. He'd visit our home two weeks a year, and I would observe him, day by day, doing practically nothing. He would sit under our big maple tree in the backyard and smoke his pipe. It wasn't much different when we visited at his home. Sadly, in his later years, he seemed to have settled for existing rather than living.

My other grandfather retired at the age of sixty-two and started what seemed like his second life. In his sixties, he attended Rutgers University and studied agriculture. Over the next couple of decades, he wrote two books, built and maintained a large garden, raised animals, helped bring condominiums to the Florida beaches to create nice places for older people, and was active in many corporate and community projects. He always reached out to help anyone who was in need.

When he visited us or we visited him, it was a much anticipated event. He planned fishing trips, days at amusement parks, and trips to New York City. He played games with us, took us to meet neighbors, helped local businessmen with tasks in their shops, and cooked us a delicious meal every night. My other grandfather didn't even help around the kitchen.

One grandfather died at age seventy-five, the other at age ninety-one. Can you guess who lived longer? Yes, the one who had a vision, the one who multiplied.

And here's an interesting fact: Not until he was eighty-nine did he receive salvation. Even so, beforehand, he still lived according to God's principles—the laws of the kingdom—and was abundantly blessed.

Before I had the privilege of leading him to Jesus, my grandfather persecuted me a lot about my beliefs. He mocked my faith almost every time we were together. After numerous attempts to share the gospel with him, I almost fell over when he finally said, "I want to receive Jesus as my Lord." It was a great day!

One month after his conversion, I again visited him. At the time, he lived only an hour away from our house. He'd just moved from his condominium on Daytona Beach to an adult community living center in Ormond Beach, where several hundred elderly people were living. On that visit, he said, "John, would you like to know my assignment? What I'm on this earth to do?"

I was amazed that a newly saved man at his age thought this way. But I simply responded, "Yes, Grandpa, what's your assignment?"

He said with a smile, "The Holy Spirit told me I'm here to tell all these people about Jesus Christ."

Two years later, my mom and her brother moved my grandfather to Oklahoma to be close to his only son. The first week there, he stayed up all night telling his newly assigned nurse his life story. In the wee hours of the morning, just before sunrise, he said to her, "It's time to go home. Tell my son to have a party on me." With that, he left his body and joined his heavenly family.

My mom was troubled and concerned that they'd put too much stress on him with the move from Florida to Oklahoma. I quickly assured her that they'd done no such thing: "Mom, when Grandpa was eighty-nine, he told me God showed him that he had two more years on earth to fulfill his assignment in Ormond Beach. This was his first week in Oklahoma; his assignment was complete." My mother was both comforted and amazed.

Although my grandfather was an unsaved man for much of his time on earth, God's principles of diligent faithfulness manifested in his life. In witnessing the different choices of my two grandfathers, even before I was a believer, I had determined that my life would follow the course of my grandfather who multiplied and lived with purpose until his last breath.

But let me be frank. Numerous times the temptation to veer the other way—to a life of ease—has arisen. It takes intentional redirecting of our thoughts to not succumb to a "maintainer" lifestyle—because merely maintaining is so much easier.

Multiplication will not result from a slothful, hesitant, careless, or apathetic motivation. We're told by the apostle Paul, "Never be lazy, but *work hard* and serve the Lord

Numerous times the temptation to veer to a life of ease arises. It takes intentional redirecting of our thoughts to not succumb to a "maintainer" lifestyle—because merely maintaining is so much easier.

enthusiastically" (Romans 12:11). Notice that this is a command, not a suggestion. Look at his words: "work hard." In order to multiply, this is one of the first traits you must exhibit. And not only are we to work hard, but we're also to be *enthusiastic* in our labor.

Don't get me wrong; faith, vision, and perseverance are three important factors of multiplying. But they're of no use without good old-fashioned hard work.

> What are some strategies you can follow to fight the common temptation to seek a life of ease and to be only a "maintainer" of your gifts from God? In what ways could you be more intentional about working harder and enthusiastically in what God has called you to do—by His power and with His giftings?
>
> To identify good strategies for this, think back to a time when you slacked off or coasted unnecessarily, rather than working hard and enthusiastically at a task God had placed before you. What influences or conditions made it easier to do this? How can you successfully resist such factors in the future?

Lisa and I have worked diligently almost from the day we became believers. It's hardwired within us—and the same is true for every believer. Our enthusiasm has been driven not by external circumstances, but by a deep passion stemming from two things: our unfaltering love for Jesus and our love for His people. This passion is based on a firm heart decision, not feelings, and it fuels a burning desire to build His kingdom. This is so important because excited emotions will not always be present. In fact, seasons may come in which those feelings aren't present at all.

One of the root words for *enthusiasm* is the Greek word *éntheos*, which means "possessed by a god, inspired."[1] Our diligence must be drawn from His indwelling presence, not from emotions or external circumstances.

MULTIPLY WHAT BELONGS TO ANOTHER

After Lisa and I got married, the first church we attended was in Dallas, Texas. It was one of the most recognized churches in our nation, with a staff of hundreds. As volunteers, we constantly signed up to do anything that was needed. I became an usher, volunteered for prison ministry, ministered in detention centers, visited nursing homes, helped in conferences, assisted church employees with menial tasks, and even gave our pastor's children tennis lessons. I never said no to any form of serving. And all this happened while I was working forty hours a week as an engineer with Rockwell International.

Eventually, upon seeing my passion to serve, the senior pastor's wife (who was the church's chief operating officer) asked me if I would be willing to join the church staff on a full-time basis. During our formal interview, however, she remarked, "John, I don't think we can afford you."

My response was, "Yes, you can afford me." I didn't care what they offered me. I was ready to accept any position for any salary.

After the interview, she offered me the position of assistant to the executive team. Lisa and I didn't need to pray too hard about it because we knew this was God's will. I accepted the offer with a salary of eighteen thousand dollars a year, which was a massive pay cut, but we felt it was a promotion. Lisa and I knew we would need miraculous provision to live off this new salary, but we didn't care. We were engaged in what we believed with all our hearts was God's calling on our lives.

This position's responsibilities were to assist my pastors, their family, and their guests. I operated with three predominate motives. First, to serve them as though I was serving Jesus. Second, to anticipate their needs and meet them before being asked. And third, when asked to do something, to never respond with "It can't be done." I would always find a way to get it done through prayer, creativity, and hard work. If something actually couldn't be done (which was rare), I would always return with the best alternative solution. Often it was an even better way of accomplishing the task.

Lisa and I didn't have children during this position's tenure. A workweek was usually fifty to seventy hours over a six-day period. She and I both felt it was important to take all possible pressures off our pastors. We wanted them to give their full attention to leading our church.

I could share many stories that illustrated our motives, but I will offer just one. My pastor had a guest who was on the ministry team of a world-renowned evangelist, now deceased. My pastor wanted to learn more about this ministry, so the two of them talked late into the evening. My phone rang at one a.m. It was my pastor asking me to come to his home (a twenty-five-minute drive from our apartment) and take his guest back to the hotel.

"I'll be right over," I said without hesitation.

I went to the house and waited as they said goodbye, then drove the guest back to the hotel. I got to bed well after two a.m.

My pastor was unaware that only a few hours later, I was due to pick up another guest from the airport who was speaking to our church the next evening; he was flying in on a red-eye flight from Hawaii. I had to get up at four thirty to pick him up on time. I never told my pastor about getting less than three hours of sleep that night. I was determined to fill any need they had, and I constantly reminded myself that it was a privilege to serve.

I told them, "I'm praying and asking God that the man who takes my place will do twice as good a job as I've done."

After serving my pastor and his wife as their assistant for four years, one day when alone with them, I told them, "I'm praying and asking God that the man who takes my place will do twice as good a job as I've done." I wanted to leave well and see my position carried on even stronger.

"That's not possible," they responded. "You've done such great work."

It was an encouraging affirmation. Their statement made all the hard work seem easy, but I wanted improvement. Eventually, they put two people in the position. My pastor released us with blessings to go serve another well-known church, this one in Florida (in the youth pastor position I mentioned earlier).

After I took this Florida position, I became frustrated that we weren't reaching more teenagers. This was the mid-1980s, when our only visual electronic medium was broadcast television. People didn't have computers, tablets, or smartphones. Streaming hadn't been invented. Simply put, daily broadcast TV was the best avenue to reach large numbers of people simultaneously.

After doing some research, I discovered that one of the most powerful television stations in central Florida had an open ten p.m. slot on Saturday night. I inquired how much it would cost to buy that thirty-minute time slot. The cost was hefty.

I approached my senior pastor and asked if we could buy the slot for a youth outreach program. "John, it just isn't in the church's budget," he said.

"Do you mind if we allow the teenagers the opportunity to give monthly in order to pay for the program?" I asked him.

"Sure, if they can afford it," he responded. He seemed doubtful that the young people could do it.

I stood before the young people and shared the vision of reaching the lost. In those days, many young people watched television late on Saturday night. On the program we planned, we would first preach the Word of God, then invite viewers to attend our church and youth group. I appealed to the young people in our group to make this possible by giving from their allowances or their pay from after-school jobs. When the pledges were tallied up, my assistant youth pastor and I were amazed. The full cost of the TV time would be covered.

My senior pastor was even more amazed. He gave us permission to start our program, which we called *Youth Aflame*. We met the budget every month, and the exciting part was that many unchurched young people started attending the youth group and came to Jesus. People have approached me decades later to say they watched *Youth Aflame* back in the late 1980s, and they tell me how much it impacted their lives.

When I left the youth pastor position, the church's youth group was divided into three different branches. The three leaders were now doing what we'd begun with one leader. Again, the grace of God, obedience, and hard work had fostered multiplication.

Jesus says, "If you have not been faithful in what is another man's, who will give you what is your own?" (Luke 16:12 NKJV). Let's restate His words according to the parable of the talents: *If you have not multiplied what is another man's, who will give you what is your own to multiply?*

For you, what is the correct answer to that rhetorical question from Jesus? And in what ways can His question be relevant to your own life at this time?

The senior pastor who allowed us to start the *Youth Aflame* program was the man who went on to declare God's plan for Lisa and me to launch Messenger International. He brought it up first, not us. When I'd started my tenure as youth pastor, I told him, "Pastor, I'll remain here until Jesus returns for me unless God shows both you and me that we're supposed to move on." Had God not prompted him in prayer about what our next place of ministry should be, I'm not sure we would have felt free to leave the church. I believe to this day this was the reason God showed him first.

BIRTHING OF MESSENGER INTERNATIONAL

Shortly after leaving the church in Florida, we were ministering in Columbia, South Carolina. It was early in the morning, and I'd found a remote place to pray.

And there God spoke to me: Son, you will reap a large harvest from the faithful seeds you've sown these past seven years in serving others' ministries. It will begin immediately and continue for years to come.

Now, as I look back, I'm in awe of that harvest.

As this personal story goes forward, be on the lookout for ways in which this journey in pursuing God's calling and purpose compares with your own journey. On that journey so far, how have you responded in the face of obstacles and difficulties?

After we were launched by our church to birth Messenger International, diligence was again a key factor in our multiplying. Lisa and I spent many evenings duplicating cassette tapes, making labels, and assembling message series. We'd have friends over on a regular basis to label and batch our newsletter or help in other areas. Lisa and I typed letters, deposited checks, kept financial records, and performed all the necessary paperwork. We made computer entries, post office runs, and supply runs—and that's the short list. We would begin working after prayer in the morning and would often labor until nine p.m. or later at night.

We did it with joy, and we considered it a privilege. Our motivation came from within, and it endured through countless disappointments and dry times. I believe the strength to not lose heart came from the time spent in prayer each morning.

The strength to not lose heart came from the time spent in prayer each morning.

In our Honda Civic, with two infant boys in their car seats in the back, we'd travel up and down I-95 (the main highway on the East Coast) and preach to small churches of eighty to a hundred people. Our first meeting was actually a church that met in a funeral home—what a glamorous start!

We would sell our cassettes and use the proceeds to expand the ministry. We made a commitment that these funds couldn't pay our salary; growing and multiplying Messenger was crucial, so we committed to not touching the money in our audio resource sales account. There were times when other funds we personally needed would arrive on the exact day they were required.

After a year and a half of hard work, the word from God came that I should write. I was so concerned that there just wasn't enough time in a day both to write and to fulfill so many other responsibilities. It seemed risky to make the commitment—but we did. And it took quite a while to write the first book. Meanwhile, unexpectedly, a few young men volunteered to help us with the menial tasks that would have pulled me away from writing. They stepped into the same role we'd taken with our pastor in Dallas. They saw a need in our lives and came forward without us asking.

I finished the manuscript for *Victory in the Wilderness* after a year of hard and sometimes frustrating work. I learned this important key: *We must grow in the grace (gifts) on our lives.* Most of us don't have fantastic results at the beginning.

Peter writes, "Grow in the grace . . . of our Lord and Savior Jesus Christ" (2 Peter 3:18 NKJV). I'm grateful that over time, my ability to write has become so much more developed than when I wrote that first book.

Lisa and I submitted the first manuscript to a well-known editor. To my utter shock, he sharply criticized it. He said I was too young and inexperienced to bring such a message to the body of Christ.

After that blow of rejection, Lisa and I immediately sought another editor. We found one, but he proceeded to botch the entire manuscript. Lisa and I were devastated when we got it back. He'd lost my voice and the strong impact of the content. And worse, his revision didn't make much sense. Simply put, it had been butchered. Yet another blow. What would we do? It had already been more than a year.

We didn't give up. We found another editor who agreed that the original manuscript had been ruined by the second editor. "John and Lisa," she said, "it's often not the right course of action to fix a botch. Take the loss on what you paid the editor and start over." She recommended that Lisa edit the original and then send it to her.

We took this editor's advice, and Lisa spent hours on the original manuscript, improving the readability of the message. The new editor then took Lisa's edits and began her process. She did an amazing job, and we felt we finally had a great manuscript.

I submitted this revised manuscript to two well-known publishing houses. Only one of them responded. They said my book was too "preachy," and since I wasn't a well-known minister, they wouldn't publish it. I then tried to get it placed with lesser-known publishers, but no one was interested.

Can you imagine our disappointment? After well over a year's worth of work and time, it now seemed we were at a dead end. I was distraught—but not willing to quit.

Self-publishing was practically unheard of in those days. Hardly anyone successful in publishing had done it, but a friend suggested we give it a try. We learned that in addition to the cost of artwork and typesetting (and of course what we'd already paid to editors), it would cost us $12,000 to print a few thousand books.

This was a massive sum of money for us. Messenger International's entire income for 1990 was $40,000. We were beginning our third year as a ministry, and we weren't bringing in much more than what we'd brought in our first year. Toward the end of our second year, I remember feeling overwhelmed when purchasing our first computer, which cost only a few hundred dollars.

So now, $12,000 seemed impossible. We needed a miracle to come up with that kind of money. We met a lady who worked in a typesetting position for a small niche publisher that specialized in outdoor sporting books. She heard me talking about writing, and she approached Lisa to offer her services to typeset and compose our book at no charge. We were so happy to not have to pay thousands of dollars for this service.

God miraculously brought in the money for the rest of what was required to self-publish, and we printed five thousand copies of *Victory in the Wilderness* (which has since been retitled *God, Where Are You?*). Our initial excitement didn't last long once we realized we had no distribution channels. Distributors and bookstores had no idea who we were, and back in those days, they purchased only from established publishing houses. No one was interested in a self-published book.

We placed copies of the book on our resource table alongside our cassette-tape series, and we sold them wherever we ministered. When I spoke on the topic of the wilderness, we would sell out—people loved the message. But that's as far as it went.

In prayer, I heard God speak to me about writing another book, so I spent another nine months writing *The Voice of One Crying*. Again, no publishers were interested, so we self-published that book in 1993. Now we had two books on our resource table, but neither was available in any retail outlet.

AN OPEN-DOOR OPPORTUNITY

A year later, a friend of mine called and asked me to lunch. "I want you to meet someone," he said.

I agreed to go. Once there, I learned it was the new leader of the publishing house that had turned me down two years earlier. The lunch went well, and the man took an interest in what Lisa and I were doing. "What's the message you've been speaking on lately?" he asked.

I began to share the hottest topic on my heart: a message addressing the importance of overcoming offenses and forgiving those who'd hurt us. He continued to probe, and I told him more of the message. After fifteen minutes, he said, "John, you know we couldn't publish a book on this. We do only a limited number of books per year, and those are written by well-known authors or ministers."

Puzzled, I said to him, "I wasn't trying to sell you on publishing me; you asked what I was speaking on in my travels."

He laughed. "Oh, yes, that's right. Keep going."

I continued to share. Fifteen minutes later, he interrupted me again. "Can you get me a manuscript in the next three months?"

I replied, "I thought you said you couldn't publish me."

"I've changed my mind," he responded. "This message needs to get out."

In June 1994, the company released the book on forgiveness, *The Bait of Satan.* I was so excited. God had opened a door I couldn't open myself. I was positive it would immediately become popular and sell well; however, that didn't happen in the first seven months. Month after month, I got discouraging sales figures from the publisher. I believed in my heart that this message was destined to go to the masses—to the nations of the world—and I refused to let go of that hope. But all indicators pointed toward yet another disappointment.

I believed in my heart that this message was destined to go to the masses—to the nations of the world—and I refused to let go of that hope. But all indicators pointed toward yet another disappointment.

A few months later, I got a call from a member of the publisher's marketing team. She said, "John, an international live talk show wants to have you on their program. They'll allot you twenty minutes, but they primarily want to talk about you and Lisa and your four sons, and about your travel ministry. However, they're willing to mention your book. It's a start—a crack in the door, so to speak. Do you want us to accept for you?"

"Definitely yes!"

I went for the interview in January 1995. A well-known couple hosted the program that evening. After the husband greeted me, the first thing he did was to hold up a copy of *The Bait of Satan* and ask, "What is the bait of Satan? What's this message about?"

I was surprised that this topic, and not our family, had come up first, but I jumped right in to speak about the book. It was as if everything came to a halt in the studio. I'd been told to watch the floor director closely, because she would hold up signs indicating the time left in the interview. It had been emphasized that I would have only twenty minutes. But then the floor director didn't hold up any signs. The hosts were captivated by what I was saying and didn't interrupt, interject, or say anything. The couple and I lost track of time; I later discovered I'd spoken nonstop for forty minutes.

The host was profoundly impacted. One of the first things he did, live on air, was invite me to come and speak on this subject at their conference, which was one of the largest in the nation.

A couple of days later, the publisher informed me that every bookstore in the United States was sold out of *The Bait of Satan*, and twenty thousand copies were back-ordered. "John, we've never seen this before," he said. "And the talk show people told us they've never seen such a response." I knew in my heart it was a divine setup, which confirmed that it was God's message being promoted.

> As you've followed the personal story here, what are the key choices and decisions you see being made, and the key attitudes? And how might these compare and relate to key choices and decisions and attitudes in this season of your own life? What helpful lessons or examples do you especially observe here?
>
> What's the strongest evidence you see of God's guidance and gracious provision in this story? Compare this with the guidance and provision you need from Him in this season of your own life—or in the days to come as you look ahead. What encouragement to your faith do you find here?

The Bait of Satan eventually became an international bestseller. It has been on and off the charts for the past three decades. At the time of this writing, it has surpassed the six-million mark in copies sold—in paperback, ebook, and audiobook.

It's ironic to look back at how this evolved. The publishing company that originally rejected me as an author now has *The Bait of Satan* as one of its top-selling books of all time. God certainly has a sense of humor.

Had I disobeyed and not written this message, it never would have strengthened so many people. Writing caused the message to multiply, because the book was reaching substantially more people than could ever have heard me speak in person.

Actually, this profound proliferation didn't start with the writing of the book. The multiplication began much earlier, as we continued on this course, even through the many blows we suffered. It began when Lisa and I worked diligently to take all pressure off our first pastor, and then multiplied our church's outreach as youth pastors. It continued through Messenger International—as we worked all hours of the day and evening, and then obeyed God's voice to write and publish.

I thought the multiplication process for the bait of Satan message was now settled and set, and that it would naturally continue to grow with book sales and as I shared the message in conferences and churches globally. I was wrong. God was about to entrust us with more.

How does this personal story help and motivate you in moving forward confidently in the face of any present or potential frustration, rejection, and discouragement?

What about your own story? How are you growing in the grace of God that is on your life? (Be encouraged by what you find written in 2 Peter 3:17–18.)

REFLECTION FOR RENEWAL

In this chapter, what statements or Scripture passages seemed most meaningful for you?

How would you restate them in your own words? (Personalize your answer as a prayer of response to God.)

What are your thoughts about what God wants you to do now in response to what you've seen and reflected upon in this chapter?

GREAT MULTIPLICATION

By his blessing they multiply greatly.

PSALM 107:38 ESV

God will often use frustration or discontentment as a catalyst to stir up our faith—either for initial multiplication or for the next level of multiplication.

An example of this is found with Abram (Abraham). God appeared to him when he was seventy-five years of age and spoke in a vision:

> Do not be afraid, Abram, for I will protect you, and your reward will be great. (Genesis 15:1)

Let's set the stage. God Almighty is the One who created and owns all the earth, including its vast resources. He has always existed and will never end. No other being comes anywhere near His greatness. He doesn't *have* life; He *is* life. All enduring knowledge, wisdom, treasures, and pleasures are in Him. There's nothing of value outside of Him.

This is the awesome Being who declares to Abram that He will *protect* him and give him *a great reward*. Let's discuss both these things.

First, *protection*. Imagine if the president of the United States assigned all the nation's armed forces to protect just you. All the generals inform their downline officers that *you* are top priority, and anything required for your safety should be implemented. If needed, they'll station every available soldier near you, with a full spectrum of advanced weaponry.

Such a scenario is almost unimaginable, but if this occurred, I'm sure you'd feel very safe and secure. But this pales in comparison to God Almighty Himself saying, "*I* will protect you."

How about a *great reward*? If your neighbor says, "I'm going to give you a huge reward," that's very kind and generous, except he may not have much to offer. If the wealthiest man in the world makes the same statement, you would get more excited. But neither matches the case here. The reward to Abram is being offered by the One who owns everything on the planet and in the universe. He declares, "The reward I have for you will be *great*." Honestly, the enormousness of this promise is difficult to grasp.

And we're still not done setting the scene.

FRUITFUL DISCONTENTMENT

The other mind-blowing reality is that the Creator doesn't send a messenger to Abram; He comes in person. God Almighty makes these unfathomable promises to him face-to-face. Can you imagine the magnitude? What would our reaction be if we were in Abram's situation? What words could possibly express the excitement, joy, happiness, and awe that any of us would feel?

But Abram's response isn't close to these emotions. In fact, he's not excited at all; he's frustrated.

> But Abram replied, "O Sovereign Lord, what good are all your blessings when I don't even have a son?" (Genesis 15:2)

Do you hear the discontentment in his response? Amazing! But could Abram's lack of enthusiasm actually be a good thing?

Suppose Abram had said, "Wow, this is awesome! Let's get this party started!" Would the eventual outcome have been different? But the better question is this: Would God have even appeared to Abram if He'd expected this kind of response? I don't believe so.

Let me explain. Let's pause Abram's story to bring clarity. Centuries later, when the Israelites were wandering in the wilderness, their discontentment stemmed from personal discomfort—which, sadly, cost them their destiny. However, more centuries later, the apostle Paul projected his own godly attitude about contentment in these words:

> I have learned how to be content with whatever I have. I know how to live on almost nothing or with everything. I have learned the secret of living in every situation, whether it is with a full stomach or empty, with plenty or little. (Philippians 4:11–12)

In both Paul and Abram, God found someone willing to endure and even embrace hardship for the purpose of looking beyond self to others. For both men, their dissatisfaction wasn't personal; rather, it was focused on *others*.

Here's a good rule of thumb: If discontentment and complaining stems from what I personally lack, it's displeasing to God. On the other hand, if my discontentment focuses on the needs of others and building the kingdom, it's pleasing to God.

Abram's frustration was that second kind. And what became of it? God enlarged his vision by highlighting the stars of the heavens and the sands of the seashore, promising that his reward would impact more than he could number. Abram's discontentment moved God to declare, "I will make My covenant between Me and you, and will *multiply you exceedingly*" (Genesis 17:2 NKJV).

Here's a good rule of thumb: If discontentment and complaining stems from what I personally lack, it's displeasing to God. On the other hand, if my discontentment focuses on the needs of others and building the kingdom, it's pleasing to God.

In what areas of your life are you sensing some degree of discontentment? Does it lead you to complain? Evaluate whether that discontentment is from a narrow, self-focused sense of personal lack, or from a wider desire to meet others' needs for the sake of God's kingdom. Which describes it best?

In what areas of your life is God clearly challenging you to grow (either through your experience of discontentment or in some other way)? How are you responding to His promptings?

What if Abram had been content with being remarkably blessed in just his own life? Would he have had a reason to believe at age seventy-five that he could father a child? *His dissatisfaction became the catalyst to multiply.*

I've learned that this discontentment is not something to ignore, but a springboard to increased effectiveness. It's what the church in the city of Laodicea lacked. Jesus sternly corrected this church for their attitude of "I . . . have need of nothing" (Revelation 3:17 NKJV). Because they were self-focused and comfortable in their plenty, they didn't feel frustrated when they didn't see others being impacted. Consequently, they didn't seek to multiply.

This describes the temptation Stan wrestled with. I, too, struggle with this at times, and I've had to fight it off. In fact, most of us do.

The longer I serve God, the more I've come to realize that one of the genuine fruits of a true believer is a deep desire to impact others for the kingdom. At the moment of salvation, we're changed into completely different people. We're reborn with a driving passion to serve. Paul writes, "For you, brethren, have been called to liberty; only do not use liberty as an opportunity for the flesh, but through love *serve one another*" (Galatians 5:13 NKJV). And Jesus tells us, "Be dressed for *service* and keep your lamps burning" (Luke 12:35).

This charge from our Master highlights the posture all believers are to maintain: *service* and the *passion* to serve. I chose the word *maintain* because this posture is already a part of our new nature. This is often overlooked due to our fear of slipping over to "works" to be saved, as opposed to salvation being a free gift. However, the saved spirit's inborn desire is to serve. Why would we avoid discussing this huge aspect of our new life? Or why would we dumb it down? Could it be that we try to reinvent Christianity as more of a consumer-based faith experience? Are we appealing to the spiritual laziness of humanity's fallen nature?

> Do you recognize in yourself a desire (to any degree) for your Christian life to be "more of a consumer-based faith experience"—something that's in sync with the spiritual laziness of your fallen nature? Discuss this honestly with God.
>
> If you recognize this attitude in yourself, communicate to God your genuine repentance.

Why would Jesus tell us, "Be dressed for service"? Why does He couple clothing with service? We find a clue in the voices of the heavenly host in Revelation 19:

> "Let us be glad and rejoice, and let us give honor to him. For the time has come for the wedding feast of the Lamb, and his bride has *prepared herself.* She has been given the finest of pure white linen to wear." For the fine linen represents *the good deeds* of God's holy people. (verses 7–8)

We see here that the bride—not God—has prepared herself. And notice the manner in which she has done so. Every bride takes a lot of time to pick out her wedding attire. It's one of her most important to-do list items for the big day. In Western cultures, she may spend considerable time shopping for and buying the outfit. In the kingdom of God, we as the bride of Christ spend considerable time *making* our outfit. Our attire is constructed from fine linen, which according to Revelation 19 is our service in building the kingdom. Serving is thus in our spiritual DNA.

Jesus says, "As the Father has sent me, so I am sending you" (John 20:21). He came for the purpose to serve (Mark 10:45)—and our mandate is no different. He also gives us (by His example) the "why" behind the importance of serving: "My nourishment comes from doing the will of God, who sent me, and from finishing his work" (John 4:34).

We wouldn't last long physically without food. Similarly, believers serving to build the kingdom will not last long without nourishment. Without it, they'll eventually backslide. This is the scenario Jesus goes on to illustrate in Luke 12, after commanding us to stay "dressed for service" and to keep our "lamps burning" (verses 35–40).

For this reason, the forces of the fallen world will work hard to make us comfortable and complacent, instead of dissatisfied in a way that leads to multiplication.

So don't despise discontentment over the level of your impact. It's most often God's way of stirring your faith to believe for divine multiplication.

> Is God stirring up your own faith to fully believe and trust Him for divine multiplication? What exactly does this mean for you now? What are you understanding more clearly about God's call?

MY DISCONTENTMENT

Once *The Bait of Satan* book took off, not only in the United States but also in other nations, you might think I would have been satisfied. I wasn't. I began wrestling with discontentment on another level.

> Again, as this personal story continues, be on the lookout for ways in which this journey in pursuing God's calling and purpose compares to the journey God has for *you*. Ask the Lord to help you recognize clearly what He wants you to pay the most attention to.

I was now speaking to much larger churches and conferences, but my frustration stemmed from the inability to get the full message communicated in a single service. It takes me roughly four hundred hours to write a book, and so much is revealed by the Holy Spirit during this time of writing. These truths are revealed for the people God loves—for the purpose of strengthening, freeing, and drawing them closer to Him.

The time allotted for a message in most churches or conferences is thirty-five to forty-five minutes. So when speaking about *The Bait of Satan*, I could cover a chapter, or at best a chapter and a half. This meant that 90 percent of the message wasn't reaching the people—unless they purchased (and read) the book, which only about one-fifth of those in attendance would do.

Out of this frustration, an idea came to me four or five years after the book was published: Why not create a curriculum and study of the book? I could teach twelve thirty-minute video lessons and cover the critical truths in each chapter. People could get the entire message not only by reading but also by seeing and hearing, whether in groups or individually. This would help expand the effectiveness of the message. We could create discussion questions for groups or individuals that would give the Holy Spirit the opportunity to probe deeper and make the message more applicable to each person.

I discussed all this with our team. One member suggested searching for an educational company to create a devotional student workbook and a leader's manual to complement the twelve videos, allowing the curriculum to be used in a wide variety of settings. We located an excellent manufacturer that did similar work for more than twenty-five hundred clients, including some of the larger corporations in the United States. We requested up front that there be no cutting corners, no compromising of quality. And we wanted the entire project to be highly innovative. We told them, "Let's aim to be years ahead both in style and technology." In those days, there weren't that many similar curriculums available for churches; the idea hadn't yet caught on.

As a side note, I was privileged to lead a Bible study for the staff of one of our presidents. When entering the West Wing of the White House, I couldn't help noticing excellence all around me. The thought came to me: *This place represents the president of the United States; we at Messenger represent the King of the universe.* Even though we'd stressed excellence at Messenger from the beginning, after this experience, we would be even more resolute about never sacrificing quality or cutting corners.

Once we had the study materials ready to go, two team members were reassigned to work full-time making telephone calls; they were instructed to contact leaders of every church we'd been to over the past ten years and inform them about the curriculum. Our heart was to come alongside them and help disciple their people, ultimately strengthening the local church.

We were so pleased when the idea resonated with leaders—the response was mind-blowing. Churches were reporting escalating attendance in small groups and their main services. We heard reports of churches doubling and even tripling in attendance. Although we initially thought only churches of less than three hundred would use the curriculum for their services, a few churches with attendance in the thousands began using the videos in this way—and they, too, were growing.

The testimonies kept pouring into our office about lives, families, and churches being changed. Pastors shared what was taking place as they spoke with their pastor friends at other churches, and many of these began calling us, seeking the curriculum. Within a few years, we had thousands of churches involved—more than twenty thousand in the United States and more than a thousand in Australia. Our church relations department grew to seven full-time workers.

Over the next several years, we did curriculum for every major book our ministry released. Within twelve years, we had more than ten different studies being used in churches all over the United States and Australia.

One aspect of the multiplication we didn't foresee, but realized later, was that a vast number of individuals who never would have purchased one of my books or heard me speak were now receiving the messages—because their church leaders had decided to take them through the materials.

"YOU'VE BEEN FAITHFUL"

Of course, we were filled with gratitude. The number of books sold now numbered in the millions, plus hundreds of thousands of copies of the studies. Nevertheless, I still wrestled with dissatisfaction. I knew these messages were for the body of Christ and were bearing much fruit, but there were still so many believers in need of the truths these messages carried.

I asked God for the privilege of giving away more books than were being sold. I knew there were pastors, leaders, and believers all over the globe who didn't have the finances or even the ability to purchase books. There were countless millions in underground churches in nations where the sale of Christian books was restricted. There were even more people in nations who didn't have the resources to import books.

How could we help them?

I knew the need was great, but connecting with these pastors and leaders seemed an impossible task. But we had to do something.

We started by responding to whatever came before us. We instructed our international director that if any group of leaders in a developing or persecuted nation needed books, we would send all they needed as gifts, or we would arrange to pay for the printing of the books in their nation.

What we were able to achieve in this was small—ten thousand to twenty thousand books per year. This number seemed like only a drop in the bucket, but we continued year after year, seizing any opportunities that came before us. My frustration continued to mount.

That day I knew a shift had taken place. We would no longer merely seize opportunities that came before us; we now had a divine commission.

Then came Memorial Day in May 2010. Lisa was in England ministering at a women's conference. I'd just finished playing a round of golf. I grabbed my Bible and went to our basement, feeling an urge to read the book of Daniel. While I was reading the second chapter, the Spirit of God suddenly filled our basement, and I heard these words in my heart: Son, you've been faithful over the English-speaking realm. Now I want you to get your messages into the hands of every pastor and leader in the world.

The presence of God lingered for several minutes. With awe and wonder, I remained still until it lifted. That day I knew a shift had taken place. We would no longer merely seize opportunities that came before us; we now had a divine commission. We would intentionally seek out pastors and leaders in need—regardless of their nation, language, or financial position.

The attention-grabber in this encounter was the Holy Spirit's use of the word *faithful*. At that time, I didn't associate "faithful" with "multiplication"; this truth hadn't been revealed to me yet. Had I been asked then to give the biblical definition of *faithful*, my reply wouldn't have included the concept of multiplication. The Spirit's words to me in the basement began to open my heart to this understanding. I knew I'd heard from God, but I still questioned how our ministry could perform such a monumental task.

During this time our team lost our international director. To fill the vacancy, Lisa and I invited a longtime friend, Rob Birkbeck, to join our team along with his wife, Vanessa. Rob had worked for the large international ministry of a famous evangelist. He was a senior director in that ministry, and one of his responsibilities was to print and distribute the evangelist's books. Rob was well-connected with publishers and pastoral networks in almost every nation of the world. At the time, none of us realized how great the impact of this partnership would be.

In January 2011, I was leading a meeting of our ministry's top leaders, including Rob and Vanessa. During the meeting, I asked, "How many books did we give to pastors and leaders in foreign nations last year?"

One of the team members looked through the year-end summary and reported the answer: thirty-three thousand books. He thought I would respond favorably to this figure—but my frustration spoke out: "That's pathetic!" I then announced boldly that in the coming year, our ministry would give a quarter-million books to pastors and leaders in developing and persecuted nations.

The entire room went dead silent. Lisa told me later that, in that moment, she tasted throw-up in her mouth. (She has a fabulous sense of humor.)

Finally, our COO, who happens to be our oldest son, spoke first. "Dad," Addison said, "are you sure you want to do that many?"

"Yes," I replied wholeheartedly. "*We will.*"

He proceeded to challenge me for the next twenty minutes. We kept going back and forth in front of everyone else, who remained quiet. He was respectful, but he wouldn't budge from contending that my directive was too lofty. In frustration he finally blurted out, "I just don't want to give our team an unrealistic goal."

At this point, I'd had enough. I proceeded to slam my fist on the table and sternly declared, "I said we're going to give away a quarter-million books this year." The room fell silent. The meeting soon adjourned, and we all left feeling uncomfortable.

The next morning, when Addison and I were alone, he said, "I was a bit uncomfortable with the way you spoke to me."

We were both calm now and wanting to reconcile. "Son, you know I love our team's input. I usually weigh out everyone's suggestions and thoughts before making a final decision. However, yesterday was different. I didn't ask the team, 'Do you think we should give away a quarter-million books?' or, 'How many books do you all think we should give away next year?' I stated that we were going to do this! But you argued with me for twenty minutes."

He acknowledged and agreed, but peacefully made one final appeal: "Dad, could you pray about this for twenty-four hours? If afterward you still believe we should do it, our team will put all its efforts into making this happen."

"Sure, I'll do it," I responded.

Honestly, I didn't pray much about it. I breathed a half-hearted prayer in order to keep my word, but because of my encounter in the basement, I already knew it was the right thing to do.

You may be wondering if I was nervous at the time. *Yes*—I was borderline terrified. I restrained myself from going down the mental path of where the finances would come from, or whether something of this magnitude would hinder other aspects of our ministry or even bankrupt it. If I allowed myself to go down that path, I would have quickly agreed with my son and backed the number down to what seemed "reasonable." The goal of a quarter-million books seemed impossible—but I was determined to stay with the directive I'd received. I knew somehow that either a creative strategy or a miraculous provision would come.

Little did I know that not one, but both would come to pass.

As you continue in this story, think about the importance of obedient faith in your own life. In what experiences has God especially taught you about obedience? Recall the lessons you learned, and thank Him for His wisdom and faithfulness.

> What special importance do you see in obeying God when others around you don't agree that the path you're pursuing is correct?

Three weeks later, I was in a hotel room in Florida writing a new book. Our team knows not to call me in the morning when I'm writing; it's my best time to concentrate. My cell phone rang, and I saw on the caller ID that it was the office. I answered, as I knew it must be something urgent or important. I heard a jovial group atmosphere on the other end. All the same people who'd been in the intense confrontational meeting three weeks earlier were in the room, and they seemed to be celebrating and laughing.

Addison said, "Dad, we haven't sent out an official communication to our financial partners about the initiative to give away a quarter-million books, but one of our team members was talking to a man he knows, and when he heard about our plan, he committed to giving $300,000 for this project!"

Until this moment, the largest gift our ministry had received from one individual was $50,000—so I joined in the celebration. After many jubilant and wonder-filled comments, I said to everyone, "Now do you understand why I was so insistent in that meeting three weeks ago?"

My son laughed and quickly said, "Dad, if you tell us to give away a million books, I'm totally on board." The others heartily agreed.

All I could do was pace the floor of my hotel room saying, "Thank You! Thank You! Thank You!"

I'll never forget that morning. I hung up the phone and couldn't write any longer. All I could do was pace the floor of my hotel room saying, "Thank You! Thank You! Thank You!" Tears were streaming down my face. All I could see in my heart were hungry pastors and leaders getting the discipleship resources they so desperately longed for.

I'm so grateful that Addison was honest and challenged me. I'm glad he didn't keep his thoughts inside but voiced what many others in that room felt. They most likely heard their own concerns being articulated in Addison's challenges, and these thoughts needed to be confronted. The whole drama caused us to overcome looming fears, which if listened to probably would have drawn us to change course and stay within our own means. Our vision would have withered, and we wouldn't have received such a large and generous gift. Maybe we would have distributed fifty thousand books or remained undecided. Instead we set a goal, and the Holy Spirit heard it. He then moved on this man's heart to give an extraordinary gift. As a team, we grew to a new level of faith.

That year, by the grace of God, we were able to give 271,700 books to pastors and leaders in forty-eight nations, including Iran, Iraq, Syria, Lebanon, Egypt, Turkey, Albania, Croatia, Uzbekistan, Kazakhstan, Turkmenistan, Myanmar, Cambodia, Vietnam, China, Mongolia, plus numerous needy African nations, and more. In previous years, we'd given tens of thousands; now it reached over a quarter-million. Our outreach effectiveness grew over eight times. Praise God—that's great multiplication!

> Again, as you've followed this personal story in these pages, what do you see as the key choices and decisions that were made? And how might they compare and relate to any key choices and decisions you're facing in this season of your own life? What helpful lessons, examples, or guidelines do you see here?
>
> What is the strongest evidence you see of God's guidance and gracious provision in this story? Compare this with your own need for His guidance and provision in this season of your life—or in further days to come, as you look ahead. What encouragement to your faith do you find here?

MORE DISCONTENTMENT

Could there be more?

In May 2011, four months after the intense confrontation in the boardroom, Rob and I were in Beirut, Lebanon, ministering to pastors and leaders who'd traveled from all over the Middle East. In the midst of the meetings,

Rob approached me with a request: "There's a pastor here from Erbil, Iraq, who would love to spend a little time with you. Would you like to meet with him?"

"Absolutely yes!"

Rob arranged for us to meet in the hotel lobby. The pastor was around thirty-five years old, and his eyes burned with passion and desire. I could tell he was serious about building the kingdom. He was dressed for service, and his lamp was blazing. He'd traveled from Erbil for one reason: to be strengthened by the teaching and meetings. I immediately sensed that he was a progressive and innovative leader who understood the importance of being relevant to the lost.

Our meeting started lightheartedly. After our conversation turned more serious, at one point he stated, "Pastor Bevere, I see you as a spiritual father. I read anything you write." (There were limited books in his native language, but he could read English.) "I even use my credit card to download your materials from Messenger International's website . . ."

At that point, I checked out. Honestly, I don't remember much of anything else we discussed. My mind was screaming: I'm looking at a pastor from the devastated, war-torn nation of Iraq—and he has to use his credit card to get materials off our website? I couldn't wait to get alone with the Lord to address this chronic need.

After saying goodbye, I went straight to my room and closed the door. I was so frustrated, I yelled, "God, You've got to show me how to get the messages You've entrusted to us to the pastors and leaders of the world who need them." I really didn't care who was in the room next to me. I had to hear heaven's plan for how to accomplish His commission and provide more accessible resources for these leaders.

Not many days after this intense time of prayer, an idea came for a strategy that would cause our outreach to become more effective many times over—in fact, exponentially more effective, without much additional work or expense.

It was a brilliant idea . . . one that could have come only from the wisdom of God. So simple, yet we hadn't considered it. Read on!

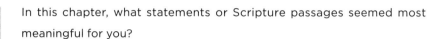

REFLECTION FOR RENEWAL

In this chapter, what statements or Scripture passages seemed most meaningful for you?

How would you restate them in your own words? (Personalize your answer as a prayer of response to God.)

What are your thoughts about what God wants you to do now in response to what you've seen and reflected upon in this chapter?

STRATEGIC IDEAS

If you don't know what you're doing,

pray to the Father.

He loves to help.

JAMES 1:5 MSG

W ith each passing year, I become more convinced of the tremendous value of an *inspired strategic idea*. Often, we look for God's provision or intervention to occur without a tactical plan, but frequently that isn't the process. What happens is a God-induced strategic idea.

There are too many biblical illustrations of these to list, but let's mention a few that support this reality:

- The strategic idea to throw a piece of wood into the bitter water so millions of people could drink (Exodus 15:22–25).
- A different inspired idea to strike a rock, providing more water for millions (Exodus 17:5–6).
- The strategic idea to quietly march once around impenetrable walls of a mighty city for six days. Then on the seventh day, a different strategic idea—to march seven times around with horns blowing, and finally to give a rousing long shout. All of this to gain entrance and conquer the city (Joshua 6).
- The strategic idea to identify a military's top warriors by having tens of thousands drink water from a spring and then separating out those

who looked down from those who kept their eye on the battlefield (Judges 7:4–6).

- The strategic idea to not attack an enemy head-on, but to circle back behind in the forest and wait to hear the marching feet in the tops of the poplar trees, signaling the Lord's assistance in the battle (2 Samuel 5:22–25).
- The strategic idea in a severe famine to ask a widow and her son to feed a prophet with their final meal, instead of eating it themselves; by obeying, they would not starve and die, as many other families did (1 Kings 17:8–15).
- The strategic idea of asking a widow in debt, who was about to lose her two sons, what she had in her house. Then instructing her to borrow empty jars from others and pour her only possession—a small amount of olive oil—into the other jars until they were full; then to sell the miraculous oil and pay the debt (2 Kings 4:1–7).
- The strategic idea to send a military officer with a disease to dip himself in the Jordan River seven times, resulting in his complete healing (2 Kings 5:1–14).
- The strategic idea to send the praise and worship team out ahead of the military troops, which produced a phenomenal victory (2 Chronicles 20:21–26).
- The strategic idea to eat vegetables, instead of the king's rich foods, to be healthier and better nourished, thus becoming standouts among the finest young men in the land (Daniel 1:8–16).
- The strategic idea to use existing water pots and fresh water to procure the best wine and save a wedding reception (John 2:6–10).
- The strategic idea to take a small lunch, then bless, break, and distribute it to feed thousands of people (Matthew 14:13–21).
- The strategic idea to spit and make mud and put it on the eyes of a blind man. Then telling him to go wash to restore his sight (John 9:6–7).
- The strategic idea to not leave a sinking ship in order to be saved (Acts 27:21–44).

Do you see common threads running through each of these events?

Choose some (or all) of the prior verses to explore on your own. What impresses you most about these strategic ideas?

In every case, the inspired idea featured divine intervention. The strategy made use of what the recipients already possessed, such as an available resource or a repositioning of themselves. And in each case, the divine provision was wrapped up in the familiar; the key component leading to the miracle didn't "magically" appear.

God often gives strategies using the ordinary, in an unordinary way, to get extraordinary results.

God often gives strategies using the ordinary, in an unordinary way, to get extraordinary results.

In your own life, how have you seen your circumstances change thanks to a God-inspired idea?

In what ways in your life—or in the life of someone close to you—have you seen God use the ordinary in an unordinary way to get extraordinary results?

All this highlights the importance of an inspired idea. We're told, "Getting wisdom is the most important thing you can do" (Proverbs 4:7 GNT). One form of divine wisdom is a strategic idea, and the good news is that God doesn't withhold wisdom. When we face uncommon challenges, the apostle James instructs us:

If you need wisdom [a strategic idea], ask our generous God, and he will give it to you. He will not rebuke you for asking. (James 1:5)

He'll make this wisdom plain, not holding back or hiding it from you. This is His promise. However, two conditions must be met for receiving an inspired strategic idea: confident faith and desperate desire.

Just make sure you ask empowered by *confident faith* without doubting that you will receive. For the ambivalent person believes one minute and doubts the next. Being *undecided* makes you become like the rough seas driven and tossed by the wind. You're up one minute and tossed down the next. When you are *half-hearted* and *wavering* it leaves you unstable. Can you really expect to receive anything from the Lord when you're in that condition? (James 1:6–8 TPT)

We must ask with *confident faith*. We don't *hope* for the tactical idea; we fully expect it. Also, we must possess a passion for our request—we must *desperately want it*. Our request doesn't come out of a ho-hum, lethargic attitude that says, "If I receive, that's great; if not, no problem." Rather, confident faith is marked by a sense of desperation and a firm determination to receive.

The *strategic idea* is a gift from God—and once received, it will open us to another realm of effectiveness. It empowers us to multiply.

In what areas of your life do you especially sense the need for more of God's wisdom? In earnest and honest prayer to the God of all grace, articulate your request for this wisdom.

In order to receive His answer—how will you approach God?

How motivated and ready are you to have God open you to "another realm of effectiveness," as He empowers you to multiply? Do any questions or doubts arise in your mind? If so, bring them before your heavenly Father, and leave them with Him.

AN INSPIRED, STRATEGIC IDEA

Getting back to the hotel in Beirut (where the last chapter ended)—I didn't go to my room and pray quietly; I just couldn't. I was at my wits' end, out of ideas. And yet I knew I'd been entrusted with the responsibility to supply these needy and hungry pastors. I don't make a practice of yelling in hotel rooms, but honestly, that day, I didn't care who heard me. It was a desperate cry to receive the *strategy* (wisdom) to multiply our effectiveness.

> Again, as this personal story continues, be on the lookout for ways in which this journey in pursuing God's calling and purpose compares with the journey God has for you.

After a time of intense prayer, peace filled my heart. I knew my request was heard—and, experiencing relief, I now believed the answer would become manifest. Thanksgiving poured out of my inner being, even though I still didn't have a strategic idea or plan.

A few days later, I had a thought: We're spending a lot of time, money, and energy in printing and distributing these books—but each leader is receiving only a single item. Why not do what we did in English years ago? Why not also make the full curriculum available in other languages to the leaders? We'll increase all our effectiveness!

But we still faced a huge challenge: How could we print and distribute so much material? Even if we paid to print all the contents of a curriculum, in most of the targeted nations, our distributors would be responsible for more pounds of weight than they could carry. The reason? Most of the distribution occurs in jungles, mountains, deserts, or waterways that are difficult to access. Often there are no paved roads. Not only this, but in hostile nations, the carriers would be easily identified by opposing authorities, and the material could be confiscated. (Note that this happened in the days prior to digital streaming.)

After more prayer and contemplation, another idea arose of putting the full curriculum on a DVD-ROM (a DVD that holds read-only data for a computer system). But this plan also presented questions: Do pastors and leaders in these nations have computer capabilities? If so, could their computers even read a DVD-ROM? On a totally different front: Was there enough space on a DVD-ROM for all the data required for a full study?

I was eager to investigate, so I first approached Rob. He was the most knowledgeable about the technical capabilities of our targeted nations since he'd been to over 160 countries. I asked him, "Do pastors and leaders in most nations, even if they're poor, have the use of computers?"

"Most do, but a few don't."

"Can their computer read a DVD-ROM? And if so, how much material can we put on a DVD-ROM?"

Rob lit up. "Yes. And as for the second question—offhand, I would guess quite a bit."

Then I threw out the idea: "Can we put a sleeve in the back of the book holding the DVD-ROM?"

"Yes!" he affirmed enthusiastically.

"How much more will it cost to do all this per book?"

Rob did the research and got back to me within days: "I've got great news. Looking at our average cost for printing and distributing a book, it will cost only another 5 percent to add the DVD-ROM."

I was excited but still a bit reserved, unsure of how much data could go on a disk.

"But here's the really good news," Rob said. "We can put not only the entire curriculum on the disk, but also the audiobook, two or three other books, a New Testament, and a PDF file so the pastors can print more books if they have the capability."

To say the least, we were jubilant and energized.

This led to another strategic idea. Again, it was conditional to the technical abilities of the seeded nations. I asked, "Do most pastors and leaders in these nations have access to the internet?"

"In most nations, yes," Rob replied.

"What if we develop a website that contains all these translated resources?

Let's give it a name that won't stand out as a Christian website; this way, governments opposing biblical teachings won't block it. We can print the website's location on the front page of the book and instruct the pastors and leaders to encourage their people to download all these resources at no cost so the entire church can go through it together."

We were like two kids in a candy store—our excitement couldn't be contained. More ideas flowed between us to help strengthen the strategy.

After completing all due diligence, we determined that, due to large quantities, we indeed could manufacture and distribute these leadership kits for roughly four dollars each. And our team at Messenger had the skill and know-how to develop the website.

Our team soon realized that this one idea from heaven provided the potential to teach, train, and strengthen entire congregations or small groups, not just individual leaders. Many small villages throughout the world have only a single church, which means we were able to significantly impact those communities for just a few dollars. What a return on investment! Could this really be possible?

At the next department head meeting at Messenger, we shared the vision. The enthusiasm caught on; each team member was ecstatic with joy and energized by the plan. I passionately declared, "It doesn't matter if it takes ten, twenty, or however many years—we're going to reach and help every leader on the planet with our God-entrusted resources."

One month later, a businessman from Texas called our office. He requested a fifteen-minute meeting with Lisa and me. He and his wife flew to Colorado. During our meeting, he began to weep. Through his tears, he trembled and said, "I know what you're doing. I know you're strengthening pastors in remote places with your resources. I want to be a part of this." He then slid a check across the table. I almost fell out of my chair; it was made out for $750,000.

I passionately declared, "We're going to reach and help every leader on the planet with our God-entrusted resources."

Over the next few months, we developed the website and worked diligently to implement the "leadership pack" plan in various countries and regions of the world. We would incur a one-time cost for each language translation of the book materials, corresponding curriculum, and extra books that would go on the

DVD-ROM. Rob hired and led teams of the best translators for the numerous languages. The two generous donations, totaling just over a million dollars, covered the needed capital for our first year.

THE IDEA TO BUILD A TEAM

At this point, let's back up the timeline and return to January 2011 and the days immediately following the decision to give away a quarter-million books. The two large donations hadn't yet been given, and I'm glad they hadn't because our lack of funds back then became a catalyst to seek God each morning for a strategy. We needed a plan to communicate the vision, and subsequently to build a huge team of men and women who would bring their gift of giving in order to sustain this massive endeavor. This would make it possible for us to resource every pastor and leader, regardless of their language, location, or financial position.

After several mornings of praying, the Holy Spirit whispered to my heart, *Son, you're well-known for your love of golf. Use it to gather. I'll draw the right men and women to come join the team and support the mission.*

My thoughts went immediately to the fact that we had one of the nicest hotels in the nation in Colorado Springs—the Broadmoor—which just happened to have two championship golf courses. So I approached Addison and Lisa with the plan.

They listened, and then asked, "When will we do this?"

"Let's do it this summer," I replied.

We were concerned we might not have enough time to pull it off. Would there be sufficient rooms available at the hotel, which just happens to be the longest-standing five-star, five-diamond hotel in the world? It's usually booked out years in advance, and we were targeting the peak season. The other concern: Would our potential guests already have their summer plans in place?

My son took the lead and within a couple of days returned with the news: "Dad, they're booked solid this summer with the exception of one week. We can reserve roughly one hundred rooms, and it just so happens you and Mom are home that week."

"Let's book it!" I said without hesitation.

"We have to sign a contract," he cautioned. "We'll be committed. Can we fill the rooms?"

Again, I blurted out, "The rooms will be full." I didn't want to think about it too much; I didn't want to reason myself out of the plan. I knew a lot of churches and businesspeople in the United States would love to support this endeavor. I called everyone I could think of, and practically everyone was eager to participate. Within a couple of months, we had enough couples to fill the committed rooms.

As we planned, our team decided not to make this just a golf tournament, but a full-blown event, a memorable experience. We determined that everything would be done with excellence and purpose to make the experience especially fun for the spouses who didn't play golf. Lisa would host special gatherings with the women. Upon arrival, we would give each couple a beautiful basket filled with snacks and gifts. There would be spectacular meals, special experiences unique to the Broadmoor, leadership sessions, and high-quality prizes to the participants—all to convey gratitude for joining the team.

Our first Messenger Cup was held in late June 2011. Before the event, I called professional athletes and well-known musicians and asked if they could donate signed items. We also got other businesses to give valuable items or experiences. We auctioned off these contributions during the banquet. We raised a little over $340,000 in our first tournament, but it was a bit awkward. We still hadn't connected with the best strategy to share the vision.

That fall, one of our team members had another inspired idea. As we were planning for the second annual tournament in the summer of 2012, he said, "We're auctioning a signed baseball, a football helmet, a signed guitar, and so forth—but the auction isn't fully funding materials for even one nation. This time, let's not auction an item; let's auction a nation. The value of a nation is much greater."

We all loved the idea, but it got even better. He continued, "We have highly competitive people coming to this event, so let's create a leaderboard, and as they fund nations, their giving will accumulate on the board. Then we'll give the golf clubs, guitars, and other prizes to those who've done the most to sponsor nations."

The creative ideas continued flowing. At one point, I protested: "I hate dragging out auctions; a few minutes of silence seem like an eternity. Let's put a small amount of time on a clock—say thirty-five minutes—and tell our participants we'll be finished with the auction once the clock runs out. Any nation whose project isn't funded will be left out. It will create a great sense of urgency."

At this point, let me briefly describe how each *project* involved two things. First was the expense to translate and interpret all the printed, audio, and video components of a leader pack, which cost roughly $18,500 per language. Second was the cost to manufacture and distribute the books or leader packs to a nation. Each country had anywhere from five hundred to forty thousand leaders. Most nations averaged five thousand to ten thousand leaders, for an average expense of $20,000 to $40,000.

In later meetings, more ideas flowed from the team to enhance the experience, communicate the vision, and pull off the second event.

That year during the auction, we witnessed the pledged funds double from the previous year. With time to spare on the clock, over fifty projects were fully funded. The momentum grew, and at the third Messenger Cup a year later, we raised over $1.3 million to fund many more projects.

Every year the cry for resources grew. More nations were sending delegates to Rob, pleading for the resources. Eventually, the number of projects passed the one hundred mark, and by the sixth Messenger Cup, there were over 140 projects and over $2 million raised. In the ninth year, we witnessed almost $3 million coming in to fund close to two hundred projects.

At the time of this book's release in 2025, the Messenger Cup team has given over fifty-five million physical resources to pastors and leaders in more than two hundred nations, and in more than 125 languages.

Throughout this time, we were all inspired by one of my heroes, Andrew Carnegie. He's one of history's best-known philanthropists, who gave most of his fortune away. In the value of today's currency, Carnegie gave billions of dollars to charitable works. A good part of this was given to build public libraries. In fact, between the years of 1883 and 1918, he built over twenty-five hundred libraries in almost every state of the US at that time.

Let me pose an intriguing question: During what time period did the United

States become a world power? It was between 1883 and 1918, the same time frame when Carnegie was building libraries. I believe his making knowledge available to the public contributed to the emergence of America as a world leader.

This principle applies to spiritual knowledge as well. God states:

My people are destroyed for *lack of knowledge*. (Hosea 4:6 NKJV)

My people have gone into captivity, because they have *no knowledge*. (Isaiah 5:13 NKJV)

After many years in our ministry, it has become evident that the most effective way to transform a village or town is *not* to construct a church building. This just keeps the local leadership dependent on us. We're much more effective if we give the indigenous leaders spiritual knowledge that will empower them to influence their village, town, or city. Such knowledge helps produce the faith needed to grow and sustain the work, which if necessary will include buildings and other resources.

In the case of our strategic initiative with resources, the amazing reality is that a church building might have cost us tens of thousands of dollars. The leadership pack, which contains hundreds of dollars' worth of resources, costs us only a fraction of that.

The fifteen years of giving leadership packs to the developing church has unquestionably been the most enjoyable of my forty years in ministry. I love being part of a team of men and women united in passion and vision to make disciples of the nations (Matthew 28:19–20). By uniting, we've far outdone what any of us could have accomplished by ourselves. This effort truly exemplifies the words, "Five of you will chase a hundred, and a hundred of you will chase ten thousand!" (Leviticus 26:8).

By uniting, we've far outdone what any of us could have accomplished by ourselves.

Our rally cry centers on this parable of Jesus:

"When you put on a luncheon or a banquet," he said, "don't invite your friends, brothers, relatives, and rich neighbors. For they will invite you back, and that will be your only reward. Instead, invite the poor, the crippled, the lame, and the blind. Then at the resurrection of the righteous, God will reward you for inviting those who *could not repay* you." (Luke 14:12–14)

The leaders we've seeded may not be crippled, lame, or blind, but our tie to this parable is that they *could not repay* us. If I minister for a church or conference in the United States, they say "thank you" by giving me or Messenger International an honorarium or offering. These leaders in the nations we've invested in can't do this. All team members—marketplace givers, church leaders, and our Messenger staff—realize we have a great privilege: to give without expecting any compensation from those we've helped.

A few years ago, Lisa and I traveled to the city of Yerevan, Armenia, where thousands of leaders from all over the Middle East had come for a conference. While there, in a separate auditorium, we gathered the pastors from Iran, Afghanistan, Syria, and similar nations. Cameras weren't permitted, and identities were kept secret. The presence of God was strong, and I kept thinking, *These leaders should speak to Lisa and me instead of the other way around.* At one point I stated, "You all see Lisa and me as the heroes. No, it's not John and Lisa Bevere, but rather the businesspeople and churches who've given millions of dollars to bless you with resources. They're the true heroes." At that point, we all broke down and wept.

After the meeting, one Iranian pastor asked, "How can people give such a large amount of money to those they've never met before?"

My reply seemed too simplistic, but it was the truth: "The love of God in their hearts." Once again, the tears flowed.

Again, as you've followed the personal story here, what do you see as the key choices and decisions that were made? And how might they compare and relate to the key choices and decisions you're facing? What helpful lessons or examples do you see?

What encouragement for your faith and purposeful vision do you find here?

EVEN GREATER MULTIPLICATION

In 2019, we realized that our in-house website for distributing the resources had limitations. It had been a good fit for 2011 when we started, but now it was clumsy and limited in its capacity. For example, the site was way too difficult to navigate on smartphones. Lisa and I, along with many of our team members, had traveled to many poor and troubled nations. We couldn't help noticing that even though people were living in tents, mud houses, or plywood shacks, the majority had some kind of smartphone. It's actually estimated, as of 2024, that over five billion people in the world have smartphones.

After numerous trips it became apparent that soon, if not already, reaching everyone on the planet via online communications would be possible. I felt we were once again experiencing a "Roman Road" moment in history.

Let me briefly explain: Scripture states, "When the right time came, God sent his Son" (Galatians 4:4). The "right time" takes many things into consideration. One important element of the right time tells us that the gospel will reach the known world. In 312 B.C., the Romans began to develop roadways and shipping routes that covered the known world. By the time Jesus said, "Go into all the world," these routes were well developed. This provided the means to quickly spread the Word of God.

I believe the right time has again emerged to make way for Jesus's second coming—the internet being the Roman Road of our day. We have the capability of spreading the Word of God to the entire world for the purpose of making disciples of all nations.

Knowing this, our team again began to pray, dream, and strategize. After months of research, we commissioned a project with one of the finest app and web developing companies in the United States. We built a discipleship platform that's high-powered, multifunctional, and user-friendly for iPhone, Android, tablets, and computers. We were determined to build the finest platform possible with today's technology. We wanted church leaders everywhere—but particularly in troubled nations—to have the very best. The remarkable reality is that we've now tracked millions of users in more than twenty-seven thousand cities in 241 nations and territories who are learning from the books, courses, and other discipleship tools available on the platform. We have only a handful of nations left to reach.

After time passed, we thought of additional ways to multiply. To expand and strengthen our platform's effectiveness, we decided to bring other notable teachers with unique, transforming messages on the platform as guests. Now leaders all over the world can use their computers, tablets, or phones to train one-on-one or in small groups or churches. Not only has this multiplied the effectiveness of the platform, but also the content will long outlive a physical book and endure for generations to come. (To learn more about how you can get involved, visit www.MessengerX.com.)

> The prophets Isaiah, Jeremiah, and Ezekiel were also servants of God who each received a unique assignment in a unique way—and with unique strategies. Look at the dramatic ways in which their callings unfold in these passages: Isaiah 6, Jeremiah 1, and Ezekiel 2–3. What do their individual stories reveal about God's character, God's ways, and God's purposes for His people? What seem to be the strategies involved in their individual situations?
>
> How might those strategies on display in Scripture relate to your own unique calling?

What if Lisa and I had decided not to write? Or what if we were content being two bestselling authors, and we never contended for the curricula? What if our team remained satisfied with reaching individuals and churches only in English? What if our staff didn't want to put the energy into gathering a team from all over the United States at the Broadmoor? Each level has presented challenges that have greatly stretched us, forcing us to depend on God's grace. At each level, it would have been much easier just to coast, never pressing on to greater effectiveness in serving others.

When we listen to God's Spirit, we'll move step-by-step into greater multiplication. At the beginning, He won't show you every step or even two or three steps ahead. In my early thirties, it would have been so much easier to look into a crystal ball and see the entire pathway to where we'd be as a team thirty years later. However, if that had been possible, we wouldn't have contended for each step so intensely in prayer and leadership. Also, we wouldn't have acquired the faith and strength of character that occurred with each step of obedience.

When we listen to God's Spirit, we'll move step-by-step into greater multiplication. At the beginning, He won't show you every step or even two or three steps ahead.

Are you seeing how important it is to learn how the Holy Spirit speaks to us personally? Our responsibility is to learn and listen for His voice, and we have a twofold starting point: First and foremost, the Spirit leads us through His written Word, and He never contradicts it. Second, He leads by peace in our hearts (Colossians 3:15), speaking to our spirits. "The Spirit Himself bears witness with our spirit" (Romans 8:16 NKJV). And so, "Since we are living by the Spirit, let us follow the Spirit's leading in every part of our lives" (Galatians 5:25).

When you're trying to fulfill your calling in your own strength, without getting a word or strategy from God through His Holy Spirit, you're setting yourself up for exhaustion. That doesn't mean you should instead do nothing. But you listen for His voice, you do what He tells you to do, and you stay faithful with what He's already given you. If you're thinking about doing something new, but God isn't speaking—then wait. He actually *is* speaking. He's saying, *Keep doing what I've already told you to do.*

People grow miserable when they try to bring forth God's call on their life through their own plans and ideas. God has not only created your calling—He's also created your path to get there. And often, it's not the straight line you expect it to be. It's all over the place, going through a wilderness, a crucible, a desert, an obstacle. Every step of the journey is giving you the character you need to handle the next step. The big key here, in whatever God has called you to, is that *you are led by the Spirit*. It is the most crucial element we've discussed so far. We have to learn to hear and understand His voice.

As you have been praying and thinking about God's specific calling on your life and how to fulfill it—what has His Holy Spirit been communicating to your own spirit?

Multiplication isn't mankind's idea; it's God's idea. Again, it was His first command to us: "Any gift I entrust to you is for the purpose of multiplying My kingdom" (my paraphrase of Genesis 1:22 and Matthew 25:14–29). Let me restate an important point: This multiplication should not put pressure on you, because ultimately, the gift comes from Him. All you have to do is pray, listen, believe, and obey what He puts in your heart.

Bottom line: He will lead you to multiply.

At this point, how strong is your confidence that the Lord God will indeed lead you to multiply?

You may be thinking, My heart is stirred from the testimony you've given in the past three chapters. But I'm only [a young mother, or a student, or a pro athlete, or a blue-collar worker, or whatever]—so how can God use someone like me to multiply the kingdom?

We'll begin discussing that in the next chapter.

REFLECTION FOR RENEWAL

In this chapter, what statements or Scripture passages seemed most meaningful for you?

How would you restate them in your own words? (Personalize your answer as a prayer of response to God.)

What are your thoughts about what God wants you to do now in response to what you've seen and reflected upon in this chapter?

INVESTING

> In his grace, God has given us different gifts [charisma] for doing certain things well. So if God has given you the ability to prophesy, speak out with as much faith as God has given you. If your gift is serving others, serve them well. If you are a teacher, teach well. If your gift is to encourage others, be encouraging. If it is giving, give generously. If God has given you leadership ability, take the responsibility seriously. And if you have a gift for showing kindness to others, do it gladly.
>
> **ROMANS 12:6–8**

The apostle Paul highlights various gifts God has given to each of His servants. Again, I don't believe it's an exhaustive list, but it covers a wide range of divine abilities. You may not agree with me on this, but allow me to explain.

I see nowhere on the apostle's list the ability to sing, to argue cases in a court, to surgically remove tumors, to paint inspiring pictures, to play instruments, and many other God-given abilities we witness on a daily basis. This is why I don't believe the list is all-inclusive. If you still disagree, I respect your position; the topic doesn't warrant extended discussion, as it isn't a major point.

Returning to the emphasis of Paul's words, I love how the New Living Translation spells out *charisma* as the ability "for doing certain things well." This identifies the main focus of this book. The past three chapters have testified to the multiplication of prophesying and teaching. Now let's turn our attention to a different gift—*giving*.

KINGDOM INVESTING

I have a friend named Mike. He became a believer in Jesus Christ when he was eleven years old, but he was unproductive in building the kingdom. He grew more and more dissatisfied with this state, and eventually—at age thirty-five—he was fed up with not making an eternal impact. Those who reach this state often try to make an immediate change without knowledge, wisdom, and faith. Wisely, Mike approached it differently. He determined that the first step to make a lasting impact was to "fill the tank." Over the next six months, he memorized two thousand verses of Scripture.

Soon after this six-month period, he decided to attend a leadership conference in Phoenix, Arizona. He was so poor he couldn't afford a hotel room and had to stay with eleven students in a two-bedroom apartment.

A special offering was taken during the conference. The leader encouraged the delegates to pray about what to give. Mike heard the Lord say, I want you to give two hundred dollars.

Mike protested: God, that's all I have!

The Lord gently replied: I'm not asking you to give any more than that.

Mike obeyed and gave all the money he had.

God then instructed Mike to give a hundred dollars a month above his tithe for the rest of the year.

Soon God started giving him strategic ideas, and his new business began to steadily increase. The next year, Mike felt he should give four hundred dollars a month above his tithe to build the kingdom. A year later, the amount went to a thousand dollars a month above his tithe. The next year, it went to four thousand dollars per month above his tithe, and the following year it went to ten thousand dollars per month above his tithe.

At this point, Mike asked the Lord for the ability to give ten million dollars to the kingdom. It seemed like a huge request, almost unattainable—but he was firm in his belief and request. However, what he heard in his heart from the Lord shocked him: Son, why are you boxing Me in?

So Mike removed the limits and believed for even more.

Soon afterward, his giving rapidly escalated, and the next year he gave close to seventeen thousand dollars per month above his tithe. Then it became twenty-five thousand dollars per month, then forty thousand, then fifty thousand. Eventually, Mike gave a hundred thousand dollars per month above his tithe to build the kingdom. The last time I talked with him, he'd hit the level of one hundred fifty thousand dollars per month above his tithe.

Mike has lived very well, but on roughly 10 to 15 percent of his income. Yes, you read that correctly; each year he gives away approximately 85 to 90 percent of what he makes. He attributes his success to learning the Bible, listening to God when he prays, and allowing himself to be discipled by those who are more mature than he is.

When it comes to multiplication, giving is often the key ingredient. Many well-meaning believers view financial offerings in this light: What am I willing to give up for the sake of others? But if that's your only perspective, it's incomplete.

When it comes to multiplication, you cannot ignore the word *giving*, because it's most often the key ingredient. In the specific area of finances, many well-meaning believers view their offerings in this light: *What am I willing to give up for the sake of others?* This is noble and godly, but if that's your only perspective, it's incomplete.

Allow me to explain.

First, to affirm the positive, God has put His love for people in our hearts; this creates the inward desire to unselfishly give and serve. This should be the preeminent desire in anyone's giving. However, a wise giver sees an offering not only as a gift of love and service but also as an *investment*. To invest is to refrain from consuming a resource in order to grow it. Specifically, regarding finances, investment is to abstain from spending now in order to lay aside funds for growth.

> Pause to give thanks to God for using His Spirit to inspire love in your heart for others. In what ways is God already using you to serve and give to others? Take a moment to give Him thanks for those opportunities.
>
> How is your attitude toward giving affected when you think of your giving as an investment? What difference does that make?
>
> Through your giving and serving, what kind of return on investment can you expect?

A few years ago, Lisa and I considered buying two plots of land. We felt they were underpriced and would grow in value over time. We possessed the cash to purchase both, and at the time decided to forgo spending the cash for personal consumption in order to make the money grow. The lots increased more in value than we expected, and our investment doubled in just two years. This resulted in our having twice as much cash two years later. We now had the ability to invest at a greater level.

Jesus says that when we invest in the kingdom, we "will be repaid many times over in this life" (Luke 18:30). He did not say "the *next* life," but "*this* life." Lisa and I were thrilled to double our investment on the lots, but what Jesus states isn't in the same ballpark; there's a huge difference between *double* and *many times over.* What's the potential of an investment that's multiplied many times over? Mike's life is a testimony to this truth.

The apostle Paul compares our giving to planting seeds. While results vary depending on the conditions, one kernel of wheat—if not consumed but rather invested in the soil—will produce over one hundred kernels of wheat on average. This falls under the category of "many times over." This is why we're told, "Give freely and become more wealthy; be stingy and lose everything" (Proverbs 11:24).

When it comes to giving, Solomon, Jesus, and Paul would not have emphasized this truth if believers were to avoid thoughts of increase and multiplication.

Most would view Mike's resolve to live on 10 to 15 percent of his income as solely a sacrifice of love. Mike, however, sees the broader picture. Since he's filled with God's wisdom from saturating his soul with two thousand memorized Bible verses, he not only sees it as an act of love; he also views the investment aspect.

He views it the same way that Lisa and I viewed those two plots of land. He approaches it no differently than a family that owns a successful restaurant. Instead of consuming all the profits personally, the family takes a good percentage of the profits to purchase more buildings, hire more personnel, buy more food, and acquire whatever else is required to grow the business. If this is done well, they may eventually have five restaurants, which ultimately would create five times the revenue. The result: They have the opportunity to be a blessing to many more than if they owned only one restaurant.

If Mike had considered his giving as something other than an investment, he wouldn't have come to understand the more profound meaning of giving. This is exactly what the parable of the talents addresses. Look at Jesus's words: "The servant who received the five bags of silver began to *invest* the money and earned five more" (Matthew 25:16). He specifically uses the word *invest* to illustrate how the servant multiplied.

ANOTHER PARABLE OF MULTIPLICATION

Let's look at a different parable Jesus used to illustrate multiplication. Here's the background:

> The crowd was listening to everything Jesus said. And because he was nearing Jerusalem, he told them a story to correct the impression that the Kingdom of God would begin right away. (Luke 19:11)

I love how this parable is introduced. The people expect Jesus to set up the kingdom and deliver them from Roman oppression and rule. He adjusts their mentality by giving the accurate perspective—which centers on His desire for us to build the kingdom after His departure. And how will this be accomplished? Through *investing*.

Listen to the story Jesus told:

> A nobleman was called away to a distant empire to be crowned king and then return. Before he left, he called together ten of his servants and divided among them ten pounds of silver, saying, "Invest this for me while I am gone." (19:12–13)

As in the story in Matthew 25, Jesus instructs us to invest. We aren't to be lazy with what has been entrusted to us; we're to work *hard* and *smart*.

Even though these two parables (in Matthew 25 and Luke 19) have similarities, they're different in important ways. Let's examine what sets them apart.

First, Matthew speaks of three servants, whereas Luke identifies ten servants. Second, in Matthew's story, each servant is given a different amount (a different quantity of "talents"); but in Luke's story, each is given an equal amount—one pound of silver.

We aren't to be lazy with what has been entrusted to us; we're to work hard and smart.

Third, in Matthew's story, the basic unit was not just one pound but a "talent"—a bag containing seventy-five pounds of silver.

In comparing the two stories, I believe Matthew's story speaks of gifts which aren't distributed evenly, whereas Luke's story portrays what all believers are equally given by God—foundational faith, the love of God, the Word of God, our covenant blessings, and so forth. However, the underlying principles in the two passages are the same.

Let's continue the story in Luke.

After he was crowned king, he returned and called in the servants to whom he had given the money. He wanted to find out what their profits were. The first servant reported, "Master, I invested your money and made ten times the original amount!"

"Well done!" the king exclaimed. "You are a good servant. You have been faithful with the little I entrusted to you, so you will be governor of ten cities as your reward." (Luke 19:15–17)

There are several points to highlight.

First, the servant invested what was given to him.

Second, he worked hard and smart—which resulted in tenfold multiplication. To work *smart* is to be in tune with the wisdom of God, and this occurs only by listening to God's counsel, as my friend Mike did.

Third, multiplication is once again directly attributed to faithfulness. There's no other action or virtue mentioned, because in God's eyes, to be faithful is to multiply.

Finally, the servant's eternal reward is proportional to his multiplication; this first servant is entrusted with ten cities to govern.

Now let's observe the second servant:

The next servant reported, "Master, I invested your money and made five times the original amount."

"Well done!" the king said. "You will be governor over five cities." (Luke 19:18–19)

This one didn't multiply ten times, but five times. His eternal reward reflected his level of investing—five cities, not ten. Why didn't he multiply ten times as the other servant? Did he not listen as closely to God's wisdom? Did he miss opportunities? Did he coast in his later years, as Stan from our first chapter was planning to do? Did he have a retirement mentality?

What are your own thoughts and conclusions about this second servant's work and the mindset behind it?

I spoke on multiplication in a leadership conference a few years back. One of California's top commercial property developers, who'd already given millions to the kingdom, came up to me after I spoke. He appeared to be in a state of shock, but also enlightened. "John," he said, "I've slipped into a mentality of coasting because of how successful I've been. It's an easy attitude to fall into, but now I see the error. Moving forward, I'll be more focused and diligent to multiply what God has given me." It's possible that his genuine repentance will alter his course from being a five-time multiplier to a ten-time multiplier.

How about the third servant in Jesus's story?

But the third servant brought back only the original amount of money and said, "Master, I hid your money and kept it safe. I was afraid because you are a hard man to deal with, taking what isn't yours and harvesting crops you didn't plant."

"You wicked servant!" the king roared. "Your own words condemn you. If you knew that I'm a hard man who takes what isn't mine and harvests crops

I didn't plant, why didn't you deposit my money in the bank? At least I could have gotten some interest on it." (Luke 19:20–23)

As in the story from Matthew, this servant had the same two major flaws. First, he was afraid; second, he didn't know the character of his master. This story once again signifies that merely maintaining what God gives us isn't faithfulness, but wickedness. Notice that the king "roared"! The servant's lazy attitude angered the master, and he showed it. Very sobering when you think about it.

What happens next only strengthens the conclusion we drew from Matthew's account:

Then, turning to the others standing nearby, the king ordered, "Take the money from this servant, and give it to the one who has ten pounds."

"But, master," they said, "he already has ten pounds!"

"Yes," the king replied, "and to those who use well what they are given, even more will be given. But from those who do nothing, even what little they have will be taken away." (Luke 19:24–26)

It's an amazing and scary reality that if we don't spend an abundant amount of time in God's Word and in communion with Him, we can easily filter God's character through the environment we live in. But when we know God and His Word intimately, we can recognize these faulty filters.

Once again, we see that God is more capitalistic in His thinking. Jesus pointedly illustrates that the bystanders protested because the first servant already had ten pounds of silver, and the master corrected their "let's be fair" mentality by declaring in essence, "To those who *invest* well, more will be given." And conversely, "Those who merely *maintain* will lose what little they have."

It's both an amazing and scary reality that if we don't do what Mike did—spend an abundant amount of time in God's Word and in communion with Him—we can easily filter God's character through the environment we live in. It may be society's filter, Hollywood's filter, Instagram's filter, a news network's filter, a harsh father's filter, a religious filter, or any other life experience or sociological mindset filter we either like or dislike. When we know God and His Word intimately, we can recognize these faulty filters.

> What kind of faulty filters do you think are most likely to influence your own mindset?
>
> What truths from God's Word have recently been helpful correctives for you in exposing wrong perspectives about life and about God's character?
>
> What need in your life do you recognize for increasing the time you spend in God's Word and in communion with Him? How can you give greater priority to this in your schedule and routines?

ALL ARE CALLED TO GIVE

Mike has the gift of giving; he excels in it. However, we should all be givers.

To help clarify, let me compare this to Jesus's commission to go into all the world and preach the gospel (Mark 16:15–16). This charge is given to every believer. All of us should be ambassadors and share the gospel with those who are lost. This is also captured in Paul's words—"Do the work of an evangelist" (2 Timothy 4:5 NKJV)—which are directed to all believers.

But there's a unique office and complementary gifting called *evangelist*. Paul writes, "And He Himself gave *some to be . . . evangelists*" (Ephesians 4:11 NKJV). Not all, but some, are called to stand in this office. This gift excels in the ability to bring in a harvest of souls. In the book of Acts, Philip is specifically called an evangelist (Acts 21:8). Billy Graham, T. L. Osborn, and Reinhard Bonnke were all gifted evangelists. They, with the help of their teams, won tens of millions of souls. They multiplied their God-given gift, just as did Mike and the others I referred to earlier.

We're all called—just as they were—to *give*, but there are some who have the *charisma* of *giving*. They excel in financial giving just as the evangelist excels in soul-winning. The message of this book focuses on multiplying our God-given gifts. However, since financial giving is such a crucial aspect of multiplication, for the rest of this chapter I want to zero in on what each of us is called to do: multiply in the area of financial giving.

> How would you honestly assess your own current faithfulness in giving? Do you understand and accept that you are called to multiply your giving?
>
> Have you already seen your giving being multiplied? If not—what obstacles to this do you recognize? How does God want you to overcome them?

In my forty years of ministry, I've witnessed two extremes when it comes to finances and giving. These extremes affect far too many in the church, and it's my sincere hope that this will change. First, there are those who only give to get; they want more for selfish reasons. If we're objective and call this out for what it is, a word to identify this motivation is *covetousness*.

Sadly, this errant mentality has helped birth the other extreme (the old pendulum swing). It occurs mostly with people who don't study the overall counsel of God's Word as purposefully as Mike did. They despise any teaching that would build people's faith toward financial giving. This attitude can even go to the extreme of resenting anything to do with offerings. In essence, advocates of this idea hinder their own effectiveness, as well as the effectiveness of those who listen to them. The result is that the overall work of the gospel is restrained.

> Which of these two extremes is more likely to snare your own thinking about giving?

After coming to Jesus, Lisa and I were members of a church that taught extensively on giving. This was in the 1980s, when many were more self-focused than mission-focused. Even though our church's teaching was mostly accurate, due to a lack of character, many people gave with motives of being rewarded with bigger homes, more luxurious cars, more expensive vacations, and various other narcissistic desires. The focus was no different from what many unbelievers pursue—except that it had a "scriptural" formula. Lisa and I knew from the start that something was out of balance, but we couldn't articulate just what it was.

Honestly, after being in this environment, it took some purging and maturing for Lisa and me to see giving in a wholesome light. The church's leader eventually succumbed to temptation and lost everything. After seeing the outcome, we were tempted to swing the pendulum, but we were committed to believing the Word of God over experiences.

We had one eye-opening encounter a couple of years after we were sent out by this church into our own ministry. I was in a service getting ready to preach when the Holy Spirit asked me, Son, do you know what a *religious spirit* is?

I'd read and spoken and even written about what a religious mindset is, and I'd heard others speak on this. But when He asked, I immediately realized there was something I didn't comprehend.

I replied, I must not know, otherwise You wouldn't ask me. What is it?

I heard the Holy Spirit's answer: A religious spirit is one that uses My Word to execute his own will. This person doesn't keep My heart's desires preeminent while carrying out My instructions. He applies My Word for his own gain.

These words were a catalyst for needed adjustments in my heart after the toxic environment I'd been in. This message from the Holy Spirit revealed that we can give and even reap the benefits—while doing it all with wrong intentions. God's laws will operate and be beneficial, even if the motive isn't correct.

Since the apostle Paul used farming as a metaphor for giving, allow me to do the same. A farmer can plant seeds for one purpose: to grow and hoard crops. Any food he can't consume, he builds bigger silos to contain; and he says to himself, "You have enough stored away for years to come. Now take it easy! Eat, drink, and be merry!" (Luke 12:19).

Here's God's response to him: "You fool!" (Luke 19:20). The principle of sowing and harvesting worked for this farmer, even though, as Jesus points out, he was covetous.

On the other hand, a different farmer may desire to help and feed other people. He experiences the same harvest as the first farmer, but his response is different. He says within himself, *Wow, not only will I eat, but also I can help my community be stronger and healthier. I can be generous!*

The laws of sowing and harvesting work equally for both men. It would be ridiculous for everyone to stop planting and harvesting after recognizing the first man's covetous motivation. Yet this is what many have done in the area of giving into the kingdom.

Let's dive deeply into Paul's words. He begins by saying:

> I thought I should send these brothers ahead of me to make sure the gift you promised is ready. But I want it to be a willing gift, not one given grudgingly. (2 Corinthians 9:5)

Paul is no doubt speaking of a financial gift or offering. He goes on, using the principle of farming to illustrate what God would do for those who give:

> Remember this—a farmer who plants only a few seeds will get a small crop. But the one who plants generously will get a generous crop. (9:6)

If our sole motive in giving is to help people, then why does Paul talk about the harvest we'll receive from giving? Is it wrong to have a secondary desire of multiplication, especially when it will increase the primary desire to build lives for the kingdom? Could it be Paul is training new believers in the Corinthian church to multiply their effectiveness, as Jesus did in the parable of the talents? Is Paul appealing to them to be moved with compassion—while at the same time investing for the purpose of being a greater blessing? I think this is indeed what Paul intends. Look at how he continues:

> You must each decide in your heart how much to give. And don't give reluc-
> tantly or in response to pressure. "For God loves a person who gives cheerfully."

And God will generously provide all you need. Then you will always have everything you need and plenty left over to share with others. (9:7–8)

Notice the two things that will be accomplished by giving sincerely and generously: Personal needs will be met, but Paul also specifically states that there will be "plenty left over to share with others." Our capacity to be generous is multiplied because we've invested or planted seed.

Here, the motive is further reinforced:

For God is the one who provides seed for the farmer and then bread to eat. In the same way, he will provide and increase your resources and then produce a great harvest of generosity in you. Yes, you will be enriched in every way so that you can *always be generous.* (9:10–11)

Paul specifically states that through our giving, God will "increase your resources"—making it possible to "always be generous." This truth is not only for those endowed with the gift of financial giving; it pertains also to every believer. God put this spiritual law in place long ago.

As I mentioned earlier, when Lisa and I started in ministry, our income was eighteen thousand dollars per year. We could barely pay our bills. I remember our first Christmas in ministry. We had to take our few spare dollars and buy supplies to assemble small baskets of homemade gifts. We didn't have enough money to purchase anything else.

> *Through our giving, God will "increase your resources"— making it possible to always be generous. God put this spiritual law in place long ago.*

A couple of years later, our pastor took up a special offering. Lisa and I wanted to be a part of the outreach. God spoke to us: Give a thousand dollars.

In the two years prior to this, we'd saved and saved so we could make a down payment on a small house. We'd accumulated eighteen hundred dollars, which represented all our assets; we had no retirement fund, no financial investments, and no other savings to fall back on. If we gave a thousand dollars for the church's special offering, we would have only eight hundred dollars left to our name. Our years' worth of savings would be significantly diminished, and it might be a long time before we'd have enough money for a down payment on a house.

However, we gave the thousand dollars because we wanted to be a part of impacting others. We also wanted to be more generous. We knew from Scripture that the only way we could increase our capacity to give was by multiplying the little we had.

As the years have passed, we've been able to give more than baskets, and more than a thousand-dollar offering. Just this year alone, we've been able to give to missions more than a hundred times that first big offering. We want to impact more lives in every way. God multiplied our ability and empowered us to be generous.

The Passion Translation brings out this truth in Paul's teaching beautifully:

This generous God who supplies abundant seed for the farmer, which becomes bread for our meals, is even more extravagant toward you. First he supplies every need, plus more. Then he *multiplies* the seed as you sow it, so that the harvest of your generosity will grow. You will be abundantly enriched in every way as you give generously on every occasion. (2 Corinthians 9:10–11 TPT)

Notice how extravagant He is toward us. For His own purpose, He'll multiply the investment we make in building the kingdom so that our generosity will grow. We build up our heavenly accounts—where moths and rust do not corrupt, nor do thieves break in and steal (Matthew 6:20)—and we'll also draw from the accounts in this life. Yes, there's an eternal reward, but there's also an account we develop for generosity in this age.

Paul made this clear when he wrote to the Philippian believers:

Not that I seek or am eager for your gift, but I do seek *and* am eager for the fruit which increases to your credit the harvest of blessing that is accumulating to your account. (Philippians 4:17 AMPC)

Just as some people have bank accounts, stock accounts, and investment accounts, all believers have a heavenly account. That account empowers us to multiply our effectiveness in building the kingdom on this earth.

> How do you imagine your own "heavenly account"? How large and healthy is it?

What would happen if all believers came to know, understand, and believe in this spiritual law? We would reach the world so much faster with the gospel! Doesn't that make it clear why the enemy of the kingdom tries in every way to keep believers from sowing financial seeds?

Lisa and I are close friends with a husband and wife named Phil and Dana who are outrageous givers. They give approximately half of their income to the kingdom. Just recently, they gave a hundred thousand dollars to a ministry for an outreach. Two days later, they gave a hundred thousand dollars to another ministry for a different outreach. I know this because Messenger International was the second ministry.

Phil started his business years ago, and it performed in an average manner—far from superior. However, twenty-five years ago, Phil and Dana made a commitment to God that they would give $250,000 to a ministry over the following three years. It seemed utterly impossible, but they wanted to make room for God's intervention.

Phil's business blossomed, but he was unaware of just how well things were going. Three months later, he discovered an unexpected $250,000 in the account. So he and Dana decided to give the pledge immediately rather than spread it out over three years. He told me, "John, that's when the ridiculous levels of giving started for us."

Just last year they were able to give more to the work of the kingdom than their income. This is an amazing reality; it means they had such reserves from the harvests of abundant giving in previous years, that they could give out more than came in during that calendar year!

Similar to Mike, they refrained from drawing back. They pressed on when it would have been easy to coast; consequently, their heavenly account was enlarged to measures they'd never dreamed possible.

Isn't this opportunity also available to you and me? Paul emphatically tells us:

> Never doubt God's mighty power to work in you and accomplish all this. He will achieve infinitely more than your greatest request, your most unbelievable dream, and exceed your wildest imagination! He will outdo them all, for his miraculous power constantly energizes you. (Ephesians 3:20 TPT)

BREAKTHROUGH

I've learned through years of ministry that we'll be tested in both our *charisma* and our financial giving. There may be a season in which no publisher is interested in talking with you about your book; in fact, that season may last years. You consider giving up because it's been a lot of hard work, the book seems to be going nowhere, and you see no possible way of changing things. But you continue in obedience. Suddenly the breakthrough comes.

Or you give and give but aren't seeing quick harvests, and it seems like your finances are too tight to do any more. Then God speaks to you, as with Mike, and you obey even when it seems impossible. You witness a breakthrough and enter another realm of giving.

When we're tempted to stop giving or stop serving—what should our response be? Can you trust God for a breakthrough? What should that trust look like?

What is a *breakthrough*? Dictionary.com defines it as "an act or instance of removing or surpassing an obstruction or restriction."[1] Picture this: Water is restricted by a wall. The water continues to rise, but the wall remains an obstruction. Then cracks suddenly appear in the wall; a short time later, a rush of water bursts through. All obstruction is eliminated, and water flows freely where it was previously restrained. That's a breakthrough.

King David declares, "God has broken through my enemies by my hand like a breakthrough of water" (1 Chronicles 14:11 NKJV). The rising water here is a picture of our continual obedience to truth; and after the breakthrough, the free-flowing water represents fruitfulness or abundance.

In regard to our friends Phil and Dana, after they gave the first hundred-thousand-dollar gift, Phil told me that their business had a record week—in just that week, they earned back the entire amount and more. This is what a breakthrough looks like. It didn't start out this way for them; they gave and gave and didn't immediately see much of a harvest. But after years of sowing continually, they experienced a breakthrough—and the harvests now seem to come almost as quickly as the planting.

It's a fulfillment of the Lord's promise recorded by the prophet Amos: "'The time will come,' says the LORD, 'when the grain and grapes will grow faster than they can be harvested'" (Amos 9:13). In the New King James Version, this truth is brought out in a beautiful picture:

> "Behold, the days are coming," says the LORD, "when the plowman shall overtake the reaper, and the treader of grapes him who sows seed; the mountains shall drip with sweet wine, and all the hills *shall flow with it*."

The harvester will have such an abundant harvest that the planter will overtake him. Those who tread grapes will still be stomping on the previous season's grapes while the plowmen begin their work for the following year.

The picture of the result is especially remarkable. The plowmen, harvesters, and those who stomp on the grapes all have the common desire to make wine. Listen to the declared outcome, as I've paraphrased it: "There shall be a continual flow of wine; it shall not stop; no more unfruitful times."

Many quit just short of the breakthrough. They've been overwhelmed by adversity or the lack of desired results.

There's a place in regard to our *charisma* and financial giving where this very thing happens. It happened with Mike, as well as with Phil and Dana. In regard to Messenger International, we have numerous testimonies of lives changed by the resources we've sown throughout the years. The grapes are growing faster than they can be harvested!

Many quit just short of the breakthrough. They've been overwhelmed by adversity or the lack of desired results. Lisa and I could have easily turned to reason and logic and ignored the voice of the Spirit of God. We needed at least five thousand dollars for a down payment on a much-needed house. Most nice apartments in our city were adult-only communities, and babies weren't permitted. We could have reasoned, "Let's first get into a house. *Then* we can save and give a thousand dollars on a future outreach." We would have missed a prime opportunity to invest in the kingdom and grow our resources.

The amazing aspect of the story is that six months later, we miraculously had the five thousand dollars. Lisa received a sum of money from an account we were unaware of that her father had set up. Additionally, two individuals (without knowing our need) gave us two thousand dollars. We were in our new house less than a year later. It was miraculous, and much better for our faith and endurance to see Him provide when it seemed "impossible." I don't believe this would have happened if we'd hung on to the thousand dollars the Holy Spirit instructed us to give.

At this point, it's wise to give a warning: We shouldn't operate presumptuously. What do I mean? We should seek the counsel of our senior partner, the Holy Spirit. He tells us, "I am the LORD your God, who teaches you to profit, who leads you by the way you should go" (Isaiah 48:17 NKJV). Maintaining a sensitive conscience (the place where the Holy Spirit enlightens us) and obedience to what He shows us is paramount, because He is the One who leads us to profit in our kingdom investments. We would not have given the thousand dollars had He not whispered the request to our hearts.

> Ask the Lord to help you honestly evaluate yourself in this regard: How sensitive is your conscience to the Holy Spirit's guidance? How quickly and fully do you obey?

Some people don't listen to the Holy Spirit's counsel. Others can't hear His counsel because they've said no too many times, and their conscience is no longer tender. If that's you, simply repent and ask Him for forgiveness for suppressing His voice. Your sensitivity will immediately return; He is quick to forgive! But then listen to His promptings, and don't let the voice of reason talk you out of it.

REFLECTION FOR RENEWAL

In this chapter, what statements or Scripture passages seemed most meaningful for you?

How would you restate them in your own words? (Personalize your answer as a prayer of response to God.)

What are your thoughts about what God wants you to do now in response to what you've seen and reflected upon in this chapter?

THE CATALYST

God has given each of you a gift
from his great variety of spiritual gifts.
Use them well to serve one another.

1 PETER 4:10

In this pivotal chapter, I'll unpack the catalyst for *effective increase*—and in using that word *effective*, I'm speaking of multiplication that endures forever.

A catalyst is a key ingredient that precipitates or accelerates an event or change. (That's my definition for it, adapted from many dictionaries.) We're all given gifts, but what triggers their enduring potential is described in these words from the apostle Peter: "Use them well to *serve*" (1 Peter 4:10). Serving is the catalyst; and genuine serving is always motivated by love, as Paul mentions as he speaks of praying for the Thessalonians:

> For we remember before our God and Father how you put faith into practice,
> how *your love motivates you to serve others*. (1 Thessalonians 1:3 TPT)

True serving originates out of a heart burning with love. It's an inner disposition that's not altered by adversity, hardship, or any other unfavorable circumstances. It manifests sometimes in word, but most often in action.

> Think about times when you've served others while being highly motivated to love them for Christ's sake. Recall the sense of fulfillment you experienced from this. How much do you trust God to do more and more of this in the future?

True serving originates out of a heart burning with love. It's an inner disposition that's not altered by adversity, hardship, or any other unfavorable circumstances. It manifests sometimes in word, but most often in action.

> "A heart burning with love" for others may sound like an experience that's rare for you. But why should that be the case? Look up Romans 5:5 and reflect gratefully on how (and to what extent) God's own love enters your heart.
>
> How confident is your faith that God will channel *His* love through *you* to *others*? Talk to Him about this.

TURKEY LADY

I'll illustrate serving with a story about some close friends. (This couple has asked to remain anonymous in their mission—so in keeping with their desire, I'll use fictional names.)

Riley and Dave live in a suburb of one of the largest cities in the United States. It was destiny for them to meet; their apartments were right next to each other.

Soon after getting married, Riley wondered why most churches, homeless shelters, and other charity organizations provide meals and gifts at Christmas, but little is done for the Thanksgiving holiday. She believes Thanksgiving is important because it focuses on family and centers on a meal. Many single moms, the disabled, and the homeless struggle to provide or participate in a suitable meal. She believes soup kitchens serve a needed purpose but lack the intimacy a home-cooked meal can provide for a family.

Riley has stated, "On our own, each of us has the opportunity to make an impact, but together the impact is greater." She's well-versed in Scripture and knows that the efforts of two working together in harmony are tenfold of what anyone can accomplish alone (Deuteronomy 32:30). She's also well aware that results keep escalating as more believers unite. Another truth burning in her heart is that true servants want to be a part of a team and don't care about getting the credit. Riley's attitude personifies these important ingredients for multiplication.

For her first Thanksgiving opportunity, Riley collected money from family and friends to purchase turkeys. With a multiplying mindset, she and Dave promised to match dollar-for-dollar all that was received. That year, she bought eleven turkeys and delivered them anonymously from the trunk of her car. The second year, the number rose to thirty-one turkeys.

The third year, she told her family and friends that they could share the vision with other friends, provided they kept it anonymous. They did, and the effort started to rapidly multiply. By the fifth year, they'd touched five hundred families and were able to add two cans of vegetables and stuffing to each donation.

It was at this point that she formally set up an anonymous distribution agreement with the Salvation Army. This charity organization is connected to social services and was able to implement an application process to help identify the truly needy. The people chosen had no other options for provision (food stamps, government programs, etc.). Riley and her team set up a drive-through and a walkup distribution site on the grounds of the Salvation Army.

Many people improvised in order to collect their needed food. They pulled wagons, rode bikes, pushed baskets, asked neighbors for rides, or just walked up and carried away the turkey, vegetables, and stuffing—sometimes for long distances—back to their trailer, apartment, or outdoor place where they lived. One homeless man had figured out how to cook the turkey outside for himself and his homeless friends using a discarded fryer and propane tank.

Eventually, the distribution became so large that a new site was needed to facilitate the volume of people. A neighboring YMCA had a large vacant lot, but relations were strained between the Y and the Salvation Army. The need prompted the two organizations to confront their differences. They reconciled, and since then, have worked together with Riley's project as well as other community efforts.

Each year, Riley and Dave set a goal to beat the previous year's distribution. They determined that no person in their entire area would go without a proper Thanksgiving meal. As the numbers grew, the distribution became more complex and difficult, especially with increased prices and some supporting friends dropping out or moving.

As a couple, Riley and Dave were stronger financially at this time and didn't want progress stalled on the Thanksgiving turkey giveaway project, so they decided to match and double every dollar donated. (And it's no wonder their financial strength increased in those six years; God was multiplying their giving so they could be more effective.)

In Riley's words, "Somehow, someway, God would always supply money from different sources, causing the totals to climb higher and higher." And what makes it more amazing is that this couple determined from the beginning that they wouldn't accept one penny from government programs or any corporations. It all had to come from family, friends, and friends of friends.

As the numbers escalated, new challenges arose. It became impossible to dispense all the turkeys in one day because the volume of people being served was so large. Riley and Dave were forced to add a second distribution day, which created a significant obstacle: Where would they store the turkeys overnight for the second day's distribution?

Riley was persistent in her search for an answer. At the midnight hour, a major grocery store chain where they bought all the turkeys stepped up and donated the use of refrigerated trucks. Now the money could be spent on food rather than storage.

They had numerous other hurdles and struggles to overcome, too many to list, but this couple's faith is strong and their resolve is unshakable. In the face of adversity, they continually prayed, cried out to God, came up with inspired strategic ideas, and found favor with people who could help.

Facing adversity, they continually prayed, cried out to God, came up with inspired strategic ideas, and found favor with people who could help.

They've been doing this now for thirty years, and as I'm writing this, last year alone they fed 12,500 families. (If an average family has four members, that would be forty-two thousand people.) They've effectively fed every needy person in their county and in a good portion of two neighboring counties. (This area includes one of the largest cities in the United States.) While doing so, they filled five tractor trailers (each forty-eight feet long) with turkeys and three tractor trailers with vegetables and stuffing. Over two hundred volunteers have been mobilized, with many of them working tirelessly over a span of several days. Many of them have been involved with Riley's project from the beginning, yet here's what's amazing: Most of the volunteers still don't know the identity of the "Turkey Lady"!

It would be impossible to list the miracles, stories, and testimonies of lives changed by their multiplication. Numerous people have come to know Jesus—including Riley's husband, Dave—and many have returned to faith. Families have reconciled, and many people have been inspired—government workers, grocery store employees, Salvation Army and YMCA employees, volunteers, and in some ways, the entire community.

Allow me to briefly highlight a few of the stories. One of Riley's friends is the treasurer of a local motorcycle club. Every year he asks the club to take up a collection for the Turkey Lady. They actually challenge each other to see who can give the most. Last year Riley received a text after Thanksgiving informing her that the bikers were increasing their donation by three thousand dollars for next Thanksgiving.

One year, the Turkey Lady team decided to donate the food overage to a local church. It inspired the church to use Riley's model to start their own program of helping the poor during Thanksgiving, as well as during other times of the year.

Salvation Army team members that have transferred to different states are eager to start programs patterned after Riley's. Others have moved into her area and couldn't wait to learn about the ministry, as they'd heard Riley's story from afar through the ranks of the Salvation Army.

Riley isn't a pastor. She doesn't work for a church, nor is she a business or corporate woman. She's a wife, mom, and devoted believer who faithfully attends church. She's well aware that she and Dave serve a mighty God who delights in their multiplication.

I'm honored to be this couple's friend.

THE NUMBER ONE EXAMPLE OF ETERNAL MULTIPLICATION

Service motivated by love is the catalyst for multiplication. Consider some of the great stories of multiplication in Scripture.

Of course, the story topping them all is that of Jesus Himself. He says:

If you want to be the greatest, then live as one called to serve others. The path to promotion comes by having the heart of a bond-slave who serves everyone. For even the Son of Man did not come expecting to be served by everyone, but *to serve everyone*, and to give his life as the ransom price for the salvation of many. (Mark 10:43–45 TPT)

The multiplication story in Scripture that tops them all is that of Jesus Himself.

Jesus clearly and strongly identifies the path to true greatness—seeking to serve, not to be served. It's no surprise that later He identifies own His supreme act of serving with these words:

I tell you the truth, unless a kernel of wheat is planted in the soil and dies, it remains alone. But its death will produce many new kernels. (John 12:24)

Once again, we hear of planting (or investing) and harvesting. Just as a single invested wheat kernel can yield a multitude of kernels, Jesus's obedience to serve produced multitudes of sons and daughters of God.

What an example! He paved the way and set the bar, showing us how to *effectively* multiply.

After giving us that picture of the dying kernel of wheat, Jesus went on in John 12 to immediately speak these startling words:

"Those who love their life in this world will lose it. Those who care nothing for their life in this world will keep it for eternity. Anyone who wants to serve me must follow me, because my servants must be where I am. And the Father will honor anyone who serves me" (12:25–26).

Take time to reflect deeply on this profound passage. How does it speak to you regarding your own unselfish serving of Jesus and others, your own closeness to Jesus, and your own pathway to pleasing and honoring God?

Jesus also tells us this:

You call me "Teacher" and "Lord," and you are right, because that's what I am. And since I, your Lord and Teacher, have washed your feet, you ought to wash each other's feet. I have *given you an example to follow.* Do as I have done to you. (John 13:13–15)

As a leader and communicator, I know the importance of the "final word"—the closing statement or message you leave with your reader, listener, student, team member, employee, child, or anyone else. It's the prevailing thought you want your hearers to dwell upon as they move forward.

In His time on earth, what was the final word from Jesus? Interestingly, it was an illustrated sermon He gave before His crucifixion—the washing of His followers' feet.

> As you think about Jesus's perfect example of servanthood, what special value do you see in the results of all the serving He did in His life on earth? How do those results include you personally?

I'm going to be honest with you. As a young believer, I intensely disliked anytime someone suggested in a small group, "Let's wash each other's feet." I'd immediately think of a trivial reason to slip out, because I just didn't like the idea of men touching my feet.

Years later, I'm relieved to know the foot washing was more of a tradition that my friends were holding on to. A parallel example is when Moses put the serpent on the pole, and all who looked upon it were healed of snakebites (Numbers 21:8–9). It was miraculous and powerful. However, many generations later, Israel made an idol of this very serpent (2 Kings 18:4). They highlighted the object instead of understanding that the original focus, years earlier, was obedience to the Lord's instruction.

In the 1980s, we followed a similar path in my Bible study groups. In my college days, we got the "foot washing" thing out of whack. We focused more on the action than what it represented.

Back in the first century, roads weren't paved. Animals were the only mode of transportation other than walking, and no one had Adidas or Nike tennis shoes. People wore sandals, or no shoes at all in many cases—so their feet were exposed to an abundance of dirt, animal feces, and other grime. It's safe to say that in that environment, stinky, dirty feet reached a level unknown to our Western world today.

When people back then entered a wealthy person's house, servants or slaves were required to clean the feet of their master, his family, and any guests. In a typical upper-class home, servants had a variety of responsibilities, such as managing stables, preparing food, and cleaning rooms. The assignment of washing feet was reserved for the lowliest servant. In some circles, the designation went even further; this nasty task was exclusively assigned to the lowest female servants, who were considered the only ones "unworthy" enough to do something so disgusting.

For the Last Supper, Jesus and the twelve disciples were in such a house, one large enough to host Jesus's entire team in a separate room. It was likely one of the most affluent homes in the city.

Perhaps many of these twelve men, hours earlier, had had their feet washed by this home's lowest servant. But shockingly, that same evening, Jesus not only grabbed the basin and pitcher of water but also disrobed—removing the symbol of His position as a teacher—and began to wash their feet. They knew exactly what was going on and what it represented.

In contrast, in my college days, I was confused and even repulsed by the popular practice of foot washing because my feet were already clean; I'd just taken a shower before the Bible study. Unsettled, I wondered, *Why is some guy I barely know attempting to wash my feet?*

Jesus's words take on a much greater meaning in light of His historical context. He was making a lasting impression, one that would stay with these disciples for the rest of their lives. It was a *final word*.

In a nutshell, in order to be great, we must voluntarily take the place of the lowliest servant. Could this be why Jesus says, "I am gentle and *lowly* in heart" (Matthew 11:29 ESV)?

> In what practical ways in your life have you already been able to "voluntarily take the place of the lowest servant," for the sake of Christ and other people?
>
> In what other practical ways can you see yourself doing this more often in the future?
>
> Set your mind for a few moments on better understanding what Jesus meant when he said he was "gentle and lowly in heart." How confident are you that he can make this more true about *you* as you continue to grow in your relationship with Christ? What specific changes might this bring to your life?
>
> For deeper inspiration on all this from the Scriptures, set aside time to actively meditate on Paul's words in Philippians 2:3–6.

It took a while for me to really grasp this. In my early days as a believer, many of us seemed to view ministry as just the opposite. Our unspoken belief was that significance isn't attained until you're leading or speaking to many. Serving was for people in the lower positions of our church. If you worked hard enough, eventually you would be a person of importance. Oh, how messed up our perception was!

I'm so grateful for the Holy Spirit's patience through my maturing process. He transformed my thinking, but it took time. As stated earlier, my first four years of ministry mostly involved taking care of our pastor's personal needs.

Higher positions will include greater serving responsibilities, with the importance of always being faithful in the smaller matters.

One day while I was running an errand, I heard a whisper from God's Spirit: Son, if I promote you, it will be to a greater position of serving. If you mess up now, you've only permanently stained a shirt. In public ministry, however, the mess will be damaged lives—lives of the people I love.

I was riveted by these words. Not only did He communicate that higher positions would include greater serving responsibilities, but He also conveyed the importance of always being faithful in the smaller matters. Serving others is always important because *people* are always important. People are the true riches.

> How open are you to being promoted to a greater position of serving? Is this something you desire? Is your faithfulness in present responsibilities preparing you for that kind of promotion?
>
> As part of your serving others—who would the Lord have you pray for today? How might they, too, grow in better understanding of their divine calling, giftedness, and purpose in life? Allow the Lord to bring these people to mind, and then lift them up in prayer.

ONE WOMAN'S EXAMPLE

One riveting example in the Old Testament of multiplication from selfless serving is seen in Rebekah. Let's briefly review the story.

Abraham sent his most trusted servant back to the country he'd left to find a wife for his heir, Isaac. The servant left promptly, taking ten camels for the long journey.

Upon arrival, Abraham's servant realized it was the time of day when young women came to the community well for water. He prayed, "This is my request. I will ask one of them, 'Please give me a drink from your jug.' If she says, 'Yes, have a drink, and I will water your camels, too!'—let her be the one you have selected as Isaac's wife" (Genesis 24:14).

Before he was finished praying, Rebekah approached with her water jug, so he asked her for a drink. What happened next was spectacular:

> "Yes, my lord," she answered, "have a drink." And she *quickly* lowered her jug from her shoulder and gave him a drink. When she had given him a drink, she said, "I'll draw water for your camels, too, until they have had enough to

drink." So she *quickly* emptied her jug into the watering trough and *ran back* to the well to draw water for all his camels. (Genesis 24:18–20)

The servant watched Rebekah in silence until she'd given all ten camels sufficient water.

In those few verses, we find many remarkable traits involved in Rebekah's serving. I'll list them one by one:

- *Eagerness.* Rebekah didn't drag her feet. She did everything swiftly, even running back and forth to the well. Slow or convenient serving is not true serving. Have you ever noticed people serving lethargically, with an attitude of "I'm tired of all this work"? That's not Rebekah—or any true servant. True servants have a willing and energetic attitude, which is evident from their actions.
- *Going the extra mile.* Servants excel. Rebekah far surpassed what was asked of her. Since most of us haven't owned camels or lived in a Middle Eastern desert, we wouldn't fully appreciate what makes Rebekah's service even more stunning. After a long trip, a typical thirsty camel can drink thirty to fifty gallons of water. Abraham's servant had ten camels. Let's do the math: If each camel drank just thirty gallons, that means Rebekah served up three hundred gallons of water to those animals! If a typical jug contained five gallons (forty pounds), she had to make sixty trips back and forth from the well.
- But there's more. In those days, there were two types of wells. With one, a rope was tied to the jug, which was lowered into the pit of the well to the water level. With the other, the water bearer walked down steps (perhaps twenty to thirty) to the water level. Rebekah was apparently using the second kind, because when the servant later related Rebekah's actions to her family, he said, "She *went down* to the spring and drew water" (Genesis 24:45). She not only made sixty trips with five gallons of water on her shoulders each time, but she did it while navigating all those steps. And keep in mind—she volunteered to do this. Which brings us to the next point.

- *Responsiveness.* A true servant doesn't wait to be asked when a need is evident; he or she moves forward immediately. In all my years of experience, it has become quite evident to me that when people consistently wait to be told, they don't multiply. Those who are always the first to act are the ones who increase.
- *Commitment.* Although the task was difficult, Rebekah was diligent in serving. Through the years I've observed a pattern: The harder the task, the more quickly great attitudes diminish. That's human nature. However, as believers, we have the nature of Jesus Christ. He never quit, even when He went through unimaginable resistance and hardship. Live from the nature of Jesus, and be inspired by Rebekah.
- *Completion.* Rebekah didn't stop until her work was finished. She was not a quitter. Doing 99 percent of a task is not finishing a task. We recall what King Saul did in the battle of the Amalekites; when he killed tens of thousands of the enemy but spared one, and therefore God did not reward these efforts of his (1 Samuel 15). Rebekah did all she did without anticipating any kind of reward for her labor—which is the true sign of servanthood. Servants don't labor for the purpose of the reward; they see the act of serving as its own reward. They love the joy, the sense of fulfillment, and the satisfaction that serving provides. Any reward is just an added blessing, not the motivation.
- The reward for Rebekah was magnificent. She didn't realize that the ten camels all bore treasures and gifts for her, and that she would be married to a godly man. But neither of these was the significant prize; the truly enduring reward was that she entered into God's promise to Abraham. She would be the mother of many nations. All nations would be blessed through her. Rebekah multiplied significantly.

From the cross, Jesus cried out, "It is finished!" (John 19:30). Later in the New Testament, we find these words of the apostle Paul near the end of his life: "I have finished the race, and I have remained faithful" (2 Timothy 4:7). Recognize that God has placed within you a desire to be able to speak these same words at your own life's end.

In time alone with the Lord, speak with Him about this. Ask Him—and thank Him—for what you will need to finish your life in this way, in fulfillment of your calling.

OTHER EXAMPLES

There are many other scriptural examples of eternal multiplication resulting from a heart to serve. Here are a few more you can investigate in detail during your own personal study time.

Ruth the Moabite was encouraged three times by her mother-in-law, Naomi, to turn back to Moab rather than go with Naomi to Israel, which was Naomi's homeland. But Ruth refused:

> Don't ask me to leave you and turn back. Wherever you go, I will go; wherever you live, I will live. Your people will be my people, and your God will be my God. (Ruth 1:16)

Ruth, much like Rebekah, was willing to go the extra mile, work hard, and stay committed, even when the going got rough. Ruth's road probably was more difficult than Rebekah's. Since she was a Moabite, after arriving at Bethlehem in Israel with Naomi, she was most likely persecuted by the locals because of her race and origin. Yet she endured any hardship to faithfully serve her mother-in-law.

What was the result? Ruth became an ancestor of many notables, including King David, King Solomon, and all the kings of Judah. Most importantly, she was in the lineage of Jesus (as pointed out on the opening page of the New Testament, in Matthew 1:5). She, too, entered into the covenant of eternal multiplication promised to Abraham.

Elisha determined to stay with Elijah and serve him, even when Elijah encouraged him three times to leave. Elijah continued serving him even when other prophets mocked and sneered that he was wasting his time. These other prophets no doubt followed logical reasoning; they'd become full-time prophets, gaining status and experience, but they believed Elisha had wasted his years serving Elijah instead of building his own ministry. But Elisha didn't listen to their logic. Instead he repeatedly and firmly told them to be quiet (2 Kings 2). He would not be deterred from serving, and he completed his assignment in serving Elijah.

Elisha's demeanor was similar to that of Rebekah and Ruth. And what was the outcome? Elisha ended up doing twice as many miracles as his mentor Elijah, and he was able to do something Elijah couldn't—put an end to evil Jezebel's dynasty. Elisha multiplied!

Gehazi had the chance to multiply Elisha's work, but he didn't have the heart of a servant. He was self-seeking and covetous, so he didn't effectively multiply (2 Kings 5).

> Considering your own personal tendencies and character traits, compare yourself to each of those four biblical characters—Rebekah, Ruth, Elisha, and Gehazi. In what ways are you like each one?

In the New Testament book of Acts, we see men who served widows' tables. They took their responsibility seriously. Hands were laid on them to ensure the task was done well. The result was impressive, for we're given this astonishing statement:

Then the word of God spread, and the number of the disciples *multiplied greatly* in Jerusalem. (Acts 6:7 NKJV)

What was so astonishing here? Say these words aloud: "multiplied greatly." And consider this: Those words were not used after Peter's classic message on the day of Pentecost, resulting in three thousand being born again. No, in that passage (Acts 2:41), the word *added* is used. In describing daily conversions, we again see that word *added* (Acts 2:47). It's the same for the five thousand giving their lives to Jesus a short while later (Acts 4:4).

The word *multiplied* is not used until the sixth chapter of Acts, when all the church became active in building the kingdom.

Today, multiplication happens when people like Stan, Mike, Phil, Riley, and Dave get into their place of serving and using their gifts. This is when we hear about *great multiplication*.

THE CRITICAL ELEMENT

Now do you understand the critical ingredient for effective multiplication? Think again about our friends Riley and Dave in light of what we've seen from Scripture. This one couple, by implementing inspired strategies and serving well, have already impacted tens of thousands of people. They've become great according to the words of Jesus.

The same is true for Stan, Mike, Phil, and Dana. They all carry the trait of being true servants.

However, please hear these important words: You can multiply *selfishly*—but your impact will not be eternal. Many people who are multiplying will one day see all their efforts burned up, because those efforts were motivated by personal gain.

This is illustrated in the parable Jesus told of the rich farmer who built bigger silos (Luke 12:13–21). The man smugly congratulated himself by saying, "Be at ease—eat, drink, and be merry, for I have arrived and now possess all I need and more" (12:19). But his story didn't end well. All his accomplishments vanished in a moment, when God took his life.

You can multiply selfishly—but your impact will not be eternal.

> Think about the root differences between serving to get and serving to give. How can we recognize when we're starting to do the first and not the second?

This book's core intent isn't to give you the faith to multiply for the purpose of heaping treasures on yourself, but rather to encourage you to give your life in service to others. Jesus declares that when we do this, all the things that unbelievers pursue will simply be added to us (Matthew 6:33). I know this, for I've experienced it firsthand.

Let's return to Lisa's and my story regarding our first church. After being in this toxic environment for six years, I had lingering unhealthy attitudes about multiplication. Soon after I left, one of many transforming and freeing encounters I've had with the Holy Spirit occurred one morning as I was driving my car. He said, Son, don't seek Me for the blessings. Let Me give them to you.

I immediately thought of Matthew 6:33: "Seek the Kingdom of God above all else, and live righteously, and he will give you everything you need." The Spirit's words brought proper perspective and helped eradicate residual selfish tendencies.

Oh, I'm so grateful to Him! I know what it's like to be selfish and covetous—the unhappiness, the stress, and the distance from the presence of God. Having learned His way and His heart—to seek first to build the kingdom—has brought so much joy and peace into everyday life, and so much of His presence!

We've come now in this book to the point where we should ask: How do we multiply when we aren't leading our own work, but serving on someone else's team?

Let's answer that in the next chapter—and see the great benefits.

REFLECTION FOR RENEWAL

In this chapter, what statements or Scripture passages seemed most meaningful for you?

How would you restate them in your own words? (Personalize your answer as a prayer of response to God.)

What are your thoughts about what God wants you to do now in response to what you've seen and reflected upon in this chapter?

IMITATE ME

I urge you, imitate me.

1 CORINTHIANS 4:16–17 NKJV

Before we move on to discuss what hinders multiplication and what fosters it, we have one more important area to discuss.

How do we multiply when we're employed by or serving someone else? For many of us—for much of our time—that's exactly where we find ourselves.

To discuss this, I'll focus on the specific area of ministry, but these principles apply to any position you may hold in the corporate world or marketplace, or in education, healthcare, government, media, athletics, the arts, or any other place in today's world.

Paul states, "It is required in stewards that one be found faithful" (1 Corinthians 4:2 NKJV). As we've established from Scripture, one of the chief characteristics of being faithful is to multiply. A few verses later in this letter, Paul sets up a key component to mass multiplication:

> For though you might have ten thousand instructors in Christ, yet you do not
> have many fathers; for in Christ Jesus I have begotten you through the gospel.
> (4:15 NKJV)

Paul is a father to the Corinthian church. As stated in this verse, a *father* is certainly one who leads another to faith. However, a father can be defined in other ways. In the New Testament, the spiritual term *father* is more frequently attached to a person who isn't involved in one's conversion.

This same Paul, in speaking to the Galatian church, makes this statement: "I advanced in Judaism beyond many of my contemporaries in my own nation, being more exceedingly zealous for the traditions of my fathers" (Galatians 1:14 NKJV). Paul isn't referring to any one person as he uses that word *fathers.*

This is also seen in Paul's phrasing when he told the Corinthians, "You do not have *many* fathers." This *many* indicates that we can have more than one father in our life.

Paul frequently refers to Timothy as his "son." However, he himself hadn't led Timothy to salvation, for we read that Paul went "to Lystra, where there was a young disciple named Timothy. His mother was a Jewish believer, but his father was a Greek. Timothy was well thought of by the believers in Lystra and Iconium" (Acts 16:1–2). It's clear that Timothy was already an established believer when Paul first met him.

If we look at the Old Testament, David refers to his harsh and tough leader (King Saul) as "my father" (1 Samuel 24:11). Likewise, Elisha refers to his leader (the prophet Elijah) as "my father" (2 Kings 2:12). Elijah himself had said to the Lord that he was no better than his "fathers" (1 Kings 19:4 NKJV).

And the long list continues.

My intention at this point is not to elaborate on what a father is, but rather to show who a father can represent. *A father is one who brings leadership, nurturing, and culture to an individual or organization.* For the purposes of our discussion, a father could hold a variety of positions—the business owner you work for, your department leader, your pastor, your small group leader, the overseer of your movement, your teacher, your coach, the doctor you serve—and that's the short list. Of course, you've probably concluded that a "father" in these situations could easily be female. Therefore, in referring to fathers, I'm also including women who stand in this role.

> Who are your father figures—those who provide leadership, nurturing, and culture to some aspect of your own life? Take a moment to give thanks to God for each of these people.

DIFFERENT OPERATIONS

Paul, as the father of the Corinthian church, instructed believers there with these words: "Therefore I urge you, imitate me" (1 Corinthians 4:16 NKJV). Later in this letter, Paul will say, "Imitate me, just as I imitate Christ" (1 Corinthians 11:1); here in chapter 4, however, the instruction is to simply "imitate me." There's a good reason for this—and it's revealed in the next statement:

> *For this reason* I have sent Timothy to you, who is my beloved and faithful son in the Lord, who will remind you of *my ways in Christ*, as I teach everywhere in every church. (4:17 NKJV)

His initial words here—"For this reason"—are significant. Paul has just told his readers to imitate him, and to ensure that there aren't any disconnects in vision, methods, culture, and convictions, he's sending them his "faithful" son, Timothy. What's the indicator of a *faithful* son or daughter? It's this: *A faithful son or daughter will multiply the ways of their father!*

> What importance do you see in imitating the ways of your leaders? (Think especially about attaining unity of vision, methods, and culture.)

I'll address this in more detail shortly, but first, consider this: When Paul writes to the Corinthian church, he doesn't tell them that Timothy "will remind you of the ways of the *apostle Peter* in Christ." Was Peter an authentic leader in the church? Most definitely. Was he a godly and anointed leader? Again, yes; he wrote two books in the Bible! Was Peter an apostle for a longer amount of time than Paul? Again, yes.

Nor does Paul tell them that Timothy "will remind you of the ways of the *apostle James* in Christ." As with Peter, James was a genuine father in the church.

He had been an apostle longer than Paul, and he was a reliable leader. He also wrote a book in the Bible, and he served as the leading overseer of the church in Jerusalem.

Did both Peter and James operate differently from Paul? Yes. Did Paul's writings and ways therefore make those of Peter and James invalid for us? Absolutely not! However, their ways were not as fitting as Paul's were for the Corinthian church, where Paul was the spiritual father.

There are different operations in the church. In other words, there are different ways of accomplishing the same goal of advancing the kingdom.

Paul was in the process of establishing his culture in the Corinthian church. His methods were different from the other "fathers," but they were all true to the fundamental beliefs and teachings of Christ. Still, each of them had different convictions and methods for accomplishing the task of making disciples of all nations.

This highlights a truth that many believers are unfamiliar with—a lack of awareness that's often the source of damaging divisions among the body of Christ. Here's the truth: There are different *operations* in the church. In other words, there are different ways of accomplishing the same goal of advancing the kingdom.

Paul instructs the Corinthian church:

> There are distinctive varieties of operation [of working to accomplish things], but it is the same God who inspires and energizes them all in all. (1 Corinthians 12:6 AMPC)

In traveling in ministry on a full-time basis for thirty years, I've witnessed firsthand the variety of cultures, methods, and convictions in the global church. And I can sense the presence of Jesus in each atmosphere.

Paul frequently uses military terms to instruct the church. It's not just imagery; we truly are members of God's military on the earth. I'll follow his lead in illustrating the different operations of ministries.

Think about this: Our United States military consists of diverse branches. We have the Army, Navy, Air Force, Marine Corps, Coast Guard, and Space Force. These branches have different procedures and methods to accomplish their goals and responsibilities. However, all these branches are on the same side when it comes to protecting and serving our nation.

An Air Force cadet will be specifically trained as a functioning member of the United States Air Force. A good amount of instructional emphasis will relate to air tactical operations, for this branch of service operates mainly in the sky. If this cadet happened to be reassigned to a battleship in the Navy, new training would be required. Of course, there are numerous fundamental techniques that overlap both branches. However, since the Navy operates primarily at sea, this former member of the Air Force would have to learn many new operational maneuvers and military strategies.

It's similar in the kingdom of God. Here's a hypothetical illustration. Let's say the names of your church's lead pastors are Joe and Terri Anderson. By God's grace, the Andersons and their team of leaders have grown the church to eighteen hundred members, and they have established approaches and methods and a culture that are unique to their leadership style. Your church's fruitfulness has affected your community in a remarkable way. The church has local recognition—but that's as far as it goes.

Now, let's say you're aware of a popular church elsewhere that's home to tens of thousands of members, and this church has attained global recognition. Their lead pastors' names are Kevin and Marissa Smith. The Smiths are setting trends and leading with fresh new tactics of ministry that are influencing many more people than your church's pastors are.

Whose ways are you going to follow—those of the Smiths, or those of your pastors, the Andersons?

You may be tempted to follow the ways of the popular global leaders and try to sway your leaders to adopt their methods. If you yield to this temptation, I would say you aren't being a faithful servant of Jesus Christ, but instead are fostering disunity, division, or even dissension. You, like the Corinthians, should seek to know and follow your leaders' methods and culture for the sake of unity. The reality is that the Smiths are not your leaders; the Andersons are.

During my years of global travel, observing the body of Christ from more of a bird's-eye view, I've witnessed frequent

For the sake of unity, seek to know and follow your leaders' methods and culture.

tragedies resulting from lack of awareness of this foundational truth. I've observed those who've gone to leadership or Bible training schools that have a different culture than the church they grew up in. Often these schools are connected to a large church, which sets the overall culture. The students experience the operations of that church in both the school and in their weekend worship experiences.

After graduation, the students return home full of passion, and they begin efforts to change their home church's culture and methods. While they may be correct in believing that the new ways are more relevant and effective, if they're too persistent, they can easily become a hindrance to the overall unity of the home church's mission.

If the methods suggested and promoted by these former students are refused by the church, it would be best for all involved for these young men and women to pray and ask God whether they should move on to another church, or else submit wholeheartedly to the culture and methods of their leader. If they move on, they should do so in a manner that wouldn't hurt their former church. It's usually best, in fact, if they move away from the region. God can always bring another leader to the area who can start afresh and avoid pulling people away from the original church due to existing relationships.

FAITHFUL SON

Now let's address the fact that the apostle Paul in 1 Corinthians 4:17 calls Timothy a "faithful son" (NKJV) As we've seen, a faithful son will seek to multiply the ways of his father. Most likely you have gifts that your leader doesn't have; the question becomes: Are you multiplying your gifts in line with your leader's heart? Does the underlying motive of your multiplication coincide with his convictions and culture, or are you fighting to establish your own way that's counterproductive and contrary to his heart?

Are you multiplying your gifts in line with your leader's heart?

This plays out practically in two ways.

First, it's demonstrated practically when you use your gifts to replicate an outcome of your leader if he were in your position with your unique gifts. This doesn't mean you should compromise your specific assignment by becoming a clone of your leader. Here's what I mean: Let's assume you're the youth pastor. You won't reach the young people of your community by copying your pastor's Sunday morning service. It's wiser to adapt your service in a way that reaches young people, but at the same time doing so with your father's heart. This can be accomplished only through good communication with him. You both should openly discuss your strategies and methods. When listening to his responses, you should truly *hear* those responses and see how his heart fits within your parameters.

Doing this effectively requires open and honest conversation. If you implement something and find yourself thinking, *I hope he doesn't notice it or hear about it,* you already know you're heading down a destructive path. If you have doubts, bring them to him; be specific so he can hear exactly what your concerns are. It may be wise to request that he sit in a service to observe your methods in operation. If he struggles with them, tell him the reasons behind your methods. If he's still uncomfortable, then immediately seek out an agreeable plan.

In the key areas of your life, who are the leaders you serve under?

How would you assess the ways in which your giftedness differs from theirs?

How closely would you say that your heart motivations are in alignment with the methods, values, and other cultural factors which are in place through your leaders' convictions, personalities, goals, and vision?

What adjustments on your part could help you become more closely aligned in this regard?

Are you able to communicate openly with your leaders about these things? Or is there a need for greater openness? If so, what steps can you take to achieve this?

The second way this plays out is by reproducing yourself. Let's assume you run the biggest youth group in the city, and God is blessing your methods;

His gift on your life is drawing people. But are you finding others with similar gifts and imparting to them the wisdom and ways you've learned? Are you raising up several potential youth pastors?

By doing so, when your "father" declares that the church will now start a new campus in another section of town, you'll already have people trained and ready to go.

I believe one reason many churches can't start campuses in other parts of their city, or can't plant new churches in another region, is that those in positions under the lead pastor are not reproducing themselves. You could be outstanding as a sound engineer, video editor, children's pastor, worship leader, guitarist, communicator, usher, or one of many other staff positions, but this alone doesn't define true kingdom success.

True significance lies in reproducing yourself. Ask yourself, *Am I praying for and seeking out others with similar gifts to mine?* Once you've located them, are you teaching, training, and drawing their gifts out while imparting your father's heart to them?

These are the two ways to be faithful when we serve another's vision. We must remember that Jesus emphatically states, "If you have not been faithful in what is another man's, who will give you what is your own?" (Luke 16:12 NKJV).

True significance lies in reproducing yourself.

Let's repeat Jesus's words by using His own definition of *faithful*: "If you have not multiplied what is another man's, who will give you your own?" Or, "If you have not multiplied your leader's ways, culture, strength, vision, resources—and most of all, your leader's heart—who will give you what is your own?" Let's say it still another way: "If you haven't given your entire strength, intellect, energy, faith, and heart to expanding your area of responsibility, who will give you the responsibility of leading an organization?"

These questions are sobering.

In my travels, those I meet who are truly successful were originally faithful with what belonged to someone else. I've frequently asked how they started out—and their answers demonstrate that they were all first faithful in what belonged to their father or fathers.

MY GREATEST STRUGGLE

When I was young in ministry, my greatest struggle was a hidden insecurity that drove me to want to be known and important. I had to prove to others—and mostly to myself—that I was a leader with original ideas. I've since learned that many potential leaders wrestle with this insecurity. If this is not dealt with at the heart level, it can lead later to their downfall.

I was a youth pastor in a large city for one of the fastest growing churches in the nation, and our team had thought of a way to reach every high school student in the area. It was a unique and good plan. Our youth group's future would entirely revolve around this initiative, for which my assistants and I had taken eight months to develop a strategy. I'd shared the vision with our youth group, and they embraced it.

But close to the launch of the plan, I discovered that it was contrary to my pastor's heart. He asked that we not execute the program. I argued with him for about twenty minutes, but he didn't budge. I finally shut my mouth when I could think of nothing else to say—but I was furious. Eight months of work down the drain, and a great plan scrapped. Worst of all, our whole vision was built around this program. We had to completely start over. How would I tell our twenty-four leaders and the entire youth group? They'd worked so hard.

Devastated, I went to Lisa for comfort. After rehearsing my frustrations, she sweetly countered, "Well, John, it looks like God is trying to teach you something." Now I was angry with both my pastor and my wife.

I proceeded to get away from Lisa, because in my eyes she wasn't being supportive. I thought this was the greatest plan ever to reach so many lost high school students. I thought, *My pastor and my wife must be totally blind.* I felt alone and frustrated and was inconsolable. *Could this really be happening?* At one point,

I even thought it was a nightmare—that I would soon wake up and all would be normal again.

In that moment, God spoke so clearly to my heart. He said, Son, when I judge you for your time of being a youth pastor, I will not judge first how many young people you won to Me. I will first judge how faithful you were to the man I put over you.

Those words riveted me, but not nearly as much as His next statement. He firmly said in my heart, You can win every high school student in the entire city to Me and lose all eternal credit and rewards for your labor because you were unfaithful to your pastor.

I suddenly began to tremble in holy fear. I immediately repented and asked for forgiveness.

I called my pastor and did the same with him.

Afterward I pondered what had just transpired, and the Lord suddenly gave me a vision. I saw myself heavy and sad, moping into the meeting with our twenty-four leaders. With distaste in my voice I announced, "Guys, you know we've worked on this for months; it's the vision of our youth group. But our senior pastor just nixed the program. Everything we've been working toward is no more."

I saw heads drop in disgust; the eyes and mouths of others were wide-open in disbelief. They were shocked and upset. In this vision, I recognized that they were all angry with our lead pastor and saw themselves as victims of his lack of creativity.

God asked me if that was the scene I hoped would come to pass. I responded, No, Sir! No, Sir! No, Sir! I knew He was addressing my attitude and my heart posture. This vision He'd given me showed that I still didn't have my father's (my pastor's) heart. I immediately repented on a deeper level.

A few days later, I walked into the meeting with my leaders. Now that I had a holy fear burning in my heart, I had a skip in my step, a twinkle in my eye, and a spark in my voice. I said with great enthusiasm, "Guys, I've got great news! Our lead pastor has spared us from birthing an Ishmael. He has declared that what we've been working on is not in the direction he wants this church to go, so we're scrapping the program!"

They all immediately responded with joy. Some smiled, others high-fived

each other, and the rest gave a shout of approval. They each caught my heart because I'd finally caught my pastor's heart.

A year later, I was tested again with another significant project we'd worked on for a few months. This time my pastor was aware of it and had agreed with our direction. However, he changed his mind three months into the project. Again, it was a drastic course change, and he was apologetic. I handled it with a totally different attitude than before. I canceled it; I didn't push back, argue, or voice any disagreement. I distinctly remember the difference I felt—the satisfaction of being able to agree, when in fact I would have stuck to the original plan had it been my choice.

Once again, I presented to my leaders the cancelation of our project, as though it had been my own idea.

God blessed our youth group. It multiplied three times in size during the two years I held the position. I'm convinced I wouldn't be where I am today had I failed these tests.

In fact, I can tell you what would have transpired, because the Holy Spirit has shown me. I eventually would have canceled the program because I wouldn't have had any choice. I would have done so with an attitude that would have spread to my leaders, thus poisoning them. Eventually I would have left the church. The gifts on my life would have impacted a small number of people, but I never would have had the ministry we now have, speaking and writing to millions of people globally. Having not been faithful in what was another's, I would not have been entrusted with a God-given mission.

Learning this lesson in faithfulness wasn't easy. As a leader with a type A personality, my tendency would have been to fight for what I thought was best. But I learned that God was more concerned about my character than my results. He wanted a firm foundation in place before He would entrust Lisa and me with our own mission.

In what ways has God taught you that He's more concerned about your character than about the results of your work and serving? How deeply has that lesson sunk in?

You are a leader too. If we walk in His ways, God has promised leadership opportunities to all His children.

My dear friend, you are a leader too. If we walk in His ways, God has promised leadership opportunities to all His children. We're "the head and not the tail"; we'll be "above only, and not be beneath" (Deuteronomy 28:13 NKJV).

Please don't kick against the goads as I did. Learn from me— so you, too, can advance in kingdom responsibility.

THE IMPORTANCE OF UNITY

An organization must be united in order to multiply. One of the most eye-opening portions of Scripture on this is found in the book of Genesis. A group of ungodly people purposed to do something that was almost unattainable for people of their time—to build a tower into the heavens. Yet listen to what God Almighty says:

> Indeed the people are *one* and they all have one language, and this is what they begin to do; now *nothing that they propose to do will be withheld from them.* (Genesis 11:6 NKJV)

Remember who's doing the speaking here: God Himself. Listen to His words: "Nothing that they propose to do will be withheld." Why did God make such a statement? Because they were "one" and had "one language." They were unified. They walked together in agreement.

If these words are spoken out of the mouth of God in regard to unsaved people, what does He say to covenant people? It's even better, for when His people unite together, "there the LORD commanded the blessing" (Psalm 133:3 NKJV). The word *commanded* here means "to order, to direct, to appoint."[1] There's no wiggle room; unity draws blessing, which includes multiplication.

This applies so much more for His New Testament children. No wonder we repeatedly see statements like these:

> Become complete. Be of good comfort, be of *one mind,* live in peace; and the God of love and peace will be with you. (2 Corinthians 13:11 NKJV)

Only let your conduct be worthy of the gospel of Christ, so that whether I come and see you or am absent, I may hear of your affairs, that you stand fast in *one spirit*, with *one mind* striving together for the faith of the gospel. (Philippians 1:27 NKJV)

Make me truly happy by *agreeing wholeheartedly* with each other, loving one another, and working together with *one mind* and *purpose*. (Philippians 2:2)

We're hearing pleas from the *father* of these churches. He wants these churches to be on the receiving end of God's commanded blessing. He knows that only then will they truly multiply in all aspects.

> In the church or ministry organization you're a part of, do you see oneness of mind and spirit as a higher priority than efficiency or outward success or effectiveness? Be further guided by the Word of God as you consider these passages: Romans 15:5–6; Ephesians 4:3–6; Colossians 3:12–15; 1 Peter 3:8.
>
> What do you see as the most important things you can do to help promote Christian unity in the circle or circles you're a part of?

Here's an excellent example of the commanded blessing reserved for those who unify: Jesus's faithful followers obeyed His command to remain in Jerusalem (Acts 1:4). Earlier, during the forty days after His resurrection, Jesus had appeared to at least five hundred men and women (1 Corinthians 15:6); yet ten days after his ascension, only 120 remained in Jerusalem. Where were the others?

I conclude that over 75 percent of those five hundred disciples didn't listen to Jesus's words. We may not know where they were, but we do know His desire was not their priority.

The men and women who stayed together in Jerusalem were unified under the authority of God's Word. The question then became: How would they respond to Peter, His delegated authority, the church *father* Jesus had put in charge?

Previously, Peter had often been impulsive and out of sync with God's will. For example, when Peter boldly stated that Jesus was the Christ, the Son of the living God, Jesus declared him to be blessed. Yet within moments—after Peter had suddenly rebuked Jesus when He foretold His suffering and death—Jesus "turned and said to Peter, 'Get behind Me, Satan! You are an offense to Me, for you are not mindful of the things of God, but the things of men'" (Matthew 16:23 NKJV).

On another occasion, Peter had walked on water while the other disciples just observed; he was leading the way once again. But within moments, he began sinking. Jesus lamented this by saying to him, "O you of little faith, why did you doubt?" (Matthew 14:31 NKJV).

In still another incident, Jesus had escorted Peter and James and John to the mountain of His transfiguration. There they witnessed His face shining like the sun, and even His clothing was transformed. Moses and Elijah appeared and talked with Jesus. What an honor!

But then, as we read in Matthew 17:4, Peter blurted out his idea that they should build tabernacles there for Jesus and Elijah and Moses. His focus was quickly corrected: "Even as he spoke, a bright cloud overshadowed them, and a voice from the cloud said, 'This is my dearly loved Son, who brings me great joy. *Listen to him*'" (Matthew 17:5). Peter was once again out of sync with God's plans and purposes.

With this in mind, let's examine one of Peter's first decisions as a leader of the inaugural church. Before we do, however, we must remember one other important fact: At this moment, only days have passed since Peter had denied ever knowing Jesus. This normally would induce many men and women to not heed Peter's leadership, especially if they disagreed with his direction or decisions.

So let's set the stage. A few days had passed since Jesus's ascension, and Peter found a prophetic word in the book of Psalms that directly related to the events of Judas's betrayal of Jesus. Peter read these words to this small congregation: "This was written in the book of Psalms, where it says . . . 'Let *someone else take his position*'" (Acts 1:20). Once again Peter saw what others didn't; but would he handle it correctly?

What you're about to read can certainly be viewed as speculative, but I hope to give enough scriptural support to validate my point. I believe Peter was once again out of sync with God in his decision-making, for he suggested that they round up all the men who'd been with them from the beginning so they could cast lots to decide who God would choose to take Judas's position.

Nowhere in the New Testament will you find God picking an apostle by a lottery system. Jesus showed these men God's way by leaving them an example: He prayed all night and heard from God before He chose the twelve original apostles (Luke 6:12–13). It would have been best had Peter sought to acquire the next apostle in a manner more similar to that of Jesus.

Remember, just a few years later, the prophets and teachers in the church in Antioch followed Jesus's example. They fasted and prayed before Barnabas and Saul were set apart for the office of apostle (Acts 13:1–4). This is yet another confirmation of the error of Peter's hasty decision.

The 120 in the upper room found two candidates: Matthias and Justus. Matthias won the lottery and was numbered among the apostles (Acts 1:23–26). However, you never find Matthias's name again in the New Testament. Why? Because Scripture would show that Paul, not Matthias, was God's choice to replace Judas. This is why Paul wrote these words about his own personal encounter with Jesus:

> He was seen by James and later by all the apostles. Last of all, as though I had been born at the wrong time, I also saw him. For I am the least of all the apostles. (1 Corinthians 15:7–9)

Paul referred to himself as though he'd been born at the wrong time; in other words, he was probably too young to be one of the original twelve. In my research, I've found different opinions of the dates of Paul's birth; the estimates from different sources range as high as fourteen years. One thing is certain: No one knows for sure Paul's birth year. So let's look at the timeline of the New Testament to get a glimpse of his age.

By most accounts, Stephen's martyrdom occurred four years after Jesus's resurrection, which means Jesus had chosen His original group of disciples seven years earlier. During Stephen's stoning, Scripture refers to Saul (Paul) as a "young man" (Acts 7:58). The *Greek-English Lexicon* states that the Greek word here for young man refers to someone just after puberty. So in subtracting the seven years, one can safely assume Paul was too young to be an original disciple.

I fully believe that Paul was God's choice. From the evidence in the New Testament, he clearly possessed the fruit and authority of an apostle, much more so than Matthias.

The main point: I believe the apostle Peter made an impulsive leadership decision that was out of sync with God's plan. Were he to make this move in today's modern church, we most likely would have a three-way church split: the "anti-lottery apostle-picking" group, the "there's no need for new apostles" group, and the "pro-lottery apostle-picking" group (which would have stood by Peter).

And yet, listen to the words recorded in Scripture after this incident:

> When the Day of Pentecost had fully come, they were all *with one accord* in one place. (Acts 2:1 NKJV)

The words *with one accord* translate just a single Greek word, *homothumadon*, defined as "with one mind, with unanimous consent, in one accord, all together."[2] From this definition, there's no room for division, either mentally or behaviorally. They were united in purpose, mind, heart, and spirit. What was the result? Scripture states that three thousand were added to the Lord that very day. If you divide this number by 120, you end up with multiplication of twenty-five times.

Think of it: The church grew twenty-five times as large in just one service. God commanded His blessing on their unity. It's a spiritual law.

To observe more of the early church's unity—and to learn from their example—explore these additional passages from the book of Acts where that Greek word *homothumadon* is used: 2:42–47; 5:12–15; and 15:22–27. (The Greek word is used also in Paul's inspiring exhortation to unity in Romans 15:5–7.)

I'm sure there were some believers in that upper room setting in Acts 1 who would have done things differently than Peter did. No doubt a better choice would have been to follow Jesus's example and first seek God for an extended time before making the decision.

Even though there was a better way of going about it, the people in that room saw the higher priority—to remain *one* by owning their leader's strategy. Each of these believers proceeded forward as if it had been his or her idea.

How often do we today divide over the silliest or smallest disagreements in our methods?

Meanwhile, let me interject this one important truth: If your leader makes a decision that's categorized by Scripture as a *sin*, this is the only time we're told not to adhere. However, most fallouts occur over methods, not sin.

> Have you ever participated in a breakup of some kind in your church or organization because of a difference over mere methods—where sin was not the issue? If so, how could the matter have been better handled on your part?

UNDERTOWS

We must remember that dissension is not limited to words or actions; it goes deeper—to the mind, heart, and spirit. As a refresher, look again at 2 Corinthians 13:11 and Philippians 1:27 and 2:2. We can be united outwardly, yet divided in our motives and thoughts.

My mother and father used to live in Vero Beach, Florida. Approximately thirteen miles north of their residence is a little arm of the Atlantic called Sebastian Inlet. It's known to the locals for its strong undertows. An undertow is a phenomenon that isn't noticeable to the naked eye. The water on the ocean's surface appears to be flowing in one direction, moving in unison toward the beach.

Dissension is not limited to words or actions; it goes deeper—to the mind, heart, and spirit. We can be united outwardly, yet divided in our motives and thoughts.

Yet underneath the surface, water is moving swiftly in the opposite direction. This contrary current grabs its victims and pulls them out to sea, sometimes taking their lives.

Are there undertows in our churches, businesses, schools, governments, athletic teams, and clubs that destructively prevent multiplication? Absolutely yes.

Why is this? Is it because we're attempting to build the kingdom of God with a democratic mindset rather than a kingdom mindset? We're citizens of a real kingdom, and our King's delegated authority cannot be overlooked. His blessing is manifested when we're submitted in heart to our leaders.

We must ask ourselves: *Is it more important to be right, or to be united?* You can be 100 percent "right" yet 100 percent wrong at the same time. If a vocal group of believers had petitioned to override the apostle Peter's choice of a lottery system and replace it with fasting and prayer (according to the pattern we've seen in Scripture), the coalition would have been 100 percent correct. However, because of the resulting disunity, the outpouring of God's blessing would have stopped.

If you recall, the next time (after the day of Pentecost) when we see extraordinary multiplication in the book of Acts is in chapter 6, after the fathers have given an operational directive. Afterward we read, "Everyone in the church loved this idea" (Acts 6:5 TPT). What was the result? "The number of the disciples *multiplied greatly*" (Acts 6:7 NKJV). Everyone took ownership of the strategy.

It is better to be blessed than to be right.

Again, I'm sure some people *could* have objected. But those believers had discovered a truth: *It is better to be blessed than to be right.* They embraced the method as if it was their own idea.

Now we must ask the most difficult question: How many of us, standing before the judgment seat of Jesus, will be shocked and bewildered by what He reveals? Will He show us, with tears, how our undertow contribution hindered the commanded blessing? Will we see the lives that would have been impacted for eternity and weep with Him as we realize the missed opportunity for us to multiply? How many of us will wish to go back and seek to be unified, as opposed to being right?

But it will be too late.

REFLECTION FOR RENEWAL

In this chapter, what statements or Scripture passages seemed most meaningful for you?

How would you restate them in your own words? (Personalize your answer as a prayer of response to God.)

What are your thoughts about what God wants you to do now in response to what you've seen and reflected upon in this chapter?

HINDRANCES TO MULTIPLICATION —PART I

CHAPTER 12

Master, I knew you were a harsh man,

harvesting crops you didn't plant

and gathering crops you didn't cultivate.

I was afraid I would lose your money,

so I hid it in the earth.

MATTHEW 25:24–25

Now we'll dive into the motives and thoughts of the lazy steward of Jesus's parable in Matthew 25. Why did the other two servants multiply, while he only maintained? Why were those other two identified as "good and faithful," while this guy was referred to as "wicked and lazy"?

Before continuing, let's take some time to establish a truth: *When someone stands in the presence of Jesus, it's impossible to lie.* Why am I mentioning this here? Let me explain with a trivial illustration. Have you ever watched an espionage movie, and at one point during an interrogation, a "truth serum" is administered to expose hidden realities? The spy or double agent then reveals what he was sworn to conceal, and the truth is uncovered.

Let's turn to a real-life situation. In the early years of my marriage, I was immature and insecure. There were incidents in which I behaved in a way that seemed acceptable at the time, until Lisa confronted me. In our discussions,

I strongly defended my actions and motives. Often in those discussions, I'd boldly defend the accuracy of my statements. Later, while in prayer and in the presence of God, I'd realize she was spot-on. I would return to Lisa in humility and admit my error.

The point: Deception, dishonesty, trickery, duplicity, and other similar behaviors cannot coexist in the royal presence of God.

Listen to what Jesus states:

> The time is coming when everything that is covered up will be revealed, and all that is secret will be made known to all. Whatever you have said in the dark will be heard in the light, and what you have whispered behind closed doors will be shouted from the housetops for all to hear! (Luke 12:2–3)

Jesus is speaking specifically of the day of judgment, when it will be impossible to think or speak in a deceiving manner; truth will permeate the atmosphere, and no lie or deceitful word will be uttered. The very fact that our stewardship parable represents this coming judgment means we can be confident that the answer given by the lazy servant is accurate. He exposes himself, even when the truth accuses him.

To review, this servant didn't *eternally* multiply for two reasons:

- He did not know the character of His master.
- He was afraid.

These two reasons are given in that order because ignorance of the character of God easily fosters fear. This will be made clear as we continue to unpack both errors.

"WHAT I BELIEVE"

Before we unpack the first error, let me tell a story. After flying eight hours to Hawaii for a conference, I learned at my hotel that my room was not yet ready, and I needed to wait. Still in my travel clothes, I found a spot to rest under a poolside umbrella. It just so happened that a businesswoman was also waiting—she was attending a different conference. We got to talking, and once she discovered I was a Christian author and minister, she began to elaborate on her relationship with God.

It didn't take more than a minute or two to deduce that she didn't know God. She kept confidently stating what she *believed*, and very little of it corresponded to what Scripture reveals.

While she was still expounding further on her beliefs, I asked the Holy Spirit for wisdom, and He showed me what to say.

When the woman finished speaking, I asked, "Do you see the man sitting across the pool?"

"Why, yes," she responded.

"Allow me to tell you about him," I said. "He's a strict vegan—he doesn't eat anything from an animal, not even honey. His dream is to swim at the Olympics for Team USA. He works out and practices three hours a day. His hobbies are racquetball, tennis, skydiving, and painting. He's married to that woman just over there by the hot tub, and she's ten years younger than he is."

The woman was intrigued but also a little confused as to why I would change the subject so abruptly, after she'd just shared her deep thoughts about God. Her curiosity got the best of her, so she asked, "Is that man here to attend the conference with you?"

"No, ma'am."

"Well, how do you know him?" she asked, even more curious.

"I've never met him."

Now looking confused and concerned, she asked how I knew so much about him. I have no idea if this is correct, but by the look on her face, I'm guessing she might have thought I was a CIA operative, an FBI agent, a detective, or even a stalker. Her curiosity had been piqued.

I paused, then said to her, "That's what I *believe* about him."

She was speechless.

I continued. "You just spoke with such confidence of your *belief* of who

God is. But almost everything you just said about Him is not true. I know this because I know Him."

Then I turned, looked her straight in the eye, and said, "What I just did with that man I've never met before is no different from what you just did with God. I told you what I *believe* about the man across the pool, and I sounded quite convincing. But chances are, most of what I said isn't true because I've never taken the time to get to know him."

The woman appeared slightly shaken but kept listening.

"God gave us His Word, recorded on the pages of the Bible, and it reveals who He is. He also sent His Spirit to reveal Jesus to us, who in turn shows us God Almighty, because He is God manifested in the flesh."

I paused, and then asked gently, "Do you think you may have made up an imaginary God in your mind—one who actually doesn't exist?"

Sadly, either she wasn't ready to confront her lack of knowing God, or she was scared to face the reality of meeting Him. We chatted for a few more minutes and soon parted ways.

You may be smiling as you read this story, and thinking, *Well, I know God. I go to church, and I've read the Bible.* However, rather than getting too comfortable in that thought, we must remember the plight of the Pharisees. They had perfect church attendance, they prayed and fasted regularly, and they could quote from memory the first five books of the Scriptures. (I certainly don't have that good a record!) Yet when the God of those Scriptures appeared in the flesh—Jesus, standing right before them—they couldn't recognize Him.

Think further about this idea that ignorance of the character of God leads to fear. In your own experience, how has any incorrect, fear-filled view of God's nature affected the way you held back from fully stewarding your gifts and calling?

KNOWING GOD

Who gets the privilege of knowing God?

All are invited, but there are established parameters. The door is open for an authentic relationship when we, from the core of our beings, make the decision to give our lives fully to Him—not in pretense, but accompanied with corresponding actions. Jesus says, "If you give up your life for my sake, you will save it" (Matthew 16:25). What does He mean by "save" it?

It's simple. True life is found only in *knowing Him.*

We don't come to know God by attending church, surrounding ourselves with Christian friends, reading Christian books, listening to worship music, repeating a "salvation" prayer, or even by doing good works. In Scripture, Jesus is frequently referred to as the groom, and we're referred to as the bride. When a bride and groom unite, the two become one. Paul writes that this "is an illustration of the way Christ and the church are one" (Ephesians 5:32). To show what knowing Him is like, God gave us that illustrative sermon about a common human relationship. On a daily basis, a clear representation of a relationship with Him can be observed: *marriage*—holy matrimony.

> *The door is open for an authentic relationship with God when we, from the core of our beings, decide to give our lives fully to Him—not in pretense, but accompanied with corresponding actions.*

When a woman walks down the aisle of a church in a white dress to the wedding march, she's making a strong statement. She's saying goodbye to the other roughly four billion males in the world. She's giving her entire heart, soul, body, and life to the one man waiting for her at the altar. Interestingly, her decision represents true "repentance." She's walking away from all opportunities to establish a marriage union with all the rest of the men on earth. She and her chosen husband enter a covenant; he's entirely hers, she's entirely his. The two embark on a journey that carries the potential of a deepening relationship, of knowing each other more than they could ever know anyone else.

I want to say something that may seem controversial, but hear me out. I personally believe that one of the great obstacles we've created to *knowing* God is the introduction of the "sinner's prayer." Our tradition typically looks like this: We sell a relationship with God, almost as if we're marketing a product to a consumer. After a message or conversation, we say, "Do you want to know God? Do you want a relationship with your Creator? Then just pray this prayer: 'Jesus, come into my life. I receive You as my Savior. Thank You for forgiving me and now making me a child of God.'"

Next, we announce the happy news to all who are present. We celebrate that our new converts are forever secure with God, and we invite them into our fellowship. However, we've said nothing about repentance—their need to walk away permanently from a self-seeking lifestyle, and to lay down their life for Him.

Yet listen to this statement from Jesus:

> If you truly want to follow me, you should at once completely reject and disown your own life. And you must be willing to share my cross and experience it as your own, as you continually surrender to my ways. For if you choose self-sacrifice and lose your lives for my glory, you will continually discover true life. But if you choose to keep your lives for yourselves, you will forfeit what you try to keep. (Matthew 16:24–25 TPT)

We can truly know God only by entering an authentic relationship with Him, which is what Jesus summarized in these verses. Knowing God is not a one-time event, but a firm decision to submit to His ways instead of what you think is best for you. This is a decision made day by day, moment by moment.

If some issue in your life is clearly revealed in His Word, there's no debating or wiggling out of obedience to God's standard. Following Jesus means you've made the decision deep in your heart to walk away from that which offends Him and to serve Him on an ongoing basis.

At this point in your life, what mindsets or behaviors might be hindering your relationship with God—blocking the authentic closeness with Him that your soul deeply craves?

The apostle James writes, "Don't just listen to God's word. You must do what it says. Otherwise, you are only fooling yourselves" (James 1:22). Those who hear from God—and yet are unresponsive in thought, word, and action—have fooled themselves. The Passion Translation of James 1:22 calls this "self-deception," which I think accurately describes the third steward in Matthew 25, as well as the Pharisees, and the woman I met at the pool in Hawaii. It's also an accurate description of many others I've encountered who fully believe they're in relationship with God because they attend church and quote Scripture while regularly speaking and living contrarily to His Word. They are sadly misled. It is *self-deception*.

Let me quickly make an important point. Lisa will tell you she's made many mistakes in our marriage (I've made more than she has, but here I'm focusing on the bride), but she has never purposefully sought her own desires at the expense of our marriage covenant. Her behavior hasn't been perfect, but her heart has never departed from steadfast loyalty.

Likewise, in our relationship with God, if we periodically disobey, He forgives. This is no different from a husband and wife not breaking their covenant relationship when a mistake is made. A relationship with our Creator and Redeemer is true loyalty from the heart, not lip service without authentic, corresponding actions.

Jesus makes the most remarkable statement: "If anyone *wills* to do His will, he shall *know*" (John 7:17 NKJV). This knowing begins in the core of our being, when we deeply desire to act on, not just hear, God's will. We do whatever He says—and then we *know*. We recognize and *know* God and His Word. The Passion Translation renders Jesus words in John 7:17 beautifully: "First be passionate to do God's will, and then you will be able to discern if my teachings are from the heart of God."

In the parable of the talents, all three stewards heard the exact same instructions before the departure of their lord. Two of them put his instructions into action, and one did nothing. It's no coincidence that the third steward really didn't *know* his master, so he regarded the importance of his instructions lightly. This steward was self-deceived.

We do whatever He says— and then we know.

HOLY FEAR

Our discussion thus far can be described with the biblical phrase "fear of the Lord." Due to all the fear that abounds, especially in this day and hour, we typically shy away from that phrase. However, we should know about *two* fears, which are totally opposite of each other. One is the "spirit of fear," and the other is the "fear of the Lord." Scripture distinguishes between the two.

Moses spoke the following words to God's people, just after they drew back from God's presence:

> "*Do not fear*; for God has come to test you, and that *His fear* may be before you, so that you may not sin." So the people stood afar off, but Moses drew near the thick darkness where God was. (Exodus 20:20–21 NKJV)

At first glance, it seems Moses contradicts himself. Let me paraphrase his statement to make it clear: "Do not *fear,* because God has come to see if *His fear* is in you." This declaration is not a contradiction, but a differentiation between being "scared of God" and having the "fear of the Lord." There's a difference. The person who is scared of God has something to hide. Recall how Adam and Eve hid from the presence of the Lord after they sinned against Him (Genesis 3:8). On the other hand, the person who fears God has nothing to hide. He or she is actually scared to be *away* from Him.

Permit me to make a firm point: *The fear of the Lord is not about being scared of God.* How can we have an intimate relationship with someone we're afraid of? As I've stated, true holy fear is to be terrified to find yourself away from God. You don't want to be anywhere other than in His presence, His care, and His love. You're immovable in that—no matter your circumstances or how bleak things may appear. You know there's no place better than being close to Him. This is evident by your obedience to Him.

To fear God is to venerate, revere, honor, and respect Him more than anyone or anything else. It's to hold Him in the highest esteem, to embrace His heart's desires as more precious and valuable than our own. We love what He loves, and we hate what He hates. What's important to Him becomes important to us. What is not so important to Him is not so important to us.

This posture places us among those who are welcomed to be close to Him. If you examine the children of Israel, their love for God was conditional. When circumstances were favorable, they worshiped, obeyed, and loved Him. When things were unfavorable, they complained. They didn't trust Him implicitly but instead were committed to self-preservation. By seeking to save their own lives, they did the opposite of what Jesus states in the Gospels; they forsook the glorious privilege of a genuine relationship with Him. Moses feared God; they didn't.

Their motives were manifested accordingly—the people "stood afar off," but Moses "drew near" to God's presence (Exodus 20:21 NKJV). They were blind to what was best, and their lives showed it. In contrast, Moses saw clearly. Moses knew God—His Word, His ways, and His wisdom. They, on the other hand, knew God only by how He answered their prayers.

How do you understand the big difference between being afraid of God and having the fear of the Lord? Express this in your own words.

How have you seen that difference in your own life?

As you understand it, why is having the fear of the Lord critical to knowing God intimately?

Take a moment to come before your heavenly Father in prayer, with special consciousness of the fear of the Lord. Reveal your heart to Him on this matter, including whatever questions or confusion you may have.

We operate appropriately in the fear of the Lord when we obey Him instantly—even if doing so doesn't make sense, and there's no apparent benefit, and it even appears harmful to our well-being. We know His character, and thus are convinced. Even though something may appear detrimental to us, it will never be so when obeying God.

Walking in the fear of the Lord is made manifest by complete obedience to Him. Abraham did exactly this when God told him to let go of what was most important to him—what he'd waited twenty-five years for. He was to surrender his son Isaac—the person he loved more than any other, and more than any possession. Abraham left early in the morning and made a three-day journey in order to do what God asked of him. God hadn't given him a "why," and it appeared this sacrifice would ruin all that Abraham had lived for. It appeared detrimental. But Abraham—the very antithesis of the lazy steward—implicitly trusted the character of God.

We operate appropriately in the fear of the Lord when we obey Him instantly—even if doing so doesn't make sense, and there's no apparent benefit, and it even appears harmful to our well-being.

Once Abraham had the knife raised to execute Isaac, the angel of the Lord stopped him and declared, "Do not hurt him in any way, for now I know that *you truly fear God*. You have not withheld from me even your son, your only son" (Genesis 22:12). This kind of love, trust, and faith is the heart of one who truly fears God.

We're told, "The fear of the LORD is the beginning of knowledge" (Proverbs 1:7 NKJV). What knowledge? We'll explore the answer shortly, but let's also examine what leads up to the answer—putting God's Word above all, which is what Abraham did.

Consider this instruction to us all:

My son, if you receive my words, and treasure my commands within you, so that you incline your ear to wisdom, and apply your heart to understanding; yes, if you cry out for discernment, and lift up your voice for understanding, if you seek her as silver, and search for her as for hidden treasures; then you will understand the fear of the LORD, and *find the knowledge of God.* (Proverbs 2:1–5 NKJV)

The answer is quite clear. The fear of the Lord is *the beginning of the knowledge of God.* Today we would phrase it a little differently. We might say, "You will understand the fear of the Lord and begin to know God intimately."

Now we can better understand the root error of the lazy steward. He lacked holy fear, which was evident by his lack of action and his final response. Just as Israel at times saw God as a tyrant, this steward saw his master no differently. He was blind to his leader's character.

Holy fear is the starting place of knowing God. David confirms this by declaring, "The LORD is a friend to those who fear him" (Psalm 25:14). Friends are those we know on an intimate level. Jesus makes a startling statement: "You show that you are my intimate friends when you obey all that I command you" (John 15:14 TPT).

Many of us often say we "love" Jesus, and it's in the same way we say we love some famous movie star, athlete, or other public figure. In early 2020, when Kobe Bryant and his daughter Gianna were killed in a tragic helicopter accident, the entire nation mourned, and many wept. People placed an abundance of balloons, cards, and flowers near the Staples Center in Los Angeles where he'd played basketball. I also mourned the tragedy and thought quite a bit about it.

But most of us who mourned didn't know Kobe like his wife, family, and close friends did. Had he seen us on the street, he would've had no idea who we were. I'd never spent time with him, yet I grieved his passing as if I did have a relationship with him. Just as Kobe wouldn't have known me when he was alive, a multitude of men and women will claim to know Jesus because they attended church, spoke of Him on social media, listened to music about Him, did things in His name, and even professed His lordship. But Jesus's reply will be, "I never knew you."

And this is why:

Not everyone who calls out to me, "Lord! Lord!" will enter the Kingdom of Heaven. Only those who actually do the will of my Father in heaven will enter. On judgment day many will say to me, "Lord! Lord! We prophesied in your name and cast out demons in your name and performed many miracles in your name." But I will reply, "I never knew you. Get away from me, you who break God's laws." (Matthew 7:21–23)

We don't ever want those words said to us by the Master. Yet if you examine this passage of Scripture closely, these people were confident in their relationship with Jesus, even emotional about it. They were self-deceived.

Kobe would have said to me, "Who are you? Where are you from? What's your name?" In this way, Jesus will say to many claiming to know Him, "I don't know you or where you come from" (Luke 13:25).

SPEND TIME WITH HIM

The fear of the Lord is the starting place of knowing Him intimately, but why camp at the starting place? Go deeper in your relationship, because He's calling you to come closer. We're told, "Come close to God, and God will come close to you" (James 4:8). Amazingly, *we* determine the level of closeness in our relationship with Him!

It surprises me how so many professing believers aren't much different from the woman I met at the pool in Hawaii. They get their "knowledge of God" from social media, worship music, blogs, conversations with friends, and their pastor speaking about Him once a week. But they don't spend personal time with Him.

Recent statistics indicate that people between the ages of fifteen and twenty-three spend well over fifty hours a week in front of screens—smartphones, tablets, computers, and television.[1] I wonder how much time they spend in the Word of God? And that question is relevant not just to young people!

Take a moment to find Isaiah 55:10–11 in your Bible and to reflect on all that God says there. Be reminded of how the Word of God is so inseparably linked to His purposes in our lives. Ponder this, and offer Him sincere praise and thanksgiving for what He says and what He does.

I've been reading my Bible for more than forty-five years, and it's still one of my favorite things to do. Before reading, I always ask the Holy Spirit to reveal Jesus to me in a fresh way. I've spent years getting up early and spending time with Him while pacing around my basement, outside in a remote place, or in my hotel room—just reading, praying, and listening. I don't want to be one of those who preached the gospel all over the world by relying solely on my gift and never getting to know the Giver of the gift.

God wants to be intimate with you. His perfect love casts out fear. Too often we find ourselves acting like the steward who was blind to his master's goodness. This is why I encourage you to pray for God to fill you with His holy fear. Then spend quality time with Him and discover who He truly is: *love*.

God sought us out, loved us, and died for us long before we knew Him. He initiated this magnificent relationship. He is *for* you. He longs to know you intimately. However, He loves us so deeply that He refuses to force us into a relationship.

So choose now. Choose life! Choose to know Him—intimately.

REFLECTION FOR RENEWAL

In this chapter, what statements or Scripture passages seemed most meaningful for you?

How would you restate them in your own words? (Personalize your answer as a prayer of response to God.)

What are your thoughts about what God wants you to do now in response to what you've seen and reflected upon in this chapter?

HINDRANCES TO MULTIPLICATION —PART II

Master, I know you have high standards
and hate careless ways, that you demand the best
and make no allowances for error. I was afraid.

MATTHEW 25:24–25 MSG

We're now ready to unpack the lazy steward's second statement: "I was afraid." Fear paralyzed him. I love The Message's paraphrase of the third servant's words to his master: "I know you have high standards . . . you demand the best and make no allowances for error."

This reminds me of a story. I played organized basketball under two coaches. On both teams I was a shooting guard, because hitting baskets from fifteen feet to the three-point range was one of the few things in the sport I could do well.

My first coach was a man who wanted the best out of us and would use encouragement and constructive correction to get us there. I knew he was for me, not against me. I made shots from all over the floor with confidence. His belief in me fueled that confidence.

My next coach was different. In his words, he said he had "high standards" and made "no allowances for error." When I took a shot and missed, the coach sharply corrected me during the next time-out, and often I was benched soon afterward. I couldn't shoot well under his coaching. In my personal practice time, when he wasn't present, I nailed shots from all over the floor. I was the same player with the same talent, but I couldn't execute when he was present.

If you look at the servant's response in Matthew 25:24–25, his perception of the master was exactly like my perception of my critical coach. But there's a big difference: In reality, the servant's master was nothing like my second coach.

Again, following up on what we learned in the last chapter, this is why it's paramount for us to take the time to know God. He's nothing like this lazy steward's perception. God is *for* us; He believes in us and has confidence in us. If we don't see Him that way, we can easily succumb to fear, and our gifts will be buried.

The Bible talks about two types of calling: general and specific.

Our continual growth in knowing God is a gracious privilege He grants as part of a general calling to all believers. This is His highest calling to salvation and righteousness—being reconciled to God through Christ. Your specific calling and assignment and gifting upon your life—something unique for each of us—will always flow out of this larger and higher calling, which is infinite in richness and blessings, and prompted by God's love.

- Delve into any of the following scriptures to see various highlights of these rich blessings. As you do, think about how they make possible your unique assignment and calling from God. You'll find abundant reasons for praise and thanksgiving as you consider these truths. John 10:3; Acts 2:39; Romans 1:6–7 and 8:28–30; 1 Corinthians 1:9 and 1:26–29; Galatians 5:13; Ephesians 1:18–19; Philippians 3:14; Colossians 3:15; 1 Thessalonians 4:7; 2 Thessalonians 2:13–14; 1 Timothy 6:12; 2 Timothy 1:9; Hebrews 3:1; 1 Peter 2:9, 3:9, and 5:10; 2 Peter 1:3; 1 John 3:1.

- We're exhorted in the New Testament to live worthy of this high calling (Ephesians 4:1; 1 Thessalonians 2:12; 2 Thessalonians 1:11; 2 Peter 1:10).

- Now think carefully: To live worthy of God's call to salvation and eternal life, how will it help to faithfully carry out your own unique calling and assignment in service to others? What deep connections do you see between these two callings?

We turn now to an entirely different root cause of unfruitfulness. As mentioned in the previous chapter, some people actually know God but still wrestle with and even succumb to fear. Scripture addresses certain reasons for this, and we'll expand on the subject for the rest of this chapter. But first, here are some insightful comments on fear and related topics:

> It's not death a man should fear, but he should fear never beginning to live. (Marcus Aurelius)

> Never be afraid of trying something new. Remember, amateurs built the ark; professionals built the *Titanic*. (source unknown)

> The greatest mistake we make is living in constant fear we will make one. (John C. Maxwell)

> One of the greatest discoveries a man makes, one of his great surprises, is to find he could do what he was afraid he couldn't do. (Henry Ford)

Let's open our discussion with a statement of unfaltering truth: *Loving God is the opposite of an unhealthy fear of God.* When we love God and people unconditionally, fear is exterminated. As the apostle John writes, "Perfect love expels all fear" (1 John 4:18).

In regard to that truth, I'll never forget an eye-opening encounter I had with the Holy Spirit in San Diego. I'd just finished a service, was alone in my room, and found myself battling fear in regard to our sons. I'd heard of ministers' children who'd been tragically killed—one by electrocution, many in car accidents, some by drug overdoses or drowning, and others for various other reasons. I'd just heard of another tragedy and was trying to eradicate the worry that was hounding me.

Loving God is the opposite of an unhealthy fear of God. When we love God and people unconditionally, fear is exterminated.

Suddenly, I heard these words in my heart: Son, fear is an indicator. It merely exposes an area in your life where you haven't submitted to Me. You're still owning that area for yourself.

The Spirit's words riveted me. I realized I'd taken on what I didn't have the power to maintain. Within moments of this enlightenment, I shouted out in my room, "Father, these sons are not mine. I'm merely a steward of those who are Yours. Therefore, whatever You desire for them is what I want done in their lives, no matter what. You may take them halfway around the world and to heaven when You're ready for them, but I boldly ask that they fulfill all You created them to do in this world."

I then shouted even louder, "But in Jesus's name, you, devil, are *not* touching them! I declare them to be God's, and I forbid you to kill, steal, or destroy what is God's!"

An overwhelming peace hit my heart, and I've never worried about our four sons since. If worry does try to creep back, I sternly say, "I gave the care of our sons to God in San Diego, and I'm not taking it back." Each time, the fear immediately subsides and the peace returns.

Fear is a horrible taskmaster. It's sneaky, it seeks to gain control, and once it has a grip on you, it's overwhelming. If not properly dealt with, fear will alter your destiny. But here's the good news: *Fear is beatable.* However, it must be addressed properly.

> In your own experience, how has fear tried to sabotage the pursuit of your calling and divine destiny? How would you characterize and describe that fear?

PAY ATTENTION TO YOUR GIFT

Paul wrote two letters to his "spiritual son," Timothy. In both, he addressed how Timothy's gift (*charisma*) was being neglected and was inoperative.

Let's establish this important point up front: Timothy was a godly man. Paul, throughout his epistles, bragged on Timothy's proven character and genuine faith. Timothy certainly doesn't fall into the category of one who's paralyzed by fear from not knowing God's character.

Paul's first letter to this young man states, "Do not *neglect* the gift that is in you" (1 Timothy 4:14 NKJV). The word *neglect* in the Greek is *ameléō*. One definition is "to overlook or regard lightly."[1] Another source defines this word as "to not think about, and thus not respond appropriately to," and "to pay no attention to."[2]

Why would Timothy—or any of us—overlook and not pay attention to a God-given gift, and in an extreme case, not even think about it? One reason could be that something isn't working or producing according to our expectations. Our thought becomes, *I tried it, and it didn't work.*

I was often tempted to think this way in my twenties and early thirties. One such occasion came after Lisa and her friend fell asleep during my message, as I mentioned earlier. I had this thought: *Why would anyone want to listen to me when those closest to me can't even stay awake when I speak?*

> Evaluate yourself carefully. In what ways have you been tempted—or are you being tempted now—to neglect your giftedness?
>
> How well do you understand the danger for anyone to neglect their gifting? How would you describe this danger?

Around the same time, another reality increased my struggle with thoughts of failure. A friend and I were each teaching a Sunday school class. In my friend's class, the attendance was over two hundred—standing room only. Meanwhile, attendance for my class averaged about twenty people; on one occasion, only one person attended.

I was tempted to question my gifts more times than I could count. I realize now that if I'd yielded to those thoughts of unmet expectations and apparent failure, I would have given up on ministry and pursued another path—ultimately becoming miserable because of leaving my life's calling.

Criticism from others is another reason we can overlook and not pay attention to our God-given gift. Without question, I was sorely tempted to stop writing after my first manuscript was ignored, criticized, and rejected by the first editor and then by publishers. Later, just after I self-published my book, a friend made disparaging remarks about my writing style. After I heard those comments, that evening I lay on our living room floor, not budging for twenty or thirty minutes, staring at the ceiling, feeling overwhelmingly dejected. I wondered if I'd wasted an entire year of my life—and a lot of money—on that book. In the face of so much criticism, I thought, *Wake up, John! Why can't you just admit it's no good and that you've failed?*

If I had succumbed to these thoughts and other remarks, I would never have written the second book, which also seemed like a failure. I remember sending it to my former Bible school teacher, and she sharply criticized it. I grew even more devastated.

After two and a half years, neither book had gained any traction.

During this time, if I at any point had listened to the criticism of others and my own thoughts of dejection, quitting would have been so easy. And I wouldn't have written the third book—which was, of course, *The Bait of Satan.*

The fear of failing is another reason we can overlook and not pay attention to our God-given gifts. Here's the ironic reality of this fear: We expect to fail before we ever begin, so we protect ourselves with inaction. We think, *Why try if it's not going to work?* How many dreams and visions have been thwarted due to the fear of failing? How tragic that God-given gifts are wasted in a manner no different from that of the lazy servant!

Concerning what the fear of failure produces, my friend Myles Munroe wrote the following in his book *Maximizing Your Potential*:

> The graveyard is the richest place on earth, because it is here that you will find all the hopes and dreams that were never fulfilled, the books that were never written, the songs that were never sung, the inventions that were never shared, the cures that were never discovered, all because someone was too afraid *to take that first step.*[3]

In agreement with Myles, my strong admonition to you is this: Don't allow your God-given gifts to be withheld from expression in this life.

What I'll say next may surprise you, since we all regard Timothy highly. But in Paul's letters we learn that Timothy is heading in the same direction of the lazy steward. His God-given gift is lying dormant, and he isn't paying attention to it. Fortunately, he has a good father in the faith who won't allow him to continue in this state.

In the second letter that Paul writes to his "son," he doesn't waste any time in speaking to this issue right out of the gate:

I remind you to *stir up* the gift of God which is in you. (2 Timothy 1:6 NKJV)

In Greek, that phrase *stir up* is just one word, *anazōpureō*, which is defined as "to revive a fire."[4] The *Greek-English Lexicon* communicates this word's meaning even more fully: "to cause something to begin again—to reactivate."[5] God's gift in Timothy was inactive and needed to be kick-started once again. So how had that dormancy happened?

Paul explains the cause in the next verse:

For God has not given us a spirit of *fear*, but of power and of love and of a sound mind. (1:7 NKJV)

The Greek word here for *fear* is *deilia*, which is most accurately translated as "timidity." Paul is saying, "Timothy, your God-given gift is dormant due to a spirit of timidity," or to put it even more plainly, "Timothy, your God-given gift is inoperative due to a spirit of *intimidation*."

This is a word we can easily relate to. To experience intimidation means being deterred from action due to fear.

But the more important aspect here is that a *spirit* is the ultimate origin of intimidation. It's a spiritual force, and if we don't address fear on a spiritual level, its roots are not fully cut off.

A spirit is the ultimate origin of intimidation. It's a spiritual force, and if we don't address fear on a spiritual level, its roots are not fully cut off.

MY BATTLE WITH INTIMIDATION

I know all about this because I battled this spirit for many years. I assumed it was a weakness in my personality. But during a set of church meetings in the early 1990s, I discovered I was completely wrong in my assessment.

These meetings were scheduled to last for only four days in a small-town church, but instead they turned into a three-week move of God. Every night, the building was packed to capacity, and many were saved, healed, and delivered. The gift of God in my life to preach was in high gear. It was remarkable. People traveled as far as ninety miles to attend the nightly services. I distinctly remember going into the empty sanctuary during the daytime, and it seemed as if God's presence had settled in the building.

But one evening in the final week, all this changed. Some of the worship leaders had criticized my ministry the night before. What they said was relayed to me by one of the church leaders just before that evening's service. The comments seemed opinionated, yet harmless. The pastor dismissed their remarks. We then prayed and went into the sanctuary, as we'd done for so many services. However, I couldn't shake the worship leaders' words from my thoughts. My focus shifted from preparing for the upcoming service to critiquing my message from the previous evening.

That evening, everything seemed dry. I tried to minister as I'd done for the previous two weeks, but I was confused, couldn't keep a thought, and hated being on the platform. I wanted to escape out the back door. I felt powerless, like a teenager in a high school speech class miserably failing to communicate before my fellow students. There was no anointing, no presence of God on me. It was horrible. I closed the service early and returned to where I was staying.

I found myself upset with God. Why didn't He help me? Why was this service so different? Why did I feel abandoned? I thought, *That message and ministry time was pathetic. Nobody will come back tomorrow night. In fact,* I *don't want to go back tomorrow.*

I went to bed hoping the next day would be different.

The following morning, I woke up heavy, depressed, and discouraged. I tried to pray but to no avail. The concern over what was wrong began to grow.

That afternoon, I spent three hours in prayer. I battled thoughts of failure the entire time. I roused myself to push past the heaviness and psyched myself up for the upcoming service.

That night in the sanctuary, the worship felt just as dry as the night before, and I felt I had nothing to give. Again, I wanted to run out the back door. Once introduced, I got up and floundered for a few minutes. I couldn't finish a thought. At one point I heard a voice in my head say, *Why did you say that? Where are you going with this message? You're pathetic!*

At that point, I'd had it. I suddenly blurted out in front of six hundred people, "I don't know what's wrong, but something hasn't been right here for the past two evenings. Can you please stand and pray with me?"

As we all prayed, God spoke to me—the first time I'd heard His voice in more than twenty-four hours. He reminded me of what Paul wrote in 2 Timothy 1:7, as I heard Him say, Son, you are intimidated by the worship team on the platform behind you. Break the spirit of intimidation and speak what I'm giving you.

I did what He said, and a bold message from 2 Timothy 1:7 immediately followed. It was the most powerful of all twenty-one services. Seventy-five percent of the people came forward, admitting they also battled intimidation. The aisles were packed with people seeking prayer for freedom.

The pastor got back with me a few weeks later to report how effective that service had been. The leaders who'd made the critical comments about me were living in blatant sin—adultery, fornication, and drunkenness. All was revealed over the next couple of weeks, and all but one of them left the church. The pastor reported that since then, his worship team had never been so unified and effective. It was a life-altering and ministry-altering experience.

For me, it ended years of fighting depression and attempting to conduct some services with my God-given but inoperative gift.

The most important discovery for me was learning that the spirit of intimidation must be directly spoken to—just like Jesus speaking the Word of God directly to Satan during the wilderness temptations. Jesus didn't ask His Father to alleviate the attacks; He Himself addressed the devil, firmly and pointedly.

In what ways have you encountered the spirit of intimidation? What is your best understanding of how this spirit must be overcome and defeated?

ELIJAH'S REPLACEMENT

I encourage you to read 1 Kings 17–19. In these chapters, you'll see a situation of intimidation (similar to mine) that Elijah experienced before Queen Jezebel of Israel.

This great prophet had boldly confronted the nation of Israel on Mount Carmel—while opposing 850 false prophets, plus King Ahab and his royal attendants. Before the entire nation, God had answered Elijah's prayer with fire. Elijah had even instructed people to execute all the false prophets. He was moving powerfully in his gifting. He then prayed, and a three-and-a-half-year drought ended. To top it off, he outran a royal chariot! All this happened in a single day. What a day of ministry!

But before the sun went down, Jezebel heard what had transpired. Then the real battle began:

> Jezebel sent this message to Elijah: "May the gods strike me and even kill me if by this time tomorrow I have not killed you just as you killed them." (1 Kings 19:2)

Before commenting on Jezebel's threat, let me say first that spirits are similar to surfers. Surfers need waves to ride on; spirits need words to ride on. We're told, "No weapon turned against you will succeed. *You will silence* every voice raised up to accuse you. These benefits are enjoyed by the servants of the LORD" (Isaiah 54:17). Notice that we're to silence every voice raised against us. This is *our* job, not God's. Jesus didn't ask God to silence Satan in the wilderness. Neither do we when attacked.

Obviously, Jezebel's words carried a massive spirit of intimidation. Once her statement reached Elijah, notice his response: "He arose and ran for his life" (1 Kings 19:3 NKJV).

This man who had confronted the nation, the false prophets, and the king now ran away. He traveled the entire length of the nation and went a day's journey into the wilderness, sat down under a tree, and *prayed to die.*

Wow, was this the same person? What was going on? Elijah was obviously confused, depressed, and hopeless, and he'd lost his vision—all of which are the symptoms of an intimidating spirit. The sad reality is that most people deal with the symptoms instead of addressing the spirit behind them.

In ignorance, I, too, fought these symptoms for years before that evening when God exposed this wicked spirit's ways. I floundered in my gifting and couldn't figure out why.

Elijah had given up, so God sent the dejected prophet on a journey. An angel appeared to him and gave him food for a long forty-day trip to Mount Sinai. Once he arrived, God asked, "What are you doing here, Elijah?" (1 Kings 19:9).

What? Hold on! God had instructed the angel to give him food for the trip, so Elijah made the journey. But upon arrival, God asked why he was there. Is God schizophrenic?

No. Here's what we must realize: If we're overcome by intimidation, often God will send us to a neutral place to minister to us, because He loves us. I was ignorant of what was transpiring in those meetings, but I don't believe Elijah was ignorant of his situation. He knew how to boldly confront opposition—but he was scared of this queen.

So what was behind God's inquiry? God was asking why Elijah hadn't confronted the queen, since she was the one spearheading all the evil. She needed to be stopped, but Elijah had run from her instead.

Rather than responding to the question behind the question, Elijah changed the subject, complaining that he was the only one left who was truly serving God. A classic sob story:

> I have zealously served the LORD God Almighty. But the people of Israel have broken their covenant with you, torn down your altars, and killed every one of your prophets. I am the only one left, and now they are trying to kill me, too. (19:10)

God completely ignored this response and once again asked the same question: "What are you doing here, Elijah?" (19:13). Once again, in verse 14, Elijah gave the exact same sob story. He'd given up and didn't want to deal with the evil behind the evil. God once again totally ignored his "woe is me" story and gave the most shocking command:

> Go back the same way you came, and travel to the wilderness of Damascus. When you arrive there, anoint Hazael to be king of Aram. Then anoint Jehu grandson of Nimshi to be king of Israel, and anoint Elisha son of Shaphat from the town of Abel-meholah *to replace you as my prophet.* (19:15–16)

How amazing, those last words! God was *replacing* Elijah because he'd succumbed to intimidation and was overcome by it.

If you continue reading in the book of 2 Kings, you'll find that Elijah spent most of his next four years training his replacement. There's also more shocking news: Elijah did *not* anoint Hazael or Jehu; his replacement, Elisha, had to do these things instead.

Elisha was not intimidated on any level. He was bold and didn't back down from any wickedness. God says about him, "Those who escape Jehu will be killed by Elisha!" (1 Kings 19:17). Between Jehu and Elisha, the evil dynasty of Ahab and Jezebel was overthrown. I believe it had originally been Elijah's assignment to do this, but due to intimidation, destiny was altered.

It's true that Elijah knew the character of God, unlike the lazy servant that Jesus spoke about. However, Elijah's battle clearly shows what fear and intimidation can do in regard to our gifting and calling.

What is most important in the face of fear and intimidation is that we firmly resolve to never back down. God will back us when we run up against this force. Intimidation is beatable, but we must hit it head-on with God's Word and promises.

I repeat: God is *for* you. He believes in you. He wants you to flourish in the gifts He's placed in your life.

So don't draw back. Don't let anyone or anything deter you from your mission and destiny.

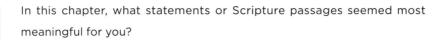

REFLECTION FOR RENEWAL

In this chapter, what statements or Scripture passages seemed most meaningful for you?

How would you restate them in your own words? (Personalize your answer as a prayer of response to God.)

What are your thoughts about what God wants you to do now in response to what you've seen and reflected upon in this chapter?

DISCOVER AND DEVELOP YOUR GIFTS

CHAPTER 14

Make a careful exploration of who you are

and the work you have been given,

and then sink yourself into that . . .

Each of you must take responsibility

for doing the creative best you can with your own life.

GALATIANS 6:4-5 MSG

We now turn to the subject of discovering and developing our God-given gifts. As I've stated, it's not my intent to discuss developing natural talents and abilities. With enough practice, almost everyone can become proficient at just about anything.

My family may argue this point when it comes to singing, and they might be right. So let me cite a realistic example: If I practiced playing a musical instrument for ten thousand hours, I might move from being a terrible musician to an average one. My time and effort might even make listening to my playing the piano or guitar somewhat enjoyable. But even after all that focused practice, it still would not be a *charisma* that propels my calling to build the kingdom of God.

When it comes to making an eternal impact, we need our Creator's assistance to uncover our calling and charisma.

GOD'S INVOLVEMENT

Let's focus now on Paul's words in Galatians 6:4 to "make a careful exploration of who you are and the work you have been given" (MSG).

There are no formulas for discovering your calling and the accompanying gifts. Various resources can help you discover what you're good at, but when it comes to making an eternal impact, we need our Creator's assistance to uncover our calling and *charisma*.

> Are you relieved and pleased to hear that "there are no formulas for discovering your calling and the accompanying gifts"? Or do would you rather follow a formula?
>
> What further or continuing need do you have for God's help, guidance, and insight regarding your calling and gifts?
>
> What clear guidance, insight, and help has God already provided you in this regard?

At times, God's direct involvement is easy to perceive in discovering our gifts, such as when He told me to write. I never would have attempted to write had I not received that word in prayer on that summer morning in 1991. No book or course could have convinced me to write, and I definitely wouldn't have stumbled into it.

As another example, King David never would have known that he was a warrior had he not protected his sheep from the bear and the lion. After these experiences, he was on the scene when the need arose for someone to deliver Israel from the Philistines. For David, the threatening predators he fought earlier were just stepping stones to fighting Goliath while the rest of Israel hid. God allowed David to discover his gifting because of the demanding needs around him.

If you consider Gideon, he was more like me. God needed to convince him through several fleeces that he was called to be a warrior.

Gideon was another servant of God who received his unique assignment in a unique way. Look at how his calling is described in Judges 6. What does his story reveal about God's character, God's ways, and God's purposes for His people?

How might those things relate to your own calling?

Let's begin at square one. It's critical to seek out and trust God's involvement in discovering your *charisma*. Scripture states in Hebrews 11:6 that God rewards those who diligently seek Him in faith; it *doesn't* say that God rewards those who *casually* seek Him in wonder and doubt.

Along the same lines, Jesus tells us this:

Keep on asking, and you will receive what you ask for. Keep on seeking, and you will find. Keep on knocking, and the door will be opened to you. For everyone who asks, receives. Everyone who seeks, finds. And to everyone who knocks, the door will be opened. (Matthew 7:7–8)

We must have a passionate desire to know our *charisma*. Hopefully, this book is fueling a burning desire in you to discover and engage your giftings. This longing will prevent you from asking, seeking, or knocking in a merely nonchalant way; instead, you'll be persistent, as Jesus prescribes above. It's not that God is holding out on you. He wants a *passion* developed in you for what you're asking for.

In high school, I wanted a high-powered telescope because I loved astronomy and wanted to study the night sky. A good scope was completely out of my price range, but I kept reading astronomy books and magazines. I would check out four or five of these at a time from the library, go through them during my spare time—sometimes repeatedly—then return them and get more. This reading developed an almost desperate desire for the telescope.

God wants a passion developed in you for what you're asking for.

Eventually my passion propelled me to devise an unusual idea to raise money for my dream scope. I was a tennis instructor for a swim and racquet club and gave lessons only during summer vacation. I did something that was never done at our club. With the permission of the club's board, I came up with a plan to offer private lessons after school in the fall season. If this worked, I could bring in enough money to buy the telescope. And it did work!

Believe me, I never took that scope for granted. And if someone had just given it to me before my desire became so intense, I might have neglected it after the excitement wore off.

God is not hard of hearing. He's not holding out. He desires that you never take for granted the gifts He gives you to build up His people. Your passion needs to be stronger than the adversity you face while on the way to your dreams. So let the desire grow, and the spontaneity will keep you fervently praying and seeking to know your *charisma*.

Next, we must acknowledge that God does not answer us in a patterned way; for each child of His, the answer is different. I'm sometimes puzzled by how we continually talk about having a "personal relationship" with Jesus, but when it comes to hearing God—in this case, for understanding our *charisma* or gifts—we want a formula. *God wants to keep it personal.* He wants to keep it special between you and Him. He doesn't answer each of His precious children's prayers the exact same way. This is why Jesus instructs us to keep on asking, seeking, and knocking. There's a "searching out" of His will that's actually quite good for us.

God wants to keep it personal. He wants to keep it special between you and Him.

In our pursuit we should ask questions of ourselves and others. This is all part of the searching process. We aren't looking for the wisdom of man, but to hear God's voice within the voices of those we speak with.

Who are the people you trust most to ask questions about your calling and gifting? How will you phrase these questions?

It's important that we know who to talk to. We must find those who are encouraging yet unafraid of speaking the truth. I would like to say that these people are in abundance, but they're rare. I know people I can go to who'll always tell me what I want to hear. Then there are those who are pessimistic, critical, and negative of seemingly everything; they lack vision. Avoid both kinds.

Instead, find the person who has faith and is mature and wise. Find a father or mother in the faith, or a wise one who has traveled the journey longer than you and has made mistakes and learned from them.

It's important that those you confide in have avoided becoming jaded or cynical, because these contemptuously distrustful attitudes are fostered in those who harbor offense. Look for a person who's quick to forgive—someone who doesn't get stuck in rote religion but rather progresses with the times and the fresh movements of God's Spirit.

Most importantly, confide in someone who sees things from an eternal perspective. When you find this person, do all you can to maintain and treasure the relationship.

Many are wise to the world but lack the eternal view. You can trust their advice only to a certain level. Be careful when listening to them, and always filter their advice through the Word of God and prayer.

Confide in someone who sees things from an eternal perspective. Do all you can to maintain and treasure the relationship.

Your parents, your spouse, and your pastors should all have your best interests at heart, and they will usually give wise counsel, although there are exceptions.

As a young man, I shared my dreams with my dad about being in the ministry. His generation was a stickler for doing it the "safe way" (which is a weakness when it comes to a life of faith). My dad said, "Son, there's no security in that path." He suggested engineering, since I was good in math and science, and he himself had been an engineer for forty years. It was a safe career choice. I didn't realize I was signing up for six years of misery, starting in college and continuing at my first job. Even though I was gifted in these subjects, I was miserable because it wasn't God's call on my life.

My first job as an engineer was working for IBM. One day my boss pulled me into his office and said, "Bevere, what are you doing in engineering? You're a people person; you should be in some field that involves interacting with people." Well-known ministers also pulled me aside in numerous meetings and said, "Son, I see the call of God on you to preach the gospel."

In my alone time in prayer, God continually drew my heart to ministry, even though I wanted nothing to do with it. All the ministers I'd ever met seemed strange. But my heart was still sensitive to our Creator.

Before I was saved, I went to a Catholic seminary for a week and began to feel as though I was called to ministry. But it scared me that, as a Catholic priest, I would never be married.

Over and over I continued receiving confirmation, which ultimately helped me put my dad's advice aside. I respected him so much, which pleased God, but I knew something was terribly off as I studied and eventually worked as an engineer. Since I'd been repeatedly asking and searching for God's direction, He wouldn't permit me to be misdirected (even by my own well-meaning dad), and He made His will abundantly clear.

When it was settled for me, I now had a burning passion that resulted from over a year and a half of searching. I was also three-quarters of the way through getting my engineering degree. I decided to finish earning my degree and then pursue the ministry after I graduated. It was a good decision, because I learned strategies that Bible school wouldn't have taught me. God will use all experiences to train us.

God will use all experiences to train us.

Another important element to discovering your gift is to be planted in a healthy local church. Scripture tells us, "Those who are planted in the house of the LORD shall flourish" (Psalm 92:13 NKJV). If you plant a cotton seed, pumpkins won't grow out of the soil. The soil is a healthy local church, and when you're committed, your God-given gifts will manifest there.

It doesn't matter whether you're called to the marketplace, education, government, athletics, or any other field. Wherever it is, you will flourish—by God's design.

QUESTIONS TO ASK YOURSELF AND WISE FRIENDS

Let's turn our focus to asking questions, both of yourself and of wise friends. The right questions asked of the right people may help awaken recognition of what you're gifted to do. Here are some examples.

What Are You Naturally Good At?

This is a good starting place. Perhaps your gift is to understand numbers, eloquently construct sentences, build things, create video stories, design clothes, or organize events. You may have natural athletic abilities, a nose for scents, or an eye for detail. Do your best to identify your strengths.

If you're able to hold a tune and have a desire to lead people into the presence of God, this could indicate that you are called to help in leading worship music or some other type of music ministry. The same would be true if you were interested in the human body and find yourself fascinated by medicine; you definitely should ask God if you're called to some aspect of healthcare. The list is endless.

But these clues should not be the final word. For example, I was a good tennis player in my younger days; I won the West Virginia state high school tennis tournament and was a starter on a team at an NCAA Division I school. I played the United States Tennis Association circuit and Junior Davis Cup, and I taught tennis professionally for three years. But in prayer, I knew professional tennis wasn't my calling.

On the other hand, I have a friend, Aaron Baddeley, who's an outstanding golfer on the PGA Tour. But in 2004—his second year on tour—he was struggling. (He barely requalified to return in 2005 when he finished 124th on the list.) Near the end of his tough year, while playing in a tournament, he was staying at our house. Sadly, he missed the cut. We got on a plane together and went to Las Vegas, where I was scheduled to minister at a conference. In that service, God spoke to his heart four times: *I did not call you to ministry; I called you to golf.*

Aaron had been resisting giving his complete efforts in golf, because he wanted to do what I did. He wanted to spend half his time traveling and speaking at conferences and churches, and the other half playing golf. He settled it in his heart that evening at the service in Las Vegas that he would give himself fully to his calling and gift.

Within a couple of years, he was number sixteen in the world golf rankings, and he eventually won four PGA Tour events and the Australian Masters. As he's been on tour year after year, his influence has grown, and he has had multiple opportunities to minister and share messages with many who wouldn't have walked through the doors of a church.

I have a pastor friend, Al, who years ago had a man in his church who loved to teach the Bible and was good at it. He wanted to be a teaching pastor, but he was also uniquely gifted to fix cars. He was promised a pastoral teaching position in a large church in a different part of the city. He took Pastor Al to lunch to inform him of this. Al is wise and shared with the man, "In praying for you, I don't feel you're called to teach the Bible on a full-time basis. You're exceptionally gifted to work on cars." The man didn't listen to his pastor's counsel and left for the other church.

A year later, the man was miserable. The teaching position still hadn't been officially offered to him, his marriage was in decline, and he was struggling financially.

In church one Sunday, the Lord spoke to him: *I never called you to be a pastor; I called you to be a mechanic who taught the Bible in your local church.*

The man returned to Pastor Al, repented of not listening to his counsel, and came back to his home church. He refocused on his business of fixing cars.

One evening God gave him a dream of hooking a computer up to a car to diagnose engine problems. He had a friend who understood computers, and the two of them built a computerized diagnostic testing device. This testing device, as it turned out, could identify problems with cars in a quarter of the time as normal methods.

This man went on to operate repair garages all over North Carolina with his unique invention. Later, the man walked up to Pastor Al, smiled, and said, "I'm called to fix cars!"

> What are you naturally good at?

What Energizes You?

One day my assistant asked me to keep a record of "energy levels" for my normal weekly work routine. She set up this rating scale: Those tasks that drained my energy would receive a–2; those that drained minute amounts of energy received a–1; those things that added minimal energy received a +1; and finally, those things that strongly energized me received a +2.

I gave several tasks—such as department meetings, travel, paperwork, packing for trips, and so forth—a rating of–2 or–1. A few I rated as +1. But the only two things that honestly merited a +2 score were speaking and writing. I was surprised by the results.

In contemplating these findings, I realized that often when I'm writing, I completely lose track of time. At times I'll start writing early in the morning without looking up before the afternoon. I'm usually mentally tired after so much writing, but I'm also energized.

The same thing happens when preaching. Back in the days when we didn't have as many time constraints, I often found myself preaching a message for more than two hours. It seemed to me like thirty minutes. (I don't know what my audiences thought.)

I've watched our creative son, Alec, work on innovative projects for hours with a total loss of awareness of time. He has excelled in our ministry's creative department. I've watched Lisa interact with ladies for hours after her women's meetings and lose all concept of time. She's energized by nurturing conversations.

What energizes you and periodically causes you to lose track of time?

Your true gifting will actually energize you, even though you may become mentally or physically tired during long stints. So that's a fairly easy way to help determine your calling. For those who've discovered their true gifting, hours of practicing, competing, or working can seem like minutes.

So ask yourself: What energizes me and periodically causes me to lose track of time? Your answer is a good indication of where your gifting lies.

Albert Einstein worked for hours and hours at a time. When he was physically exhausted, he would grab a metal tray and sit in a chair holding the tray in his hands by his knees. Just before he hit deep sleep, the tray would slip out of his hands and hit the floor. The loud crashing sound would awaken him, and he would get back to work.

> What energizes you?

What Are You Drawn To?

What grabs your interest? What causes you to come alive? When you sing, is your heart full? Do you find yourself singing when no one else is? I know when I sing, it's a complete labor for me and tires me quickly. Singing is not my gifting. I couldn't sit in a room and harmonize and write music with others. I have no interest in doing that, but I know some people who love it.

What magazines interest you? What YouTube videos do you get excited about? What stops you when you're going through Pinterest? What subjects were your favorites in school? What books do you gravitate toward when walking through a bookstore?

Here's an important question: What would you be drawn to do even if you were never paid for it? Most professional athletes would play their sports even if they weren't paid for them. My dad would sit me down on Saturday mornings and tell me how a steam engine or some other machine worked. I recall one Saturday morning when he spent over an hour drawing and explaining a boiler. These times would bore me nearly to tears, and I should have figured out right then that my calling was not to be an engineer.

What would you be drawn to do even if you were never paid for it?

I loved my dad so much that I never had the heart to tell him I hated those sessions. I made the huge mistake of pursuing engineering for financial security; don't make the same error I did.

How many people are miserable in their job because they do it for one reason only—to get a paycheck?

As I mentioned earlier, years ago when my pastor's wife told me they couldn't afford me, my response was, "Oh, yes, you can!" I was willing to work for lower pay because I was drawn to that type of ministry. Once on the job, the seventy hours a week of serving my pastor and his guests seemed like nothing. I often commented to Lisa that I should be paying my pastors for allowing me to serve them instead of them paying us.

I hesitate to write the following, because there's a risk that you may think I'm bragging—but I hope you'll choose to believe that my motive is to be helpful. When we first started the ministry, Lisa and I decided that my royalties for writing would go to Messenger International. I've now written more than twenty books, and each one averages between 400 and 450 hours of time to write and edit. This means I've invested almost nine thousand hours in writing. That's over three years of writing eight hours a day, including weekends. In essence, I've not been paid for those three years. I've done it because it's my gifting that enhances my calling.

I can honestly say that if I had to choose between doing this and being paid two hundred thousand dollars per year as an engineer, I would do this again in a heartbeat.

This is why the apostle Paul writes:

I am entrusted with the stewardship of the gospel whether or not I'm paid. So then, where is my reward? It is found in continually depositing the good news into people's hearts, without obligation, free of charge, and not insisting on my rights to be financially supported. (1 Corinthians 9:17–18 TPT)

What are you drawn to? What would you enjoy doing even if you were not paid to do it?

Who Are You Drawn To?

Recognizing who you're drawn to also reveals a lot about your calling and gifts. Certain people awaken and unlock the gifts within you. Find your tribe—those who share similar giftings and callings as you. They'll become pivotal for understanding who you are and how God has gifted you. Your tribe should be people who accept and understand you.

Certain people awaken and unlock the gifts within you.

I love sitting with other ministers and discussing adventures and challenges of ministry, and of course the Word of God. I also love sitting with entrepreneurs and businesspeople. These are all areas of strength in my life.

Running a ministry organization has many similarities with running a marketplace business. Lisa and I have had to be entrepreneurs. When we were young, there were no known ministries quite like what we were called to do—at least, none we could pattern ourselves after. We had to blaze a trail. For this reason, entrepreneurs in the business world have always awakened things in me that help me do what we're called to do in a more proficient way.

If you love interior design, you'll find yourself comfortable around other designers. If you're a doctor, you'll be stimulated by conversing with other physicians. If you're a musician, other musicians will help stir up your gift. I could go on and on. Finding your tribe can help you identify, and even draw out, your gifting.

Who are you drawn to?

Again, it's important to remember that none of the answers to these questions can ever stand alone and apart from your personal time of seeking God for what He's specifically called you to do. If I'd listened to the majority of the ministers who spoke to me in my formative years, I would have picked a city and started a church as a pastor. Very few could see the unique and different callings and gifts that were on Lisa and me.

On the other hand, a handful of wise ones helped steer us in the direction we felt in our heart.

DEVELOP YOUR GIFT

Now let's turn our attention to the second half of Paul's statement in Galatians 6:5: "Each of you must take responsibility for doing the creative best you can with your own life" (MSG). God has given each of us the potential to build our life, which helps build His kingdom. However, at one time or another, we all must face the fact that merely possessing potential is not enough; that potential must be realized.

At one time or another, we all must face the fact that merely possessing potential is not enough; that potential must be realized.

How sad would it be for you or me to come to the end of our life knowing we still had more to contribute? At the judgment seat, the pain of regret could be unbearable as we learn what could have been—or worse, we learn about the lives that were never impacted because of our negligence to develop what God has entrusted to us.

Settle it now—that you'll die empty, *holding nothing back*. You'll have poured out everything in you so you're empty.

The world needs what you have—your God-given gifts.

> Think again about the fundamental things at stake here. Why, in reality, is it important for you to develop your gifts, and to hold nothing back in pursuing them?
>
> What can you expect to happen when your gifts are intentionally and completely developed?
>
> What can you trust God for in this regard?

An interesting insight of the reality of our God-given gifts is found in this verse: "A man's gift makes room for him, and brings him before great men" (Proverbs 18:16 NKJV).

Your gift "makes room" for you and brings you before "important people." To "make room" means to create space. The space we're talking about here is twofold. First, your gift makes room for you to fulfill your potential—bridging the space between where you *are* and where you *could be*. Second, your gift makes room for you to be promoted to new levels of your destiny.

Keep in mind that with every promotion, a higher standard of skill is required. Again, Solomon writes: "If you are uniquely gifted in your work, you will rise and be promoted. You won't be held back" (Proverbs 22:29 TPT).

Consider David. In 1 Samuel 16 we find the account of King Saul being tormented by an evil spirit, because the Spirit of the Lord had departed from him. Desperate for relief, Saul ordered his servants to seek out a skilled musician to be brought to him.

One of the young servants responded, "I have seen a son of Jesse the Bethlehemite who plays *skillfully*" (1 Samuel 16:18 AMPC). David wasn't just a gifted musician; he was a *skilled* one. What made him skilled? His gift was developed, and therefore room was made for him to advance in his calling.

Could it be that many are not progressing in their calling because their gifts are underdeveloped? Could the degree to which our gifts are developed determine the extent to which we can be promoted?

Let's return to Paul's words to Timothy that we quoted in the previous chapter. But this time we'll continue on to his suggested remedy for his spiritual son:

> Do not neglect the gift which is in you, [that special inward endowment] which was directly imparted to you . . . *Practice* and *cultivate* and *meditate* upon these duties; *throw yourself wholly into them* [as your ministry], so that your progress may be evident to everybody. (1 Timothy 4:14–15 AMPC)

There's so much to learn from these wise words. When we observe men and women who excel in their field, sometimes we may find it easy to in essence diminish their success by stating, "They were born with a special gift." The fact is, they (like you) were indeed born with a gift—and they *chose to develop it.* Just because we didn't witness them perfecting their gift doesn't mean they haven't worked hard to do so.

We neglect our gift by giving little attention to it.

As we noted earlier in this passage, Paul began by warning Timothy to not neglect his God-given gift. We neglect our gift by giving little attention to it. Timothy was told that his progress would become evident by fully investing in his gift's development, which Paul wrote would be accomplished through *practice*, *cultivation*, and *meditation*.

Let's briefly examine each of these.

Practice

To *practice* means "to perform or work at repeatedly so as to become proficient," according to *Merriam-Webster*. Private practice determines our public performance, because we'll always perform according to the level at which we've practiced. It's easy to marvel at a spectacular public performance but lose sight of the weeks, months, and years of training and hard work that went into this level of consistent practice.

According to experts in the science of human behavior and performance, it takes approximately ten thousand hours of practice to become proficient in, or to master, a particular skill. However, Professor K. Anders Ericsson of Florida State University and science writer Robert Pool challenge traditional beliefs that "practice makes perfect." They take it a step further by revealing that it's not enough to practice for ten thousand hours unless those hours of practice are done with focused intention to improve, rather than just going through the motions. They've coined this type of practice as "purposeful practice":

> So here we have purposeful practice in a nutshell: Get outside your comfort zone but do it in a focused way, with clear goals, a plan for reaching those goals, and a way to monitor your progress.[1]

Unless we push ourselves beyond our level of comfort and skill, we'll never grow. If we aren't "purposeful," the danger is that once we reach a level of "good enough," we can easily become complacent. Then it's only a matter of time before we become sloppy in our practice, which will ultimately have a negative effect on our performance and hinder further multiplication.

Developing your area of strength is liberating, not limiting. It increases your potential to multiply. This doesn't mean we don't work on our areas of weakness or acquire new skills; it means we're focused and invested in the areas that will yield the greatest return on our potential.

Developing your area of strength is liberating, not limiting. It increases your potential to multiply. It means you're focused and invested in the areas that will yield the greatest return on your potential.

I recommend learning new skills, but never at the neglect of your areas of calling.

Here's the bottom line: Growth is not automatic; it requires intentionality. Unless we're consistently practicing so we can become "skilled" in our gifts, we'll never realize our full potential. That's why we must remain committed to personal growth. Most people want to do great things with their lives, but not everyone is willing to put in the necessary work to become great. Practice is paying the price that produces great rewards.

> For you, what does practice look like regarding your area of calling and giftedness?

Cultivate

Practice is practical, while cultivating is more educational. To *cultivate* means "to develop or improve by education or training; to promote the growth and development of."[2]

When you consider the word *cultivate*, think "coaching." Coaching is critical to your personal growth and development in many areas. A coach provides constructive criticism and guidance that you cannot acquire on your own. Anyone who has excelled in their gifting has had coaching and guidance from others along their journey. The wonderful element of coaches is that they see your potential and are committed to drawing it out of you—even if that includes being hard on you.

Coaching can come through a variety of relationships: mentor-mentee, parent-child, teacher-student, plus apprenticeships and internships, and indirectly from books, courses, study groups, seminars, and other resources available to us in abundance.

Another way to receive education in your area of gifting is to gather with those who share similar giftings. Again, this is often referred to as "finding your tribe." When you're in the presence of those who share similar talents and passions, you're fostering the opportunity to collaborate and innovate together, whether the setting is formally structured or more casual.

During the 1930s and 1940s, a group of creative writers—known as the Inklings—met in a private room in a pub near the grounds of the University of Oxford. Among these literary enthusiasts were C.S. Lewis and J.R.R. Tolkien. The purpose of these gatherings was to read and critique the members' unfinished works—from which were inspired the creation of Tolkien's *The Lord of the Rings* and Lewis's *The Chronicles of Narnia*. Talk about a great tribe!

> For you, what does cultivation look like in regard to your area of calling and giftedness?

Meditate

To *meditate* means to reflect or contemplate. Certain growth can occur only when we take the time to stop and reflect on the lessons we're learning. When we honestly monitor our growth and allow ourselves time to evaluate our progress and performance, we position ourselves to become aware of specific areas that need attention or improvement.

Reflection time is never wasted time.

Reflection time is never wasted time.

My friend John Maxwell often reminds his audiences and readers that experience is not the best teacher; *evaluated experience* is. As you reflect on your progress, take to heart the feedback you receive from coaches and peers. Think also about innovative ways to improve and utilize your gifts. Ask yourself (and God) the right questions: *What do I need to change? What have been my biggest areas of growth? What areas deserve more of my attention? What's required for me to break through to a new level?*

> For you, what does meditation or reflection look like in regard to your area of calling and giftedness?
>
> Take a moment to consider the biblical instruction for self-evaluation

and self-testing in 1 Corinthians 11:28, 2 Corinthians 13:5, and Galatians 6:4. What will be your personal commitment to continue this kind of checking up on yourself throughout the rest of your life?

HOLD NOTHING BACK

Finally, let's revisit Paul's words to Timothy:

> Practice and cultivate and meditate upon these duties; *throw yourself wholly into them* [as your ministry], so that your progress may be evident to everybody. (1 Timothy 4:15 AMPC)

Everything we've discussed in this book is contingent upon giving ourselves gladly and completely to what God has called and gifted us to do. Your calling demands your full commitment. As we give ourselves wholeheartedly to what God has entrusted to us, our progress will become evident to all, and we'll multiply our potential.

Each of us is responsible for stewarding our gifts and doing the creative best we can with our own lives. By now we've seen that the degree to which our gifts are developed will determine the degree to which we can advance in our sphere of calling and multiply our effectiveness.

We have one shot give this life everything we have. Let's hold nothing back, and let's be emptied, pouring ourselves out completely as a gift back to God.

This is living. This is how we'll truly experience life to its fullest.

And this is how we'll honor Him who is worthy of all praise and glory.

REFLECTION FOR RENEWAL

In this chapter, what statements or Scripture passages seemed most meaningful for you?

How would you restate them in your own words? (Personalize your answer as a prayer of response to God.)

What are your thoughts about what God wants you to do now in response to what you've seen and reflected upon in this chapter?

ANOINTED

Now He who establishes us with you in Christ
and has anointed us is God.

2 CORINTHIANS 1:21 NKJV

During a recent Thanksgiving holiday, our family was sitting around the dining room table. Lisa had made a remarkable feast. We were all basking in its afterglow and enjoying each other's company. As the dad, I felt that I needed to say something to my family, as well as to a few of our team members who joined us. After I uttered an inward prayer, a word came to my heart:

"Guys, I'm now sixty years old, and in more ways than one I feel my father-role responsibility of sharing a bit of wisdom. If you were to ask me to state the most important thing Lisa and I have done in walking with God during the past forty years, it would be this: *Staying consistent.*

"We've had many opportunities over the years to throw in the towel, so to speak. Also, many opportunities to compromise truth for personal gain or self-promotion, or to alleviate a trial we were experiencing. But we've chosen to make truth our anchor, holding on to it no matter how painful the circumstances.

"Here's a very wise statement Job made in his turmoil: 'I can take comfort in this: Despite the pain, I have not denied the words of the Holy One' (Job 6:10). When I've made mistakes—and I've made a lot of them—I've been quick to repent and ask forgiveness, both from God and man. I look now at the blessings that abound from consistent obedience to truth, and they're mind-blowing. God is so very gracious."

THE ANOINTING

A great blessing that has resulted from consistently submitting to truth is "the anointing." To understand this, let's turn to the great ordination—the day when God the Father inaugurated Jesus as King of heaven and earth. The author of Hebrews quotes these Old Testament lines addressed to God's Son:

> For you have cherished righteousness and detested lawlessness. *For this reason,* God, your God, has *anointed* you and poured out the oil of bliss on you more than on any of your friends. (Hebrews 1:9 TPT)

Pay attention to those words *for this reason;* they're crucial to understanding a key truth. Jesus's immovability on two particular issues resulted in a great benefit, and His example should be our standard. First, Jesus loved *righteousness.* This is the Greek word *dikaiosúnē*, defined as "conformity to the claims of higher authority."[1] And at the same time, He hated *lawlessness.* Many Christians may *dislike* lawlessness, but this is not the heart of Jesus; He *hates* it. This Greek word for lawlessness is *anomía*, which in essence means "disobedience to the authority of God." Jesus hated anything to do with departing from God's authority. Period. Jesus's steadfast obedience, no matter the difficulty, was the reason the anointing on His life was more powerful than that of any of His companions.

The anointing is what fuels our God-given abilities to eternally multiply. Think of it as an enhancer to what you're gifted to do.

Why do I close this book by discussing the anointing? The answer is simple, yet important: *The anointing is what fuels our God-given abilities to eternally multiply.* Think of it as an enhancer to what you're gifted to do. Let me give two quick examples.

I've heard people with tremendous voices that I appreciated, but then I've heard those with less magnificent voices who moved my heart more deeply, which resulted in change. The difference was the anointing. I've also heard people utter messages with profound content, while other less notable messages have affected me deeply at the heart level, which brought behavioral change. The difference was the anointing.

The same effect is true for all God's servants, no matter the field of calling, whether government, business, the arts, education, and so forth. King David made this statement:

> But my horn (emblem of excessive strength and stately grace) You have exalted like that of a wild ox; I am anointed with fresh oil. (Psalm 92:10 AMPC)

His words are so revealing. In examining a few of the leading commentaries on this verse, I found widespread agreement that the emphasis is not on the "wild ox" but rather on the idea of being made strong by God. The anointing brings joy. God calls it the oil of bliss or of joy—and according to Scripture, "The joy of the LORD is your strength" (Nehemiah 8:10). In essence, the psalmist declares that the anointing makes us strong. It enhances and strengthens the gifts on our life to bear eternal fruit.

I believe this is one of the unspoken, game-changing aspects of the parables of the talents and minas: The labor of the two multiplying servants was enhanced by the anointing. I say "unspoken" because this truth is gleaned from the various scriptures we've looked at. For the servants to multiply, it was important to consistently obey the instructions of their master, and to hate disobeying those instructions—thus attracting the anointing to enhance their gifts.

David makes mention of the oil being *fresh*. Anointing is not a one-time occurrence, but rather the blessing that begins and continues in one who consistently walks in submission to God. It's not something gained at one point in time and then taken for granted because "now I've got it." Samson had the anointing, but he didn't keep it fresh. He compromised and disobeyed; he did not hate lawlessness. He got away with lawlessness a few times, but eventually his sin caught up to him. And so we read:

Anointing is not a one-time occurrence, but rather the blessing that begins and continues in one who consistently walks in submission to God.

> *His strength left him.* And she [Delilah] said, "The Philistines are upon you, Samson!" So he awoke from his sleep, and said, "I will go out as before, at other times, and shake myself free!" But *he did not know that the LORD had departed from him.* (Judges 16:19–20 NKJV)

Samson was unaware that the anointing had lifted.

This sobering truth is why David, after his disobedience regarding Bathsheba, passionately prays these words:

> Create in me a clean heart, O God. Renew a loyal spirit within me. Do not banish me from your presence, and don't take your Holy Spirit from me. Restore to me the *joy* of your salvation, and make me *willing to obey you*. (Psalm 51:10–12)

David's heart cry, his great plea, was that the anointing would not be removed from his life—and he knew this would depend on a loyal and consistent life of obedience to God.

> What is your understanding of this "anointing"? How is it cultivated, according to your present comprehension of this?
>
> How can the anointing remain fresh in your life?
>
> What can you expect to happen if you take the anointing for granted?

Let's continue to examine the anointing and to whom it's given. Look again at Paul's statement highlighted at the opening of this chapter:

> Now He who establishes us with you in Christ and has anointed us is God. (2 Corinthians 1:21 NKJV)

The Greek word for anointed here is *chríō*, defined as "to assign a person to a task, with the implication of supernatural sanctions, blessing, and endowment—to anoint, to assign, to appoint."[2] There are key words in this definition that cannot be overlooked.

The word *sanction* is defined as "authoritative permission or approval, as for an action." Simply put, the anointing is the divine approval to *act*. Jesus says,

> The Spirit of the LORD is upon me, for he has *anointed* me to bring Good News to the poor. He has sent me to proclaim that captives will be released, that the blind will see, that the oppressed will be set free, and that the time of the LORD's favor has come." (Luke 4:18–19)

The anointing was God's approval upon Jesus *to do something*.

In the same manner the apostle Peter states, "God *anointed* Jesus of Nazareth with the Holy Spirit and with power, who went about *doing good*" (Acts 10:38 NKJV). Again, the anointing is for action.

Other key components of the meaning of *chriō* are the words *assign* and *appoint*. In serving God, there's always a testing period. We're tested in obedience before we're appointed or anointed.

In the story of Mike that I mentioned earlier, his critical test occurred when God asked him to give his last two hundred dollars. Regarding Lisa and me, our test was whether we would stay committed to the divine directive to write—even when no publishers were interested in our first two books, and there was very low interest from the general public.

Jesus says more than once, "Many are called, but few chosen" (Matthew 20:16 NKJV). I believe the word *many* here refers to all who belong to Him. Each of us has a divine calling. However, the word *chosen* means "appointed" and, according to Jesus, that number, sadly, is "few." Why? An approval process must be passed.

Read carefully these words of Paul: "Greet Apelles, that one *tried* and *approved* in Christ" (Romans 16:10 AMPC). Apelles was put on trial—as is true for all who desire to journey toward our destiny. He obviously passed the test, and he therefore was *chosen* or *approved*. From the principles of the Scripture, we know—without being told—that Apelles was anointed because his gifting had the enhanced touch of God upon it.

There are so many who prematurely self-appoint in the actual area they're called to. But what they should strive for is not their own approval, but divine approval:

For it is not the man who praises and commends himself who is approved and accepted, but it is the person whom the Lord accredits and commends. (2 Corinthians 10:18 AMPC)

Let's circle back to my spoken words after that Thanksgiving dinner. I wanted my family and team members who were present to know that *consistent obedience*—loving righteousness and hating lawlessness—is crucial to the fulfillment of our destiny, because such consistency positions us for His anointing.

In looking back over our lives, Lisa and I have obeyed God in some difficult times; often this obedience appeared counterproductive, even detrimental, to our growth and well-being, as well as other personal benefits we were seemingly walking away from. But what looked to be disadvantageous to us in the short run actually ended up being the very key that opened a significant door to our destiny.

In Luke 10:2, as Jesus sends out His disciples for ministry, He tells them, "The harvest is great, but the workers are few." Why are the workers few? Because few will pay the price to position themselves to fulfill their calling.

Take a moment to look in your Bible at what was happening in the verses just prior to this—in Luke 9:57–62—where Jesus has three encounters with individuals who were thinking about following Him. Notice carefully their interactions with Him. How do you see this passage illustrating various roadblocks that can keep us from fulfilling our calling?

Those roadblocks can include, for example, our giving less importance to following Jesus than we do to cherished relationships, or to a pursuit of money and possessions, or to our craving for security. In what ways could these things be potential roadblocks to your own fulfillment of God's calling on your life?

YOUR COMMISSION

You are *called* as much as anyone—including even your greatest heroes of the faith. More than likely, your calling is not in the organized church world, because only some—a small number—are called to this sphere. You're privileged to excel, to stand out in the arena of life you're sent to.

- Daniel distinguished himself in the government offices of Babylon (Daniel 6:3).
- Joseph distinguished himself in the great nation of Egypt (Genesis 41:39–40).
- Phoebe stood out as a minister of the gospel in Cenchrea (Romans 16:1).

Your calling is no different. *You are uniquely gifted.* God has placed on you the abilities required to fulfill your mission.

> How can you honestly expect the anointing to distinguish you within your sphere of influence, the arena of life to which you are called?

Listen to Scripture's record of Bezalel and his team of workers:

The LORD has gifted Bezalel, Oholiab, and the other skilled craftsmen with wisdom and ability to perform any task involved in building the sanctuary. (Exodus 36:1)

These men didn't possess the ability to speak the Word of God and minister to the people, as Moses or Aaron and his sons did. But these craftsmen were gifted with hands that could build the tabernacle.

You, too, have been gifted to build God's tabernacle with the skills He has given you. However, this sanctuary isn't made of gold, silver, bronze, precious stones, fine linen, acacia wood, or any other materials used to build the tabernacle of the Old Testament or the temple in Jerusalem. Today, God's tabernacle is made of living stones—human beings—and these living stones are being built up as a habitation of God (1 Peter 2:5; Ephesians 2:20–22). You're gifted to build people for God's glory.

> **You are empowered to multiply.** We're stewards of the gifts God gives us, and His desire is for you and me to return to Him multiplied fruit that has been produced by these gifts. To multiply, we must seek out the strategies of heaven. Principles can be taught by leaders, but these unique and heavenly strategies are personal; they aren't studied from a book or learned in a classroom.
>
> We leaders can only encourage you to seek Him and listen to His voice. Obey Him, even when it seems insignificant. What ends up multiplying is usually something that seems trivial. Remember, a mustard seed is smaller than all other seeds, but it grows into one of the largest trees.
>
> **You multiply through investing.** This takes on many forms, but when we release, we receive a harvest of blessings. If the seed remains unplanted (uninvested), it remains alone, but when invested, it produces a multiplied harvest. At any point, your harvest can be either hoarded or reinvested. Don't ever stop investing; it's the key to your next level of effectiveness.
>
> **Your catalyst is serving.** If your motive is anything other than to serve, you'll end up in a place where you don't want to find yourself. You may be well off in the eyes of others, but you'll be drained of passion. Your lamp will continue to diminish, even to the point of going out. But be comforted—He will not quench a smoking lamp. He'll continually seek to gain your attention, to rekindle your fire (Isaiah 42:3). No matter what you do, seek to serve, love without hypocrisy, and endure any hardships you face.
>
> **Desire the anointing.** It's your enhancer. It will propel your work to become eternal. The anointing will exalt your strength and make you stand out in your field of calling. It will separate you from those in the world—and even in the church—who use their God-given gifts for selfish or worldly purposes.

You must have faith. It's the only way to multiply your God-given potential. Without faith, "it is impossible to please God" (Hebrews 11:6). In order to grow it, you must hear His Word. We're told, "Faith *comes* by hearing, and hearing by the word of God" (Romans 10:17 NKJV). It's hearing, then hearing, then hearing again that causes the Word of God to be firmly embedded in the heart.

That's why it would be wise to read this book again, and then again. But don't just read it; put the book down and meditate on how these truths apply to you—then act on them. Absorb into your spirit the Word of God which is systematically laid out in this book. Do this through reading, meditation, and prayer—to the point that you believe you're called to multiply, no matter what life around you looks like. This conviction inside you to multiply should grow bigger than your outward circumstances would dictate.

Absorb into your spirit the Word of God as laid out in this book. Do this through reading, meditation, and prayer—to the point that you believe you're called to multiply, no matter what life around you looks like.

Finally, remember: God is *for* you!

"For I know the plans I have for you," says the LORD. "They are plans for good." (Jeremiah 29:11)

And again, we're emphatically told:

If God is for us, who can ever be against us? Since he did not spare even his own Son but gave him up for us all, won't he also give us everything else? (Romans 8:31–32)

Listen to these words, not the discouraging statements that originate from the god of this world—the chief accuser and discourager. Your Creator is your Father, and He desires your success in the labor He's called you to.

As a father in the faith who has now passed his sixtieth year, I am also for you! I'm cheering you on to go further than my peers and I have gone. We serve one King; we are citizens of one kingdom, and members of one household;

we have one faith, one mission—to build the house of God that He'll inhabit for all eternity.

Let's work together. Let's become one and maintain unity. Let's see His glory fill His dwelling place once again. There's no other solution for the world's problems.

I love you—but most importantly, God the Father, Jesus Christ the Son, and the Holy Spirit deeply love you. And their love for you endures forever.

Now to Him who is able to keep you without stumbling or slipping or falling, and to present [you] unblemished (blameless and faultless) before the presence of His glory in triumphant joy and exultation [with unspeakable, ecstatic delight]—To the one only God, our Savior through Jesus Christ our Lord, be glory (splendor), majesty, might and dominion, and power and authority, before all time and now and forever (unto all the ages of eternity).

Amen (so be it).

Jude 24–25 AMPC

REFLECTION FOR RENEWAL

What teachings and Scriptural principles highlighted in this book have been most meaningful for you?

How would you restate these things in your own words? (Personalize your answer as a prayer of response to God.)

What are your thoughts about the most important things God wants you to do now in response to what you've seen and reflected upon throughout this book?

SALVATION, AVAILABLE TO ALL

If you openly declare that Jesus is Lord and believe in your heart that God raised him from the dead, you will be saved. For it is by believing in your heart that you are made right with God, and it is by openly declaring your faith that you are saved.

ROMANS 10:9–10

God wants you to experience life in its fullness. He's passionate about you and the plan He has for your life. But there's only one way to start the journey to your destiny—and that is by receiving salvation through God's Son, Jesus Christ.

Through the death and resurrection of Jesus, God made a way for you to enter His kingdom as a beloved son or daughter. The sacrifice of Jesus on the cross made eternal and abundant life freely available to you. Salvation is God's gift to you; you cannot do anything to earn or deserve it.

To receive this precious gift, first acknowledge your sin of living independently of your Creator, for this is the root of all the sins you've committed. This repentance is a vital part of receiving salvation. The apostle Peter made this clear, on the day when five thousand were saved after he proclaimed the gospel of Christ and then said, "Repent therefore and be converted, that your sins may be blotted out" (Acts 3:19 NKJV).

Scripture declares that each of us is born a slave to sin. This slavery is rooted in the sin of Adam, who began the pattern of willful disobedience. Repentance is a choice to walk away from obedience to yourself and to Satan, the father of lies—and to turn in obedience to your new Master, Jesus Christ—the One who gave His life for you.

You must give Jesus the lordship of your life. To make Jesus "Lord" means giving Him ownership of your life—spirit, soul, and body, everything you are and have. His authority over your life becomes absolute. The moment you do this, God delivers you from darkness and transfers you to the light and glory of His kingdom. You simply go from death to life—you become His child!

If you want to receive salvation through Jesus, pray these words:

God in heaven, I acknowledge that I'm a sinner and have fallen short of Your righteous standard. I deserve to be judged for eternity for my sin. Thank You for not leaving me in this state, for I believe You sent Jesus Christ—Your only begotten Son, who was born of the Virgin Mary—to die for me and to carry my judgment on the cross. I believe that Jesus was raised again on the third day and is now seated at Your right hand as my Lord and Savior. So on this day, I repent of my independence from You and give my life entirely to the lordship of Jesus.

I confess You, Jesus, as my Lord and Savior. Come into my life through Your Spirit, and change me into a child of God. I renounce the things of darkness that I once held on to, and from this day forward I'll no longer live for myself. By Your grace, I'll live for You who gave Yourself for me, that I may live forever.

Thank You, Lord; my life is now completely in Your hands, and according to Your Word, I shall never be ashamed.
I pray all this in Jesus's name, Amen.

Welcome to the family of God! I encourage you to share your exciting news with another believer. It's also important that you join a Bible-believing local church and connect with others who can encourage you in your new faith. You have just embarked on the most remarkable journey. May you grow every day in revelation, grace, and friendship with God!

CALLED TO SALVATION

Here are just a few of the many promising verses in God's Word that can reinforce your peace and encouragement in accepting and embracing the Lord's offer of salvation.

For God loved the world so much that he gave his one and only Son, so that everyone who believes in him will not perish but have eternal life. God sent his Son into the world not to judge the world, but to save the world through him. (John 3:16–17)

Everyone who calls on the name of the LORD will be saved. (Acts 2:21)

If you confess with your mouth that Jesus is Lord and believe in your heart that God raised him from the dead, you will be saved. (Romans 10:9)

He will keep you strong to the end so that you will be free from all blame on the day when our Lord Jesus Christ returns. God will do this, for he is faithful to do what he says, and he has invited you into partnership with his Son, Jesus Christ our Lord. (1 Corinthians 1:8–9)

Even though we were dead because of our sins, he gave us life when he raised Christ from the dead. (It is only by God's grace that you have been saved!) (Ephesians 2:5)

God saved you by his grace when you believed. And you can't take credit for this; it is a gift from God. (Ephesians 2:8)

He saved us, not because of the righteous things we had done, but because of his mercy. He washed away our sins, giving us a new birth and new life through the Holy Spirit. (Titus 3:5)

There is only one God and one Mediator who can reconcile God and humanity—the man Christ Jesus. He gave his life to purchase freedom for everyone. This is the message God gave to the world at just the right time. (1 Timothy 2:5–6)

For God saved us and called us to live a holy life. He did this, not because we deserved it, but because that was his plan from before the beginning of time—to show us his grace through Christ Jesus. (2 Timothy 1:9)

Let all the world look to me for salvation! For I am God; there is no other. (Isaiah 45:22)

ACKNOWLEDGMENTS

The book in your hand is a team effort, so I want to acknowledge some of the coworkers who contributed to it:

Bruce Nygren: Thank you for your expertise in the content editing. Once again, you've taken my writing and, without losing my voice, made it a much better read. And thank you for the challenging questions you asked that ultimately made the book stronger and more accurate.

Cory Emberson, Laura Willbur, and Loran Johnson: Thank you for ensuring that the grammar, punctuation, and style of this message stayed accurate and consistent. I admire your gift.

Chris Pace: Thank you for your unending encouragement in reading this manuscript as it progressed chapter by chapter. Thank you also for helping me shape chapter 14. Your input was invaluable.

Addison Bevere: Thank you for your editing skills and your challenging questions, which made the message a better and more accurate read. Most of all, thank you for being a faithful and encouraging son.

Allan Nygren: Thank you for your brilliant design of the layout of this book and the cover. I admire your gift!

To the Messenger International Team: Each of you does so much behind the scenes to build God's kingdom. I'll rejoice with you on the day we witness Jesus greatly rewarding your selfless service.

Holy Spirit of God: My greatest gratitude goes to You! This message would never have been possible without Your guidance and wisdom. I'm exceedingly thankful for Your ongoing revelation of my Lord and greatest love, Jesus Christ. I love You deeply, and it's an honor to serve You and partner with You.

NOTES

Chapter 3

1. Spiros Zodhiates, *The Complete Word Study Dictionary: New Testament* (Chattanooga, TN: AMG Publishers, 2000), under "ekklēsías."
2. Frederick William Danker, ed., *A Greek-English Lexicon of the New Testament and Other Early Christian Literature* (Chicago: University of Chicago Press, 2000), under "ethnos."

Chapter 4

1. Johannes P. Louw and Eugene A. Nida, *Greek-English Lexicon of the New Testament: Based on Semantic Domains* (New York: United Bible Societies, 1996), under "oikonomos."
2. Louw and Nida, *A Greek-English Lexicon*, under "ouaí."
3. Zodhiates, *The Complete Word Study Dictionary*, under "ouaí."
4. Zodhiates, *The Complete Word Study Dictionary*, under "diakonéō."
5. Louw and Nida, *A Greek-English Lexicon*

Chapter 5

1. Zodhiates, *The Complete Word Study Dictionary*, under "oknērós."
2. Louw and Nida, *A Greek-English Lexicon*, under "oknērós."
3. Louw and Nida, *A Greek-English Lexicon*, under "ponērós."

Chapter 6

1. *Merriam-Webster Dictionary*, "enthusiasm," accessed October 20, 2024, https://www.merriamwebster.com/dictionary/enthusiasm.

Chapter 9

1. Dictionary.com, "breakthrough," accessed May 5, 2020, https://www
.dictionary.com/browse/breakthrough.

Chapter 11

1. Warren Baker and Eugene Carpenter, *The Complete Word Study Dictionary:
Old Testament* (Chattanooga, TN: AMG Publishers, 2003), under
"commanded."
2. Zodhiates, *The Complete Word Study Dictionary*, under "homothumadon."

Chapter 12

1. "Digital Babylon: Our Accelerated, Complex Culture," Barna Group,
October 23, 2019, https://www.barna.com/research/digital-babylon.

Chapter 13

1. Zodhiates, *The Complete Word Study Dictionary*, under "ameléō."
2. Louw and Nida, *A Greek-English Lexicon*, under "ameléō."
3. Myles Munroe, *Maximizing Your Potential* (Shippensburg, PA: Destiny
Image, 2013), 145.
4. Zodhiates, *The Complete Word Study Dictionary*, under "anazōpuréō."
5. Danker, *A Greek-English Lexicon*, under "anazōpuréō."

Chapter 14

1. K. Anders Ericsson and Robert Pool, *Peak: Secrets from the New Science of
Expertise* (New York: Houghton Mifflin Harcourt, 2016), 22.
2. Dictionary.com, "cultivate," accessed October 23, 2024, https://www
.dictionary.com/browse/cultivate.

Chapter 15

1. Zodhiates, *The Complete Word Study Dictionary*, under "dikaiosúnē."
2. Louw and Nida, *A Greek-English Lexicon*, under "chríō."

ABOUT THE AUTHOR

John Bevere is a minister known for his bold, uncompromising approach to God's Word. He's also an international bestselling author who has written more than 25 books that have collectively sold millions of copies and been translated into 130 languages.

Along with his wife, Lisa, John is the cofounder of Messenger International—a ministry committed to revolutionizing global discipleship.

When John is home in Franklin, Tennessee, you'll find him loving on his g-babies, playing pickleball, or trying to convince Lisa to take up golf.